The ABCs of Managing Your Money

By Jonathan D. Pond, CPA
with Michael A. Dalton, Ph.D., JD, CFP, CPA
and O'Neill Wyss, CFP

NATIONAL ENDOWMENT FOR FINANCIAL EDUCATION

About NEFE

The National Endowment for Financial Education^SM (NEFE^SM) is an independent, nonprofit organization whose primary purpose is to improve the well-being of the general public by advancing the knowledge and competence of professionals throughout the financial services industry. NEFE was established in 1992 as the parent corporation of the 20-year-old College for Financial Planning®. Along with the College, the divisions of NEFE include the Institute for Tax Studies^SM, the Institute for Wealth Management^SM, the Institute for Retirement Planning^SM, the Public Education Center, and NEFE Press^SM.

This complimentary copy of *The ABCs of Managing Your Money* is being provided to your library as a public service of the National Endowment for Financial Education.

The National Endowment for Financial Education intends this publication to be used as an educational supplement only. No financial, legal, tax, or investment advice is intended or implied. All concepts expressed herein should be discussed with a financial advisor, attorney, accountant, and/or tax consultant. In no event shall NEFE be liable for any consequential, incidental, or punitive damages whatsoever, whether based on breach of warranty, contract, negligence, or other liability based on a theory of tort.

Library of Congress Catalog Card Number 93-086164

ISBN 1-884383-00-9

The ABCs of Managing Your Money

Table of Contents

(Continued on the next page)

Table of Contents *Continued*

About the Authors

Jonathan D. Pond, CPA

The primary author of *The ABCs of Managing Your Money* is financial expert Jonathan Pond, a nationally known author, lecturer, and columnist. Pond has written nine books on personal financial planning, including the *Personal Financial Planning Handbook, Safe Money in Tough Times,* and *The New Century Family Money Book.* In addition to writing award-winning newsletters, Pond contributes to *Cosmopolitan, Newsweek,* and other national publications. He is a regular guest on NBC's "Today" Show, and has his own weekly radio talk show, "Your Money With Jonathan Pond." Educated at the University of North Carolina, Emory University, and the Harvard Business School, Pond is president of Financial Planning Information, Inc., in Boston.

Michael A. Dalton, Ph.D., JD, CFP, CPA

Coauthor Michael Dalton is an Associate Professor of Accounting and Taxation at Loyola University. An expert in taxation, personal finance, and the valuation of closely held corporations, Dalton has written six financial planning software packages published by FinPlan, Inc. and two textbooks, *Cost Accounting: Traditions and Innovations* and *CPA Review.* He also has written numerous articles on accounting, tax issues, and financial planning and has taught in-house financial planning courses for such businesses as Exxon Corporation, ITT, Federal Express, and The New Orleans Saints NFL football team. His Ph.D. was from Georgia State University and his JD from Louisiana State University.

O'Neill Wyss, CFP

O'Neill Wyss, also a coauthor, is an investment professional who has had the CFP professional designation since 1981. He helps individuals and organizations solve their specific money management problems and attain their financial goals. The author of the book *Strategic Financial Planning for the 1990s,* Wyss has been a member of the National Speakers Association since 1984. He conducts education and motivational programs for associations, corporations, and professional organizations.

Introduction

You can increase your financial planning savvy so that you can achieve financial security. The more you understand about financial planning, the better able you will be to achieve your financial goals. This chapter will show you why taking action today is in your best interest.

Introduction

Financial planning is a must for everyone—young and old, single or married, with or without children. Financial planning can begin with your children's first allowance, and continue throughout their entire lives.

You don't need to be rich to reap the benefits of financial planning. The best way to achieve financial security is through careful financial planning. At first glance, the task might seem to be overwhelming. But the truth is that it's easy to do—once you get the hang of it.

This book will help you do just that. All you need is to be willing to focus on your current financial condition and compare it with your current and future expectations and objectives. Are you saving enough money to sleep comfortably at night—even if you are unsure about your job security? Have you begun to invest your savings regularly and wisely? Have you established clear-cut objectives: purchasing a home, having and raising children, putting aside money for college tuition, establishing retirement-oriented savings?

Many people find talking about their personal financial objectives difficult, even though they spend many of their waking hours thinking about it. The difficulty is in taking the first few steps in being honest with yourself about your financial condition. In doing so, it's important to remember that not facing up to the facts about your financial condition won't prevent you from constantly worrying about it. Dealing with these important issues directly will help you think more clearly about the range of available solutions which, in turn, will help diminish the constant worry. Since worrying about money is unproductive and self-defeating, your most productive and self-fulfilling option is to learn all you can about financial planning. However, just as we fear the sting of the doctor's needle, many people fear the dose of financial reckoning that seems as if it will hurt more than it will help. In truth, the sting is temporary, but the benefits are long-lived.

Like a good road map, a successful financial plan can help you determine where you want to go and how to get there with a minimum of unforeseen, untimely, and costly detours. You will be surprised to find how easy it is to actually plan a swift and sure

> "Financial planning can begin with your children's first allowance."

journey in reaching your financial goals. One reason is that most events that affect your finances can be planned for—this book will show you how.

Moreover, time is on the side of those with a well-thought-out financial plan. For example, if you know that your daughter will be attending college in 10 or 15 years, you can start now investing a modest but adequate amount of money each month. Your current life-style will not be significantly changed, and when the time comes, you will be able to afford the cost of higher education.

Another area where financial planning can save the day is insurance. Without adequate insurance coverage, your hard-earned financial resources could be lost. With proper planning, you can save money on your current insurance premiums, and you also can ensure that you and your family have the coverages you need.

Affording a long-lived and comfortable retirement—perhaps the single most important financial planning goal—is another area where financial planning proves itself to be invaluable. All of us who do not die will retire someday. Are you saving enough money today so that you will be able to retire comfortably and securely?

This book will assist you along the road to financial security by showing the key elements of successful personal financial planning. You *can* achieve financial security! Taking control of your financial future, making the right financial planning decisions, and, when necessary, having a professional financial advisor help you make those decisions are what this book is about. For example, do you know that two essential ingredients to achieving your life's financial goals are regular saving and wise investing? Many people do not pay sufficient attention to saving and investing their hard-earned money. If you save, you can invest. However, if you don't invest, you will risk falling short of your financial goals.

While money is the focal point, successful personal financial planning requires attention to a variety of areas, including:

- Planning to meet your financial objectives
- Organizing your financial records
- Using credit effectively
- Saving regularly and investing those savings wisely
- Accumulating enough assets to meet your lifetime needs
- Minimizing your income taxes
- Planning to retire comfortably and securely
- Preparing an appropriate estate plan

How to Use This Book

This book will assist you and your family to meet many of life's financial challenges. It is divided into nine chapters:

Each of the nine chapters provides essential information and advice about a particular personal financial matter. The financial snapshots and other examples in this book indicate times in an individual's life when research and action are warranted regarding steps that need to be taken to move toward the goal of achieving financial security. Seeking qualified professional advice is often advisable during these key life events or in anticipation of them. Also included at the end of this book is an appendix full of useful financial planning work sheets and checklists—which appear within the individual chapters—to help you on your way.

You can use this book in a variety of ways:

• **As a helpful guide to personal financial planning.** You will uncover many ideas that you can quickly and easily put to use in your own personal financial planning.

• **As a tool to review your current financial situation and to uncover areas that need attention.** Each chapter presents common questions pertinent to the financial area being discussed and a financial snapshot which explores relevant themes. Each chapter also contains key words, work sheets, and checklists you can use to understand and evaluate your financial situation and determine what actions to take.

• **As an easy-to-use reference to help you answer many of your most important financial planning questions.** One of the largest obstacles people encounter in their financial planning is gaining access to timely and objective information. This book provides unbiased and understandable answers and guidance. Successful personal financial planning cannot be done overnight. If you begin to gradually make some changes, you will be well on your way to achieving everyone's primary financial goal—financial security.

Getting Your Financial Plan Started

Up to now, you may not have paid a lot of attention to financial planning, or you may think your finances are adequate. Either way, this book contains a wealth of information that will help you manage your wealth, no matter how modest it might now be. Even if you're starting from scratch or if indebtedness has you in financial difficulty, you'll find many ways to improve your financial well-being so that you will be able to enjoy financial peace of mind. The following financial planning objectives are important to most people. Each objective is referred to a particular chapter. Which of these are important to you?

Objectives

	Very Important	Somewhat Important	Not Important
• Improving personal record keeping (Chapter 2)	☐	☐	☐
• Reducing debt (Chapter 2)	☐	☐	☐
• Ensuring complete insurance coverage (Chapter 3)	☐	☐	☐
• Investing more regularly (Chapter 4)	☐	☐	☐
• Reducing income taxes (Chapter 5)	☐	☐	☐
• Assuring a comfortable retirement (Chapter 6)	☐	☐	☐
• Making sure your estate is properly planned (Chapter 7)	☐	☐	☐
• Buying a home (Chapter 8)	☐	☐	☐
• Meeting college education costs (Chapter 8)	☐	☐	☐

For most people, financial security means *financial independence*—the ability to meet all foreseeable financial needs out of your own resources. In other words, financial security means being able to own a home, to afford your child's college tuition, and to retire comfortably when you want to retire. Whatever financial demands you may face—buying a home, educating the children, surviving the death of a breadwinner—this book will help you plan ahead so that you can overcome financial obstacles and meet your financial goals.

CHAPTER 2

Getting Your Personal Finances in Order

Taking control of your financial life is as easy as reading this chapter—Really! Here you'll find what it takes to achieve successful personal financial planning, how to plan realistically to improve your spending and saving habits, how to avoid common personal financial mistakes, and when you can benefit most from the services of professional financial advisors.

Getting Your Personal Finances in Order

Questions

What is personal financial planning?

What is net worth, and why is it important to me?

How can I avoid making personal financial mistakes?

What credentials should I consider when hiring a professional financial advisor?

When should I engage a financial advisor?

This chapter introduces several critical first steps toward achieving financial security. You will learn the key areas of personal financial planning, including how to determine your net worth, prepare a budget, avoid mistakes, and when and how to select a professional financial advisor. This chapter provides a thorough introduction to financial planning basics.

Key Areas of Financial Planning

Successful personal financial planning involves three distinct yet interrelated key areas: getting organized, saving and investing money, and planning for retirement. Each area contains several important matters to consider, as listed on the following page.

Financial Snapshot | *Sarah Melton*

Sarah Melton recently was divorced; now that she is on her own, she is struggling to put her financial affairs in order. After having been out of work for several years, Sarah has just been hired as a paralegal. It's a good job with flexible hours and generous benefits, but her paycheck is quickly consumed by living expenses and tuition for law school, which she attends at night. In addition to juggling a job and her schoolwork, Sarah also must care for her three-year-old daughter, Melissa. Melissa spends her days at a local day-care center, and two nights a week—when Sarah's at law school—with a babysitter.

Sarah's former husband was completely responsible for the couple's financial affairs. Now that Sarah is divorced, she's starting over financially. The balances on her three credit cards are all overdue, and she's not sure how she's going to pay for her next car insurance premium. Sarah feels as though she's up against the wall, especially given how much she has to pay for child care. Her salary, supplemented by child support payments, doesn't seem to go far enough to meet current expenses, let alone allow her to start saving for Melissa's college education.

Luckily, Sarah is not entirely without savings: she has a small nest egg, most of which consists of money that she inherited from her grandmother. Her nest egg is deposited in a savings account. While Sarah is scared to invest for fear of losing it, she realizes that the interest earned on her savings account doesn't even keep up with inflation.

Before Sarah can really focus on earning that law degree, she must take control of her finances. Indeed, developing a workable financial plan—one that includes a budget to keep costs under control—is Sarah's number one priority. It's also her number one challenge.

Getting Organized
- Setting financial objectives, strategies, and priorities
- Determining where you stand financially
- Putting your personal records in proper order
- Finding competent advisors in the legal, insurance, and investment areas
- Acquiring and maintaining comprehensive and cost-effective insurance coverage
- Planning to meet major expenses
- Managing your debt effectively
- Bringing your spending under control

Saving and Investing Money
- Saving and investing regularly
- Accumulating an emergency fund that will see you through lean times
- Setting realistic investment objectives
- Learning to take advantage of the numerous investment alternatives available
- Building an investment program that meets your special needs
- Reviewing your investment portfolio
- Minimizing current income taxes
- Planning to reduce future income taxes

Planning for Retirement
- Starting to plan early for a comfortable retirement
- Projecting retirement income and expenses
- Taking advantage of tax-advantaged retirement plans
- Coordinating your retirement income needs with your personal and pension plan investments
- Making sure your estate planning documents are valid, up-to-date, and appropriate
- Dealing with the problems of old age—both yours and those of your parents

Key Words

Asset Any item that has financial value—i.e., house, personal property, car, investment, etc.

Capital gains tax Money owed to the Internal Revenue Service (IRS) on an investment or a house, under certain circumstances, sold at a profit.

Liability A debt that must be repaid.

Net worth The amount by which assets (for example, your savings, investments, and/or property owned) exceed liabilities (debts owed).

This chapter and the ones to follow will discuss each item in detail to help you take control of your personal finances. Be assured that personal financial planning really isn't as complicated as many people fear. All it takes is some discipline, time, and the willingness to take charge of your financial life.

Establishing and Prioritizing Goals
Many people don't achieve financial security until they retire. There's nothing wrong with that. However, some people *never* achieve financial security—not by the time they retire, not by age 75.

Achieving financial security requires planning and sacrifice. The only way you're going to be successful in attaining financial security (short of marrying or inheriting a bundle) is to save regularly and invest wisely. The only way to save regularly is to spend less than you earn. The only way to spend less than you earn is to plan ahead and, if necessary, forgo some nonessential purchases.

The more specific and realistic you are about your financial goals, the greater are your chances of achieving them. You must establish your goals before devising strategies, or detailed plans, to achieve them. Devising goals requires more effort and diligence than creating them. In other words, it's a lot easier to say "I want to retire by age 55" than it is to actually be able to design a plan to do it.

Some goals are more urgent to achieve than others. For example, achieving financial security by retirement may be your ultimate goal. However, you probably will have other financial goals that need to be met earlier in life.

Setting priorities is an important part of successful goal setting. You need to prioritize your goals so that the pursuit of one goal doesn't interfere or detract from the pursuit of another goal. For example, many people rank securing adequate insurance coverage pretty far down the list of priorities, yet adequate coverage is essential to financial security. Since insufficient insurance may jeopardize years of accumulated savings, adequate insurance coverage should be a top priority.

Assessing Your Current Financial Status: A Closer Look

The following items will help you get a handle on your current financial situation.

Set Up a Record-Keeping System

To find out where you actually stand, you first need a good record-keeping system. This will allow you to prepare a statement of assets and liabilities and a personal budget. All of these will help start you down the right financial planning path.

Many of us keep good records at work, but our personal records are not as good. An effective home record-keeping system can be simple to set up and easy to maintain. A good system is comprehensive enough to be useful, yet simple enough to encourage regular use. Here's the way to go about it. Organize personal records around the following three basic files:

1. **Active file.** Use this to monitor your current budget, organize bills, keep track of important papers, and help prepare the current year's tax return. Remember: if your filing system is not easy to use, you will end up postponing filing items, sometimes indefinitely. A good home active file could consist of nothing more than a cardboard box with manilla file folders. You'll save money as well as time, since you can keep track of valuable tax deductions if your records are well organized. Good personal records also will help you avoid problems if you are ever audited by the IRS.

2. **Inactive file.** Use this to store past tax returns in the event you're ever audited. This file should contain important papers—formerly stored in your active file—that are more than three years old. As a general rule, after six years, you can discard most of your records. However, home improvement receipts are important to save because some improvements increase the original value of the property, potentially reducing any gain on the sale of the property. Receipts also can be used to help prove claims for deductions.

3. **Safe-deposit box.** This should store most of your legal and important personal papers, ownership records, and estate planning documents. Keep an updated list of the contents of the safe-deposit box in your active file. Since the bank probably doesn't insure valuables stored in your safe-deposit box, if you store jewelry or rare coins you should obtain a safe-deposit box insurance floater through the company that handles your home-owners or renters insurance.

Determine Your Net Worth

Personal financial statements are important in showing an individual's financial well-being. Two types of statements should be prepared. The first is a statement of personal assets and liabilities (personal balance sheet), which will summarize your assets and liabilities, and determine your net worth. Your net worth is the amount by which your assets (for example, your savings, investments, property owned) exceed your liabilities (debts owed). Periodically determining net worth helps you to gauge your financial progress. The second statement is a personal budget, which summarizes where your income comes from and how it's spent. A budget is an essential part of any successful financial plan because it provides a moving picture of your financial situation.

You don't need an accountant to prepare your personal financial statements. But, you will need to gather your financial records. A Statement of Personal Assets and Liabilities Work Sheet appears at the end of this chapter.

Statement of Your Personal Assets and Liabilities

Preparing this statement is an excellent way to gauge your financial progress. The statement should list assets at their current fair market values (what they are worth if you were to sell them today). Try to be realistic, especially when valuing real estate and personal property (such as jewelry or a sailboat)—two areas where many people are prone to overvalue. If you have some common stock or real estate that has appreciated considerably in value, remember that your net worth might not be as high as it now appears once you sell those assets. Why? You may have to pay income tax on their appreciated value. Be sure to list all liabilities and avoid inflating or understating their value.

Once an up-to-date personal balance sheet has been prepared, you can make plans to increase your net worth. If you have recently begun your career, don't be dismayed if your net worth is small or negative. The important thing is to take action to improve it. Also, periodically review and revise your statement of personal assets and liabilities so that you can monitor the gradual improvement of your net worth.

Personal Budget

Budgeting is crucial to managing your day-to-day finances. The purposes of budgeting are (1) to define possible problems in spending patterns, (2) to identify opportunities to overcome these problems, and (3) to help you plan realistically to improve your spending habits. (A Personal Budget Planner appears at the end of this chapter.)

Your budget should carefully balance the various needs of all family members. One way to keep everyone happy is to establish a personal allowance for each family member. Whatever form your own budget reconciliation takes, however, remember to leave a comfortable margin for unexpected expenses. A budget that cuts too close to the bone will be too hard to follow.

The following checklist will guide you through several steps necessary to develop a useful and user-friendly budget.

☐ **Select—or design—a budget form that suits your needs.** Budgets come in a variety of formats and styles. One is bound to suit your needs. The sample budget form at the end of this chapter will help you understand how budgets are organized. You can use it as is, or modify it to suit your particular needs. If you are looking for a comprehensive (and complicated) system, several family budget systems are available in books or computer software.

☐ **Forecast your income.** The budget work sheet will help identify your various sources of income. Be sure to be realistic in estimating your income, particularly items that might be uncertain in amount or nonrecurring, like annual bonuses. It is always better to estimate on the low side when projecting income.

☐ **Summarize past expenses.** Before you can estimate future expenses, you should summarize your past expenses on one of the columns of your budget work sheet. Don't simply estimate your past expenses. The more precise you can be, the better your budget will work out. Summarize and categorize cancelled checks and then make an honest estimate of how you spend your cash. One way to get a handle on how you spend money is to carry a notebook to record each item paid for in cash.

☐ **Estimate future expenses.** Now that you have forecast your income and estimated your past expenses, you should estimate your future expenses over whatever period you are budgeting—a month, a quarter, or a year. The objective is to budget your expenses so that, at a minimum, they don't exceed your income. You should strive, of course, to spend less than you earn to get into the habit of saving regularly.

Nonrecurring expenses (in other words, those that don't reoccur every month) present a special problem. These expenses include insurance payments, vacations, and individual retirement account contributions. Summarize them separately, and set money aside to avoid periodic crises in cash flow caused by large expenditures. Each month, you should put one-twelfth of the estimated total annual amount of these infrequent bills into a separate account. The money should be withdrawn when these bills come due.

☐ **Compare your actual expenses with your estimated expenses.** At the end of the budgeted period, compare the amount of income you actually earned with the expenses you actually paid with your budgeted amounts. Once you've prepared and worked with a few budgets, you will become more proficient at identifying the areas where you can reduce your expenses further. Before you know it, you will be well on your way to putting your financial house in good order.

Using Professional Financial Advisors to Assist in Your Financial Planning

The payoff of budgeting well is increased savings and/or improved consumption. Increased savings creates the need to determine good from bad investments. Certified Financial Planners can help you make such decisions. Certified Public Accountants and attorneys also can assist you with other aspects of your personal financial planning.

However, many people either fail to select appropriate financial advisors or neglect to work with them effectively. Taking a more active role in making sure your advisors are providing the best possible advice and service will help make your professional relationship work. Remember, it's up to you to define the role that your family financial advisors will play.

Avoiding Common Personal Financial Mistakes

The road to financial security is paved with good intentions. In personal financial planning, one of the best ways to achieve financial security is by successfully avoiding mistakes. With this in mind, the following 10 common errors many people make in the course of their financial life are included—so that you can detour around them.

1. **Neglecting to cover gaps in insurance coverage.** The surest way to wipe out years of hard-earned accumulation of capital is to suffer an uninsured loss. Deficiencies in any area of insurance can be financially disastrous.

2. **Mismanaging credit.** Since credit is very easy to obtain, many people lack the self-discipline necessary to manage it effectively. Financial institutions are no help, because they promote high-limit credit cards, five-year car loans, and large home equity loans with overly liberal repayment terms.

3. **Failing to save regularly.** Regular saving is essential to achieving financial security. As income increases, savings also should increase. Nevertheless, many people do not save regularly. Somehow, they mistakenly think that the equity buildup in their home, an inheritance, or their company pension plan will provide them with long-term financial security. They're wrong.

4. **Making inappropriate investments.** Whether it is caused by ignorance or greed, or both, many people make an inappropriate investment at least once in their lifetime. Unfortunately, some people consistently invest their money in the wrong areas by taking either too much—or too little—risk.

5. **Using inappropriate planning strategies.** There are many complex financial strategies available to anyone who wants to use them, but they often make little or no sense. Generally, basic, straightforward strategies produce the best results.

6. **Failing to take full advantage of tax breaks.** Failing to take advantage of available tax deductions as well as other legal tax reduction techniques is another mistake many people make. Reducing taxes is one of the most painless ways of reducing expenses so that savings levels can be increased.

7. **Overspending.** Many successful people increase their spending in the plenty years to such a high level that when a lean year occurs—income declines, or an unforeseen expense arises such as the death of a loved one—they end up in a financial bind. Living beyond your means always puts your finances in jeopardy.

8. **Failing to accumulate sufficient retirement resources.** Many people work for companies providing few or no pension benefits. Some people change jobs frequently. If their employers do offer retirement plans, many people fail to maximize contributions. Many companies are cutting back on their pension plans; therefore, many workers must take the initiative to accumulate sufficient resources to assure a comfortable retirement.

(Continued on the next page.)

Avoiding Common Personal Financial Mistakes *Continued*

9. **Neglecting to prepare a will and other estate planning documents.** While not around to witness the havoc, people who do not prepare basic estate planning documents do their heirs a disservice. Inappropriate or nonexistent estate planning can end up costing heirs a great deal in terms of both inconvenience and money.

10. **Not shopping around for the most appropriate financial planning products and services.** While the types of investment, insurance, and other financial products are abundant and bewildering, you *can* find the right products to meet your needs. However, many people are unwilling to take the time to ensure that they are making the most of each dollar they spend or invest.

No one can avoid making mistakes in personal financial planning. Some, however, make too many mistakes and, worse, repeat them. As you review the above list, you will probably identify areas where you need improvement. Pay close attention when they are addressed later in this book.

Financial Planners: Their Role and How They Are Compensated

A financial planner can help you deal with many matters that affect your financial well-being, including insurance, investments, credit management, retirement, and estate planning. If unable to help you directly, he or she should be able to steer you in the right direction. As a result, selecting a good financial planner is very important.

The fact that a planner *is* a certified member of a financial planning organization is a good starting point and demonstrates that he or she took the initiative to learn about the diverse field of financial planning. There are three main certifications that financial planners can earn:

1. **Accredited Personal Financial Specialist (APFS).** This certification is conferred by the American Institute of Certified Public Accountants (AICPA) and can be held only by CPAs. The vast majority of people with the APFS designation operate on a "fee-only" basis. (Fee-only planners will be discussed later.)

2. **Certified Financial Planner (CFP).** The CFP designation is granted to individuals who have completed an intense study program, passed a comprehensive examination, and have fulfilled an experience requirement. The CFP designation is awarded by the Denver-based International Board of Standards and Practices for Certified Financial Planners, Inc. (IBCFP).

3. **Chartered Financial Consultant (ChFC).** This certification is awarded by the Bryn Mawr, Pennsylvania-based American Society of Chartered Life Underwriters (CLU) and Chartered Financial Consultants (ChFC) to individuals who complete a 10-section course of study and who have passed two exams.

Note: In addition to the above certifications, many planners are Registered Investment Advisers. These individuals are registered with the Securities and Exchange Commission, which is required by law for people who give investment advice.

Many people can and do benefit from the services of a financial planner. If you have a complex financial planning matter that needs evaluation, a consultation with a planner who is experienced in your particular area of concern may well be worthwhile. In addition to evaluating specific concerns, financial planners can comprehensively review your total personal financial situation, either on a one-time or an ongoing basis. Other professionals—such as bankers, insurance agents, and stockbrokers, to name a few— who practice in specialty areas of financial planning also may be able to assist you in attaining your specific goals.

Financial planners are compensated for their efforts on your behalf through fees, commissions, or a combination of the two. A fee-only planner is paid on an hourly or retainer basis. If a fee-only planner spends 10 hours devising an investment strategy for you, you are billed for 10 hours' work at an hourly fee. Alternatively, the planner may arrange a fixed fee.

A commissioned planner earns his or her income by commissions charged on investments and insurance products that you buy through the planner.

Some planners combine these two sources of compensation, earning income through both fees and commissions. Fees are earned by providing a review of your financial situation together with specific recommendations. If you decide to accept them, the planner will then earn commissions on the investment and insurance products that you purchase through implementation.

CPAs and Their Role

Certified Public Accountants, or CPAs as they're more commonly called, practice in practically every town in this country. A CPA provides a variety of services, and most are well qualified to advise you on tax matters and/or prepare your income taxes. If your tax situation has become complex—for example, you've started a business, just sold your house, or received a lump-sum pension payout—then you may benefit from the help of a CPA come tax time.

Many CPAs also have become proficient (and even certified) in personal financial planning. The APFS degree previously discussed designates a CPA who is qualified to help you with your personal financial planning needs.

Attorneys and Their Role

A family attorney is essential for preparing necessary estate planning documents such as wills and powers of attorney. It is often best to use an attorney who is approximately your age or younger, because you don't want to be burdened with having to find a new attorney when your current one retires. However, you may outgrow your attorney's expertise if your estate grows to a level that will require more sophisticated estate planning techniques. Larger estates require the expertise of an attorney who devotes all or most of his or her time to estate planning matters, rather than general practice.

Finding competent advisors is well worth the effort. There is no ideal way to locate these professionals, but word-of-mouth recommendation referrals can be an important first step. You should expect your financial planner and attorney to be responsive to your needs and to conduct their work ethically. If you are unhappy with one of your advisors, it may be because you have not taken an active role in establishing the relationship. First, try to resolve the problem with your advisor. But if the problem persists, don't hesitate to make a change.

At the beginning of this chapter, we met Sarah Melton, a recently divorced mother who was struggling to keep her finances in order. Sarah needed to quickly devise a plan that would allow her to pay bills on time and to begin a savings and investment program.

Sarah realized that getting her finances in order was going to take some time, so she decided to devote her next three-day weekend exclusively to developing a sound financial plan. When the time arrived, Sarah arranged to have Melissa stay with her grandmother so that she could focus on her financial situation. The first thing Sarah did was to make the following list of her short- and long-term goals.

Immediate goals:
1. Set up an income and expense budget covering the next year.
2. Pay off credit card balances.
3. Pay off the balance on this year's car insurance premium.
4. Set aside three months' salary as an emergency fund.

Longer-term goals:
1. Using her nest egg as a beginning, start a regular investment program for retirement.
2. With the assistance of her former husband, establish a college education fund for Melissa.
3. Finish law school in three years.

Having developed a coherent set of goals, Sarah proceeded to determine exactly how she was going to meet them. After summarizing her income and expenses for the past six months, she prepared a budget for the next six months. She found areas where she could cut back without too much pain. She could substantially reduce her credit card charges without giving up any necessities. With discipline, Sarah could pay off all three credit cards within the next four months. With those accounts out of the way, Sarah could then pay off the balance on her car insurance premium. While the insurance company's monthly payment plan was convenient, the interest charged on the unpaid balance inflated her already high premium.

Sarah realized that within six months she would be in good enough financial shape to begin depositing at least $250 in her savings account each month. Once she had accumulated three months' salary in an emergency fund—which would take about a year-and-a-half from now—she would be ready to begin contributing to a retirement fund for herself and a college-education fund for Melissa. Since the divorce agreement made Sarah and her ex-husband equally responsible for Melissa's education, Sarah was confident that he would agree to establishing—and would contribute to—the education fund.

Once short-term goals had been met, Sarah was confident that she would be on the right road to achieving her longer-term goals. By the end of her three-day weekend, Sarah had already taken the first step to financial security. A good deal of work lay ahead—she needed to learn how to properly invest her savings, for instance—but Sarah had started moving in the right direction. It would be appropriate for Sarah to seek professional assistance to learn how to invest her savings.

Statement of Personal Assets and Liabilities *Work Sheet*

Use this work sheet to summarize your assets and liabilities. Three columns are included so that you can periodically monitor your progress. Prepare this statement at least once per year. Many people prepare it more frequently.

Assets and Liabilities

	19	19	19
Assets			
1. Cash in Checking and Brokerage Accounts	$	$	$
2. Money Market Funds and Accounts			
3. Fixed-Income Investments			
• Savings account			
• CDs			
• Government securities and funds			
• Mortgage-backed securities and funds			
• Corporate bonds and bond funds			
• Municipal bonds and bond funds			
• Other fixed-income investments			
4. Stock Investments			
• Common stock in publicly traded companies			
• Stock mutual funds			
• Other stock investments			
5. Real Estate Investments			
• Undeveloped land			
• Directly owned, income-producing real estate			
• Real estate limited partnerships			
6. Ownership Interest in Private Business			
7. Cash Value of Life Insurance Policies			
8. Retirement-Oriented Assets			
• Individual retirement accounts			
• Salary reduction 401(k) plans			
• Keogh or simplified employee pension plans			
• Employee thrift and stock purchase plans			
• Vested interest in corporate pension and profit sharing plans			
• Tax-deferred annuities			
• Other retirement-oriented assets			

(Continued on the next page)

Statement of Personal Assets and Liabilities *Continued*

Assets and Liabilities

	19	19	19
9. Personal Assets			
• Personal residence(s)	$	$	$
• Automobile(s)			
• Jewelry			
• Personal property			
10. Other Assets			
•			
•			
•			
11. Total Assets	$	$	$
Liabilities			
1. Credit Cards and Charge Accounts	$	$	$
2. Income Taxes Payable			
3. Miscellaneous Accounts Payable			
4. Bank Loans			
5. Policy Loans on Life Insurance Policies			
6. Automobile Loans			
7. Student Loans			
8. Mortgages on Personal Residence(s)			
9. Mortgages on Investment Real Estate			
10. Broker's Margin Loans			
11. Limited Partnership Debt			
12. Other Liabilities			
•			
•			
•			
13. Total Liabilities	$	$	$
14. Net Worth (total assets less total liabilities)	$	$	$

Note: Assets should be listed at their current market value. Be realistic in valuing those assets that require an estimate of market value, such as your home and personal property.

Personal Record-Keeping Organizer *Work Sheet*

The following Personal Record-Keeping Organizer serves two purposes. First, you can indicate next to each item where that particular item is now located. Second, you can organize your personal records by consolidating your documents into the three files noted below.

I. Items for Storage in a Safe-Deposit Box

Personal

1. Family birth certificates	
2. Family death certificates	
3. Marriage certificate	
4. Citizenship papers	
5. Adoption papers	
6. Veterans papers	
7. Social Security verification	

Ownership

1. Bonds and certificates	
2. Deeds	
3. Automobile titles	
4. Household inventories	
5. Home ownership records (e.g., blueprints, deeds, surveys, capital addition records, yearly records)	
6. Copies of trust documents	

Obligations/Contracts

1. Contracts	
2. Copies of insurance policies	
3. IOUs	
4. Retirement and pension plan documents	

Copies of Estate Planning Documents

1. Wills	
2. Living wills	
3. Trusts	
4. Letters of instruction	
5. Guardianship arrangements	

(Continued on the next page)

Personal Record-Keeping Organizer *Continued*

II. Items for Storage in Home Active File

Current Income/Expense Documents

1. Unpaid bills	
2. Current bank statements	
3. Current broker's statements	
4. Current cancelled checks and money order receipts	
5. Credit card information	

Contractual Documents

1. Loan statements and payment books	
2. Appliance manuals and warranties (including date and place of purchase)	
3. Insurance policies • Home • Life • Automobile • Personal liability • Health and medical • Other:	
4. Receipts for expensive items not yet paid for	

Personal

1. Employment records	
2. Health and benefits information	
3. Family health records	
4. Copies of wills	
5. Copies of letters of instruction	
6. Education information	
7. Cemetery records	
8. Important telephone numbers	
9. Inventory and spare key to safe-deposit box	
10. Receipts for items under warranty	
11. Receipts for expensive items	

Tax

1. Tax receipts	
2. Paid bill receipts (with deductible receipts filed separately to facilitate tax preparation and possibly reduce taxes)	
3. Brokerage transaction advices	
4. Income tax working papers	
5. Credit statements	
6. Income and expense records for rental properties	
7. Medical, dental, and drug expenses	
8. Records of business expenses	

(Continued on the next page)

Personal Record-Keeping Organizer *Continued*

III. Items for Storage in Home Inactive File

1. Prior years' tax returns	
2. Home improvement records	
3. Brokerage advices (prior to three most recent years)	
4. Family health records (prior to three most recent years)	
5. Proof that major debts or other major contracts have been met	
6. Cancelled checks (prior to three most recent years)	

Taking Control   **2**   *Work Sheet*

Personal Budget Planner *Work Sheet*

Individuals and families should prepare budgets just as businesses do. Use this Personal Budget Planner either to record your past cash income and cash expenses and/or to budget future income and expenses. You may want to use the first column to record your past income and expenses, the second column to list your budget over the next month, quarter, or year, and the third column to compare your actual future income and expenses against your budget in the second column. If you budget over a period of less than one year, be sure to consider those expenses that you pay less frequently than monthly, such as insurance, vacations, and tuition. You should be setting aside an amount each month that will eventually cover those large bills.

Indicate at the top of each column whether the amounts in that column are actual or estimated past figures or budgeted future figures. Also indicate the time period in each column, e.g., "March 1995" or "Year 1994."

Budget Planner

Indicate if actual or budgeted			
Indicate the time period			
Cash Income			
1. Gross salary	$	$	$
2. Interest			
3. Dividends			
4. Bonuses/profit sharing			
5. Alimony/child support received			
6. Distributions from partnerships			
7. Income from outside businesses			
8. Trust distributions			
9. Pension			
10. Social Security			
11. Gifts			
12. Proceeds from sale of investments			
13. Other • • •			
14. Total cash income	$	$	$

(Continued on the next page)

Personal Budget Planner *Continued*

Budget Planner

Cash Expenses			
1. Housing (rent/mortgage)	$	$	$
2. Food			
3. Household maintenance			
4. Utilities and telephone			
5. Clothing			
6. Personal care			
7. Medical and dental care			
8. Automobile/transportation			
9. Child-care expenses			
10. Entertainment			
11. Vacation(s)			
12. Gifts			
13. Contributions			
14. Insurance			
15. Miscellaneous out-of-pocket expenses			
16. Furniture			
17. Home improvements			
18. Real estate taxes			
19. Loan payments			
20. Credit card payments			
21. Alimony/child support payments			
22. Tuition/educational expenses			
23. Business and professional expenses			
24. Saving/investments			
25. Income and Social Security taxes			
26. Other • • •			
27. Total cash expenses	$	$	$
Excess (Shortfall) of Cash Income Over Cash Expenses	$	$	$

Establishing Goals and Objectives

Checklist		
Current Status		
Needs Action	**OK or Not Applicable**	
		1. Set some realistic financial planning goals, and plan how you are going to achieve them.
		2. If you experience any major changes in your personal or financial status (major life events), review how your new circumstances will affect your overall financial planning.
		3. Discuss money matters openly and regularly with your spouse.
		4. Create a personal record-keeping system that is comprehensive enough to be useful yet simple enough that you will use it.
		5. Prepare a statement of personal assets and liabilities periodically to measure your financial planning progress.
		6. Select your financial advisors with care, and be aware of potential conflicts of interest they may have.
		7. If you are not satisfied with any of your financial advisors, don't hesitate to make a change.
		8. Be particularly careful in selecting a financial planner. Be sure he or she has the qualifications that are necessary to meet your needs.

Comments:

CHAPTER 3

Assuring Comprehensive Insurance at a Reasonable Cost

How to protect your hard-earned assets from unforeseen disasters including, fire, theft, or a costly illness is what this chapter is all about. In it, you will find out how you, your family, and your property can be adequately insured—for a price you can't afford to do without.

Assuring Comprehensive Insurance at a Reasonable Cost

Questions

How do I know how much life insurance I need?
Is there a quick way to review whether I am adequately insured against all risk areas?
What is a floater policy?
Is umbrella liability insurance necessary or optional?
What is noncancellable insurance?
Which automobile insurance options are important?

Assuring Comprehensive Insurance

Make no mistake, sufficient insurance coverage is essential in taking control of your financial life. Without it, your financial aspirations may go up in smoke, and your best plans for saving and investing could be ruined.

Life is uncertain and risky. Fortunately, there are several types of insurance designed to protect against the risks associated with our day-to-day activities. After you have read the following discussion about insurance, you can use the Insurance Coverage Work Sheet at the end of this chapter to evaluate your current or contemplated coverages.

Important Facts You Should Know

• You have a 55% chance of being involved in an automobile accident in the next three years.

• Eight out of 10 men and women between the ages of 25 and 65 will suffer from an accident or illness that keeps them away from work for an average of 90 days.

• One out of four people suffer a disability of six months or longer at some point before they retire.

Financial Snapshot *Susan Kniser*

"I was so excited when I got my new job, but when my parents told me about the insurance I'd need, it seemed like they were raining on my parade," says Susan Kniser. (She just graduated from college a few months ago, and had landed her first job in a tough job market as an architectural assistant.) "My parents will be delighted to find I'm leaving home to get my own apartment. But I'm beginning to wonder what insurance coverages I will need and if I'll be able to afford them."

Susan may be shocked to learn that insurance can be a big expense, particularly for people starting out in the work world. Even if her company provides good insurance benefits, she can still easily spend 10% to 15% of her income on coverages that her employer doesn't provide. Nevertheless, Susan, like the rest of us, needs adequate insurance coverage—it's essential—even if she doesn't have much in the way of savings and other assets.

> "Sufficient insurance coverage is essential in taking control of your financial life."

When planning the types of insurance and amount of coverage you need, there are several important matters to keep in mind:

• **Cover all essential areas**. You and your insurance agent must make certain that all foreseeable areas of catastrophic risk are insured. The four most common gaps in coverage are (1) inadequate long-term disability coverage, particularly if you are self-employed; (2) inadequate life insurance coverage; (3) lack of an umbrella liability policy; and (4) insufficient coverage on valuable personal possessions such as jewelry and silverware. These are discussed later in this chapter.

• **Obtain the correct policy coverage**. Carefully evaluate each insurance policy before you purchase it so that you are assured of receiving the kind and amount of coverage that you need. Sometimes, you don't need to purchase the most comprehensive policy, but you should be certain that the coverage you receive meets your own specific needs. Also, you should be able to pay any deductibles or policy limits out of your savings.

• **Adjust coverage to meet your changing needs**. Even though you may have adequate coverage now, your needs will change in the future. Therefore, you should review the adequacy of your insurance coverage at least annually. For example, if there is an obvious change in your status, such as marriage, the birth of a child, or a job change, update your coverage as soon as possible.

• **Minimize the cost of insurance**. Studies have shown that many people pay too much for their insurance coverage. Fortunately, companies in the insurance industry are intensely competitive. The premiums they charge for similar coverage can vary dramatically. Thus, you may be able to achieve significant savings by carefully shopping and comparing policy features offered by different companies.

Key Words

Beneficiary The person or persons who will receive payment resulting from a policy claim.

Death benefit The actual coverage or face value of the policy.

Deductible The amount of money you must pay on a policy before your insurance coverage actually takes effect. If, for instance, your policy has a $200 deductible, you would pay the first $200 in claims before the insurance policy pays anything. The higher the deductible, the lower the premium. Deductibles may be annual or apply on a per cause basis.

Insured The person who is insured under the policy.

Owner The person who actually owns the insurance policy.

Premium The amount you pay an insurance company for the coverage you request.

Types of Personal Insurance Coverage

To help you make the best insurance decisions, the following sections will describe the six main categories of personal insurance coverage:
- Life insurance
- Health insurance
- Long-term disability insurance
- Automobile insurance
- Homeowners and renters insurance
- Umbrella liability insurance

Life Insurance

Life insurance provides a way to protect your dependent family members from a loss of income due to the death of one or two breadwinners.

How much life insurance coverage do you need? Determining how much is directly related to making sure your dependents are taken care of if you should die. This can be complicated, but is a necessary calculation. Life insurance companies can provide projections. You can use the work sheet at the end of this section to make the calculation. You also can make a rough estimate from the following general rule of thumb.

First, assuming that you need life insurance, you should start with a bare minimum of four to five times your annual salary. If you have more than one family member who will be financially dependent, you should have six to seven times your annual salary. This minimum would allow your family time to get back on their feet financially after your death. Most importantly, you should provide funds for your children's college education, a lump sum to pay off the home mortgage, and money to provide a lifetime income supplement for your surviving spouse.

"Life insurance provides a way to protect your dependent family members from a loss of income due to the death of one or two breadwinners."

Note: Family insurance needs follow a cyclical pattern. Thus, purchasing insurance that allows you to change the level of coverage is often a good idea. For example, many people's life insurance needs decline significantly once the children have left home and are out on their own. Keep in mind, however, that inflation alone reduces the value of insurance, and other needs and opportunities may arise which justify keeping all the insurance you have.

Life Insurance Policy Alternatives

Life insurance policies can be divided into two broad categories: term and cash value. The basic distinction between them is that term insurance is pure life insurance protection. In other words, your premium buys coverage for only a specified period of time. Cash value insurance provides both insurance protection and a special savings/investment feature. Let's look at each category for a better understanding.

Term Insurance. Term insurance is designed for one purpose only: pure protection for your dependents if you die within the term specified. When comparing policies, you should be aware of three basic types.

1. Level term is a policy in which the death benefit remains level and the premium increases throughout the life of the policy. The premium may remain level for five to 15 years but will eventually increase. It is very practical for people on a fixed budget. It is also the cheapest type of term insurance, but it becomes more expensive as the insured gets older.

2. Decreasing term is a policy in which the premium remains the same each year, while the death benefit declines. People who do not need as much insurance as they get older sometimes own this type of policy.

3. Convertible term policies give you the option of transforming your insurance from term to whole life with no questions asked. This feature may not seem important now, but should your health condition decline, owning a convertible insurance policy could be advantageous since you could convert the term policy before it expires, thereby providing you with insurance for the rest of your life.

With newer term policies, you can increase or decrease coverage as your needs for protection change. Also, you should always request a policy that is guaranteed renewable so that you can keep the coverage even if your health deteriorates.

Cash Value Insurance. Your cash value premium not only buys insurance protection, but part of it is applied to a cash reserve which supports the policy in its later years. Over a period of time, the cash reserve grows and can be used as collateral for a loan from the insurance company or taken as a lump sum on surrender of the policy. One of the most attractive features is that this cash value accumulates tax deferred inside the policy. There are many varieties of cash value policies: whole life, universal life, and variable life.

1. Whole life. A whole life policy is designed to have a level premium as long as you live, which provides a guaranteed death benefit. However, current policies have either dividends or an interest-sensitive design which may increase the death benefit or decrease the premium over the life of the policy.

2. Universal life. This type of insurance product combines the protection of a conventional term insurance policy with the current yields available from short-term investments. But, unlike a whole life policy, the cash value of a universal life policy grows at a *variable rate*.

Universal life's advantage is the flexibility it offers. For example, you can buy additional insurance with the built-up cash value should the need arise. (A medical examination may be necessary.) You also can vary premium payments within the limits established by the policy—a useful feature if your income is subject to periodic fluctuations.

3. Variable life. As with whole life and universal life insurance, a portion of your variable life premium buys pure insurance protection, while the rest is invested by the insurance company on your behalf. The variable life policyholder may choose from a range of investments. For example, you can direct the company to invest your premiums in a combination of stock, bond, and/or money market mutual funds.

There are two kinds of variable life policies. Straight variable life has a fixed annual premium, while universal variable life allows more flexibility to vary the premiums that are paid. In addition to deciding how the money will be invested, you can choose the amount of premiums you can afford to pay in a universal variable life policy.

But you should realize that there are increased risks since stock and bond mutual funds fluctuate in value from time to time. The death benefit of a variable life policy is paid for by the pure insurance part of the policy and will never fall below a specified amount. However, the policy could lapse. The amount of cash value is not guaranteed, and it could be reduced if the investment portfolios perform poorly. The policyowner assumes all of the investment return risk.

Which Kind of Life Insurance Best Meets Your Objectives?

Basically, it depends on your need for protection. For example, parents of young children often need so much protection that term insurance may be their only cost-effective alternative. Also, coverage on the life of the breadwinner(s) may be needed to provide a fund for education purposes. Decreasing term insurance also can be used to pay off a large home mortgage balance.

Sometimes, using a combination of term and cash value insurance can provide both protection and a tax-deferred savings program. People who can't tolerate stock or bond market risks can use this approach.

Before purchasing any type of life insurance, be sure to compare financial ratings on insurance companies. This can be done through the A.M. Best's *Insurance Reports*, available from your local library. Preferably, consider purchasing policies only from financially strong companies rated A++, A+, or A by A.M. Best, Moody's, Standard & Poor's, and Duff & Phelps. Look for the top ratings from the three out of the four rating services.

Health Insurance

Health insurance is designed to take care of major medical expenses—from initial hospital and surgery costs to the medical supplies needed for recovery. This also includes doctor visits and prescriptions. Most importantly, you need to make certain that you and your family members maintain continuous and comprehensive health insurance coverage, whether you enjoy the security of an employer-sponsored plan or pay for your own insurance.

Everyone knows the cost of medical care has risen dramatically over the past few years. Insurance companies have been hit with rising medical claims. As a result, they are very select on whom they will accept for coverage, and the types of medical care they will pay for.

As a general rule, employees of large companies enjoy the best in employer-paid health insurance, while coverage in smaller firms can range from being nonexistent to comprehensive. As insurance companies struggle to meet their ever-increasing costs, even well-insured employees are likely to experience further limits on employer-paid health insurance coverage. More and more employers are requiring their employees to pay part of the premiums for comprehensive group coverage.

Typically, employer-sponsored group plans offer savings of 30% to 40% over equivalent individually purchased plans. For this reason, if your employer offers major medical coverage, by all means take advantage of it and enroll in the plan. Even though you can buy your own medical insurance, it will cost you a lot more money, and your coverage may be much more limited than that provided by an employer-provided policy. Nevertheless, it is crucial to have health insurance coverage for you and your family.

Fortunately, there are several routes to finding an individual policy should it be needed. You can affiliate with a group to get coverage reasonably similar (not as good, but better than an individual plan) to that offered by an employer-sponsored plan. Another choice is to buy it as an individual, whether from an insurance company, health maintenance organization (HMO), or preferred provider organization (PPO).

> "Health insurance is designed to take care of major medical expenses—from initial hospital and surgery costs to the medical supplies needed for recovery."

Basic coverage. Basic medical coverage usually includes hospital room and board; hospital services such as diagnostic services, surgical care, anesthetics, drugs, medical equipment, and supplies; regular health care service to a maximum limit; and sometimes outpatient care. Coverage of medical expenses is provided on an indemnity or service basis.

Coinsurance. Unlike a deductible, which is a stated dollar amount, the insurer pays a fixed percentage share of a major expense. A policy might, for example, pay 80% of daily hospital bills, with the policyholder paying (coinsuring) the remaining 20%. Coinsurance kicks in after the annual or per cause deductible is met. Coinsurance payments are limited by stop-loss clauses, if any.

Excess major medical. This is special insurance designed to take effect when ordinary benefits have been exhausted. If your medical plan has a benefits ceiling, supplemental coverage is a *necessity* in order to protect your financial security.

Guaranteed renewable. Whatever type of policy you buy, make sure that it is guaranteed renewable. This means that your policy can be cancelled only if you fail to pay the premium. Even if your health deteriorates, the insurance company may raise your premium, but it can never cancel your policy.

Indemnity benefit. An indemnity benefit repays the insured for medical expenses incurred in a predetermined fashion.

Major medical. Major medical insurance picks up where basic coverage leaves off. The maximum benefits provided by a major medical insurance plan may be as low as $10,000 or as high as $1 million, and sometimes have no maximum. But if your maximum major medical benefits are under $250,000, you should obtain an excess major medical policy to protect you against a catastrophic accident or illness that could run up medical bills that exceed your maximum coverage.

Scheduled benefit plan. Also known as an indemnity benefit, this plan pays a *fixed sum* toward the amount of each covered medical bill. For instance, an indemnity policy might pay you $275 per day toward daily hospital charges for a semiprivate room.

Service benefit. A service benefit pays a *percentage* of each covered medical bill. Should you get sick and your medical bills balloon, a service benefit will leave you in better shape financially than an indemnity benefit.

"Stop-loss" clause. Most medical insurance plans include a stop-loss clause, which limits the amount of money you will have to spend on coinsurance, cost sharing, or deductibles during the benefit year. For example, a $1,000 stop-loss ceiling means that, once you've paid $1,000 in deductibles, cost sharing, or coinsurance, the insurance company picks up all your remaining expenses for that year. The stop-loss clause usually covers expenses beyond the deductible.

Health Insurance Alternatives

Health Maintenance Organizations (HMOs). HMOs can provide excellent total health care services including doctor appointments (i.e., routine physical exams), hospital stays, operations, prescription drugs, eyeglasses, and podiatry. As with a conventional insurance company, an HMO usually charges a monthly premium. However, HMOs are not insurance companies and are not regulated by state insurance departments.

HMO members must go to a designated health center or centers for treatment. They usually see only those physicians who are part of the HMO. Sometimes employers offer a choice of health care plans. An HMO may be one of these alternatives.

The drawback of any HMO is that your choices are limited. Once you've chosen a doctor, he or she determines what sort of treatment you'll receive and whether you'll need to see a specialist or go to a hospital. Make sure your HMO provides the following health-related coverage and/or services: (1) it allows you to select your own doctor; (2) it provides coverage for unlimited hospital stays, annual physical exams, and preferably for eye care and contact lenses; (3) it provides coverage for emergency care from a non-HMO provider, especially if you require care outside of the HMO's region; and (4) it allows you to change doctors if you're not satisfied with the service or treatment.

Preferred Provider Organizations (PPOs). PPOs are comprised of a group of physicians who band together to provide medical care at discount rates. PPO participants generally pay less to see member physicians and hospitals, but pay at a higher rate if they go outside the PPO for treatment. Membership in a PPO also can be obtained on an individual basis.

COBRA

This is a federal law that ensures continuing group health coverage for most former employees and their dependents. (Most employers must provide an opportunity for a former employee to keep group health insurance.) Passed in 1985, the Consolidated Omnibus Budget Reconciliation Act (COBRA) directs businesses with more than 19 employees to provide continuing group health coverage for at least 18 months after employee termination or resignation. The only exception is for employees who have been fired for gross misconduct.

Long-Term Health Care Insurance. The numbers are staggering: well over $80 billion (nearly 21% of America's total health care expenditures) is being spent on nursing home care costs. And, given our aging population, this number seems destined to skyrocket. Statistics show that 40% of all Americans age 65 or older will spend at least some portion of their lives in nursing homes. Moreover, half of all couples exhaust their entire life's savings within a year of one spouse's being admitted to a long-term care facility. The average annual cost of a nursing home stay is $25,000, a figure that can reach $50,000 or more in some large metropolitan areas. Nursing home care costs have historically risen at a 5.8% annual clip. That means the average annual nursing home cost will be around $118,000 by 2019.

Medicare, even when coupled with private Medigap coverage, generally pays only for posthospitalization stays in skilled nursing facilities. Custodial and intermediate care, the kind that most people in nursing homes receive, is not covered by either Medicare or Medigap.

Long-term care coverage is one way to prepare for possible institutionalization. Faced with these alarming statistics, many people age 50 or older may want to consider a relatively new and increasingly popular type of insurance known as long-term care (LTC) coverage. Offered by private insurance companies competing in an increasingly aggressive market, policy features and benefits have improved considerably in recent years.

- **Who can be covered?** Long-term care insurance is issued to those as young as 40 and sometimes as old as age 84. Level premiums are based on the current age of the insured when the policy is issued. Generally, discounts are available for married couples.

- **How benefits work**. A long-term care policy usually covers four basic types of care: skilled, intermediate, custodial, and home. The first three types of care are usually provided in a hospital-like institution, with different floors or wings dedicated to specific types of care. At-home care requires the services of a paid nurse or attendant: depending on the individual's condition, the care giver might be on duty anywhere from around the clock to only a few hours each day.

Long-term care policies provide daily benefits ranging from $50 to $100 or higher for the first three types of care; benefits for home care are usually half that for nursing home care. The maximum benefit period is usually five years. In place of the deductible required by most standard medical policies, most LTC policies impose an elimination period, or a time period after admission to a long-term care facility during which no benefits are paid. Elimination periods vary from policy to policy, but some insurance companies offer policies with no elimination period at all. The following example shows how a typical long-term-care policy works.

> "Long-term care coverage is one way to prepare for possible institutionalization."

EXAMPLE: At age 73, a male resident of New England pays $2,300 a year for a policy covering a nursing home stay including all levels of care. After an elimination period of 120 days, the policy pays $110 a day for up to four years. Starting in the second year, the benefit increases by 5% annually.

Most policies are guaranteed renewable and include a waiver of premium during the benefit period. Other items a standard LTC policy should include are:

1. A fixed amount of each day's cost of care. Factoring in some inflation protection, a good daily rate is $80 to $100.

2. No prior hospitalization requirement (such as three days) before you can enter a nursing home and get coverage.

3. A waiting period of only 20 days.

4. A preexisting conditions clause which states a minimum number of days. Preferably, you should eliminate this type of clause altogether.

5. Home care at a reduced rate, with maximum payout equal to about half the amount paid for nursing home care. It is essential for you to also have home care since this is becoming a more popular trend for the future.

6. A level premium based on your age when you purchase the policy. Make sure the rate cannot go up unless the increase applies to every policyholder in your state.

7. A guaranteed renewable clause, which means your policy can be cancelled only if you fail to pay the premium.

8. Coverage for three types of care—skilled, intermediate, and custodial—so that no matter what type of care a doctor prescribes, the insurance will pay for it.

9. No prior hospitalization requirement for Alzheimer's disease. Even though most policies say they will cover Alzheimer's, a prior hospitalization requirement could mean you are not covered because the condition doesn't always demand in-patient care.

10. At least three years of maximum coverage, and four to six years if you can afford it. The average stay in a nursing home is currently two-and-one-half years. Unlimited benefits is obviously the best coverage.

Long-Term Disability Insurance

Long-term disability insurance is used to protect you and your family against the loss of income due to a prolonged illness or crippling injury. Generally, the shorter the term of disability, the less the expense. But the longer the term of disability, the greater the need for adequate coverage.

> "Long-term disability insurance is used to protect you and your family against the loss of income due to a prolonged illness or crippling injury."

When it comes to disability insurance protection, age is a very important factor. The younger you are, the more disability insurance protection you are likely to need—even if you're feeling fit as a fiddle. Why? Younger people usually have limited investments, so they have to rely almost entirely on their productive money-making years to make ends meet and to achieve financial security. If a younger person's earning power is interrupted by an uninsured long-term disability, the potential to achieve financial security later on may be seriously impaired.

Is this kind of insurance really necessary? *Yes.* Statistics show that you are seven times more likely to become disabled before you retire than you are to die. Most people assume that Social Security and worker's compensation will provide an adequate safety net. But they don't. Neither is likely to provide the amount you'll need if you become disabled. Numerous cases show the Social Security Administration denies disability benefits to nearly two-thirds of the individuals who apply. Likewise, worker's compensation pays *only* for job-related disabilities. Unfortunately, most accidents and illnesses are *not* job-related.

How much disability insurance do you need? Depending on how much income your asset base can generate, your disability coverage should provide benefits that equal 60% to 70% of your current gross salary. Moreover, your coverage should guarantee benefits until you either recover or reach age 65—when you will be eligible for Social Security retirement benefits. Most importantly, if you determine that all gross income is needed to pay monthly expenses, make sure that income from your disability policy(ies) plus income from other assets will cover them.

Important Disability Insurance Considerations

The two main types of disability insurance are any occupation coverage and own occupation coverage. The first kind will take effect only should your disability prevent you from working at even the simplest, most menial, or low-paying job. The second kind takes effect if your disability prevents you from working at your own occupation. For obvious reasons, you should be sure that your disability insurance provides own occupation coverage.

Some insurance policies define disability as any condition leading to a loss of income. These policies are the most comprehensive, but they are also the most expensive. Make sure that any policy you buy covers disability from both accidents and sickness.

Be sure to check the benefits period. The longer policy benefits cover you (such as 10 years, to age 65, or for life), the higher the premium you will pay.

You also need to know about the elimination period. This is the time that elapses between the onset of disability and the beginning of the benefit period. During the elimination period, you must be able to pay for your own expenses. These periods generally range from 30 days to one year. As long as you can afford to cover a period of disability out of your own savings, you can opt for a longer elimination period. The longer the period, the lower the premium.

Durable Power of Attorney

This is a separate legal document that enables you to name someone to handle your affairs should you encounter long-term or permanent disability. You can empower this person to handle tax matters, direct income to dependents, continue your business affairs, manage investments, and make medical decisions. The importance of having a durable power of attorney is that should you become incompetent from your disability, a trusted person will automatically be appointed to make decisions in your best interest. Durable power of attorney is discussed in more detail in Chapter 7.

Like most insurance products, disability insurance can be enhanced by purchasing riders, such as the following, that broaden your coverage.

- **Noncancellable and guaranteed renewable**. The best policies offer these features. They mean that as long as you pay the premiums to keep the policy in force, the insurance company cannot cancel your protection or increase the premiums, and it must renew your policy on the anniversary date.

- **COLA (cost-of-living adjustment).** The COLA rider is designed to index your benefit to inflation so that your benefit will rise as the cost of living rises. Without it, you would be forced to watch the buying power of your fixed monthly benefit slowly erode.

- **Guarantee of insurability rider.** This means that, when it comes time to renew your existing policy, the insurer will have to sell you a new policy, regardless of the condition of your health, assuming that your income or foreseeable income is adequate to justify additional insurance.

Insurance

3

Sources of Disability Insurance Coverage

Company-Provided Group Insurance.
Your employer may or may not provide some disability coverage (in addition to worker's compensation). If so, take a careful look at the policy and answer the following questions: How much does it pay? How long do you have to be disabled before benefits begin? What other policy provisions determine how, where, and when you receive disability payments?

Association Insurance. If you find that your company insurance is inadequate, you may still be able to get some of the advantages of group disability coverage, similar to what employers provide, by acquiring insurance through professional groups or fraternal organizations. For example, self-employed people may be able to obtain disability coverage for themselves through the local chamber of commerce, or small-business organizations or trade associations. Even if you are not self-employed, it may be worth your time to investigate group disability coverage offered by various organizations that you already belong to or may be able to join.

Individual Insurance. If your employer doesn't provide adequate coverage, you may find that you will need to purchase a disability policy on an individual basis. Even though this option can be very expensive, you usually can obtain much more comprehensive coverage to meet your exact needs. However, make sure that any individual policy is coordinated with your company-sponsored plan so that you don't pay for more coverage than you really need.

Automobile Insurance

Isn't all auto insurance the same? *No.* Automobile insurance provides different coverages for different vehicular-related losses—from personal bodily injury to physical damage to your car. Driving an insufficiently insured vehicle is a shortcut to financial disaster. It also may be illegal. The law in all states requires certain coverage amounts.

Automobile Insurance Policy Provisions

Automobile insurance policies should contain all or most of the following provisions.

Bodily Injury and Property Liability Insurance. This insurance covers injury to pedestrians and occupants of other cars, and damage done by you to the property of others. Automobile insurers routinely categorize bodily injury and property liability insurance with a numerical code. For example, in a policy coded 10/20/5 (or $10,000/$20,000/$5,000), the first number is the highest amount the insurer will pay for bodily injuries suffered by one person, the second is for all persons injured in one accident, and the third is for damage to property.

The amount of bodily injury and property liability insurance you need depends in part upon how much you've accumulated in the way of assets and in part on your earning power. For example, if you are beginning to accumulate investments, you probably want at least $100,000 in coverage for each injured person, with a maximum of $300,000 per accident, and $50,000 for damage to property. Many insurance companies offer a single-limit policy that covers total payments for both property damage and personal injury.

Medical Payments Insurance. This insurance covers medical payments for the policyholder and his or her family members. Also included are other passengers in the insured's car, no matter who caused the accident. This is relatively inexpensive, optional insurance that may be unnecessary if you have adequate health insurance. However, make sure you have enough protection from the medical claims of other injured persons.

Uninsured Motorist Coverage. Uninsured motorist coverage protects you from the hazards of becoming involved in an accident with an uninsured or underinsured driver. This insurance covers the policyholder and any passengers riding in your car at the time of the accident. It also covers the insured and any members of the family if hit by an uninsured motorist while walking or riding a bicycle. Reasonably priced coverage is commonly available.

Collision Insurance. This covers damage to your vehicle no matter what or who caused the accident. Premium costs vary with the amount of the deductible, the type of car, and the extent of coverage. Generally speaking, the older your car, the less sense it makes to have collision coverage.

Comprehensive Coverage. This coverage protects your vehicle against theft, damage from falling objects, vandalism, earthquakes, floods, collisions with animals, and a host of other risks.

Eleven Ways to Reduce Automobile Insurance Premiums

The following pointers can help you prevent your premiums from ballooning out of control.

1. Drive safely. Unsafe drivers are penalized with increased premiums, so avoid speeding tickets and drive defensively.

2. Buy a conservative car. A boring sedan costs less to insure than a flashy sports car that is more likely to be stolen. Check with the insurer prior to purchase to compare premiums on alternative cars.

3. Make your children take driver-training courses. If your child takes an approved driver-training course and receives a grade of B or higher, the insurance company should lower the premium. You also may be able to save on premiums if your child makes good grades in school.

4. Put all family vehicles on one policy. You can reduce your per vehicle premium by about 15% when you insure several vehicles on the same policy.

5. Raise your deductible. Just as with medical insurance, if you are willing to pay a higher deductible, you can usually qualify for a lower premium.

6. Take a defensive driving course. Some states require automobile insurers to reward even seasoned drivers for taking defensive driving courses.

(Continued on next page)

Eleven Ways to Reduce Automobile Insurance Premiums *(Continued)*

7. Buy an antitheft device. Insurers will often reduce premiums for car owners who safeguard their cars with antitheft devices.

8. Join a car pool. An increasing number of insurance companies reduce premiums if you join a car pool.

9. Do your own comparison shopping. Automobile insurance rates are very competitive, so check the rates offered by several quality companies before purchasing your policy.

10. Don't duplicate medical coverage provided by your health insurance policy when purchasing auto insurance. If you have an adequate health insurance policy, you may not need to take the medical-payments or insured-motorist coverages in those states that do not require such coverage.

11. Eliminate comprehensive and collision on cars where the cost benefit justifies such elimination.

"Automobile insurance provides different coverages for different vehicular-related losses—from personal bodily injury to physical damage to your car."

Homeowners and Renters Insurance

Homeowners and renters insurance is designed to insure your property and possessions against loss due to fire, theft, or other risks.

Although most homeowners are aware of the need to insure their home, many remain unwittingly underinsured. The majority of renters, however, tend to be uninsured. Whether you are underinsured or uninsured, the results can be financially disastrous.

Basic Homeowners Coverage

The following items are minimums for basic homeowners coverage:

• The house structure.

• Other structures on the property, for example, a garage or outbuilding.

• Personal property and the contents of the main dwelling, usually up to 50% of the coverage on the main dwelling.

• Living costs incurred while repairing damages caused by an insured risk, usually up to 20% of the coverage on the main dwelling.

• Losses of personal property while away from home, including the possessions of children residing at school, usually with a limit and under certain conditions.

• Personal liability up to a maximum for each occurrence, usually at least $25,000.

• Medical payment for injuries that occur on the premises, up to a maximum per occurrence, usually set at $500 per person.

• Damage to trees, shrubs, and plants up to 5% of the coverage on the main structure.

• Damage to property of others, usually up to $250.

Note: With the exception of areas pertaining to the structure itself, most of the above items are included in standard renters policies.

"Homeowners and renters insurance is designed to insure your property and possessions against loss due to fire, theft, or other risks."

Levels of Coverage

There are three levels of private residency (home) insurance: HO-1, HO-2, and HO-3. The higher the number, the broader the coverage. Renters coverage is HO-4, and condominium coverage is under HO-6. HO-3 policies are the most popular choice for homeowners because of their broad-based coverage and because the cost is only slightly more expensive than HO-2. The following table summarizes the various levels of coverage.

Comparison of Risks Covered Under Various Homeowners Insurance Plans

Comparison of Risks

Risks	Basic HO-1*	Broad HO-2	Special HO-3	Renter's HO-4	Unit Owner's HO-6	Older Home HO-8
Fire or lightning	A,B	A,B	A,B	B	B	A,B
Windstorm or hail	A,B	A,B	A,B	B	B	A,B
Explosion	A,B	A,B	A,B	B	B	A,B
Riot or civil commotion	A,B	A,B	A,B	B	B	A,B
Damage from aircraft	A,B	A,B	A,B	B	B	A,B
Damage from vehicles	A,B	A,B	A,B	B	B	A,B
Damage from smoke	A,B	A,B	A,B	B	B	A,B
Vandalism and malicious mischief	A,B	A,B	A,B	B	B	A,B
Theft	A,B	A,B	A,B	B	B	A,B
Damage by glass or safety glazing material that is part of a building	A,B	A,B	A,B	B	B	A,B
Volcanic eruption	A,B	A,B	A,B	B	B	A,B
Falling objects		A,B	A,B	B	B	
Weight of ice, snow, or sleet		A,B	A,B	B	B	
Accidental discharge or overflow of water or steam from within a plumbing, heating, air-conditioning, or automatic fire protective sprinkler system, or from within a household appliance		A,B	A,B	B	B	
Sudden and accidental tearing apart,cracking, burning, or bulging of a steam or hot-water heating system, an air-conditioning or automatic fire protective sprinkler system, or an appliance for heating water		A,B	A,B	B	B	
Freezing of a plumbing, heating, air-conditioning, or automatic fire protective sprinkler system, or household appliance		A,B	A,B	B	B	
Sudden and accidental damage from artificially generated electrical current		A,B	A,B	B	B	
All perils except flood, earthquake, war, nuclear accident, and others specified in policy			A			

Notes: A = Dwelling   B = Personal Property   *HO-1 coverage, while still available in some states, is being phased out.

Insurance

3

38

Note: Condominium or cooperative owners need to know the legal responsibilities that come with these forms of ownership. Condo owners, for example, are liable if the condominium association is sued and is not able to cover the full settlements. In such an instance, each unit owner is assessed to cover the gap. Check the adequacy of the association's master policy to ensure there is a loss-assessment insurance endorsement. If none exists, the association should add it. Otherwise, one can be added to your own insurance policy for a minimal fee.

Take a Personal Inventory

Taking an inventory of your personal possessions is crucial to assuring that you get back what you deserve in the event you suffer a loss. Your insurance agent should be able to provide you with a work sheet to help you make a complete listing. Record all identifying information, including serial numbers, as well as the complete description of your personal possessions. Photographs of furniture, appliances, etc., will be a big help. Another alternative is to videotape all your possessions. (Don't forget the garage.)

Store your inventory (videotape and photographs) somewhere away from your house—preferably in your safe-deposit box, which is fireproof. Also, when acquiring new possessions, remember to keep your inventory up-to-date by adding receipts and recording the proper information.

Optional Coverage

Many homeowners and renters will benefit from selecting one or more of the following coverage options.

Replacement Cost Coverage on Your Home. Homeowners/renters insurance should cover at least 80% of the replacement value of your home, allowing for annual inflation. Replacement cost coverage is more expensive (usually 10% to 15% higher) than the basic coverage, but it's worth it. The reason is simple: it offers much more protection in the event you suffer a major or total loss.

Replacement Cost Coverage for Household Contents. This option allows both homeowners and renters to avoid disputes with the insurer over the actual cash value of losses. For example, if your seven-year-old television set worth only $75 is stolen, it is much better to have the insurance company pay you $500 to replace the set, rather than its actual cash value of only $75.

Floater Policy. A floater provides extra coverage for specified valuable possessions such as jewelry. If you keep these valuables at home or use or wear them, they should be covered under a floater policy. This will require a professional appraisal unless they have just been purchased. A floater provides a specific amount of insurance for each object on an itemized basis—guaranteeing full replacement value and eliminating deductibles.

Likewise, be sure that the floater policy provides all-risk coverage. This means that you will be reimbursed no matter what the cause of the loss. This even includes a "mysterious loss," in which you might not have any idea how an item was lost.

Safe-Deposit Box Coverage. The contents of safe-deposit boxes are not insured by the bank, and insurance coverage under a regular homeowners policy is limited to only $500 or less. Therefore, if you store valuables there, a rider on your safe-deposit box would be advisable. Be sure to maintain an up-to-date inventory of its contents in a separate place.

Insurance

3

Business-Related Property Inside the House. Personal computers and other equipment used to operate a home-based business must be insured separately. Basic home office coverage is often available as a rider to the regular homeowners policy. Be sure to see if your occupation qualifies for the coverage. These riders also extend homeowners liability to include business-related injuries and reimbursement for damage to business equipment. Basic home business policies are available separately.

Host Liquor. Liability for alcohol-related accidents incurred by someone who consumed too much alcohol at your home or apartment may not be covered unless you have added host liquor coverage or have a comprehensive policy. Be sure to check with your insurance agent about this type of coverage.

Earthquake. A standard homeowners insurance policy does not cover either an earthquake or a flood (although fire caused by an earthquake is covered). These disasters may be covered by an addition to the homeowners policy. Costs of these riders vary according to the region's vulnerability to earthquakes and to the type of house to be insured.

Flood. A flood is another frequently over-looked event that could cause catastrophic damage to your property. Flood insurance is available from the federal government for flood-prone areas. Some private companies also offer coverage.

When to Review and Revise

No homeowners or renters policy should go beyond three years without updating. Ask your insurance agent to periodically review your policy, especially after you move to a new area.

Umbrella Liability Insurance

Personal liability umbrella policies will protect you and your family from claims arising out of nonprofessional activities. For example, if your dog bites a neighbor or if your car rolls into the street and hits the mail truck, umbrella insurance will protect you. It is usually coordinated with your automobile and homeowners/renters insurance policies, and is designed to take over when your homeowners or renters and automobile policy liability limits have been exceeded. In our lawsuit-crazed society, this is a policy few should go without.

Note: Umbrella insurance does *not* cover any liability resulting from your professional activities.

A good umbrella policy will protect you, family members living in your home, children attending school away from home, and even pets. In addition, the policy should cover legal defense costs, critically important since even the successful defense of a lawsuit can be very costly. The *best* protection against the threat of a lawsuit is to purchase a personal liability umbrella insurance policy.

An umbrella policy can be obtained at a reasonable cost. Naturally, the premium will vary depending on your personal circumstances, such as the size of your family, number of homes you own, etc.

> "Personal liability umbrella policies will protect you and your family from claims arising out of nonprofessional activities."

Professional Liability and Malpractice Insurance

Professional liability insurance isn't something only doctors and lawyers need. This coverage—also called errors and omissions insurance—is used for a diverse array of professionals, including veterinarians, medical technicians, nurses, accountants, architects, insurance and real estate agents, and engineers.

Most often, the company that handles your homeowners and automobile policies is the one to turn to for this type of protection. Your company may require you to boost the liability limits on your homeowners (or renters) and automobile policies. So, in addition to the umbrella insurance premium,

you also may have to pay somewhat increased homeowners and auto insurance premiums to boost those policies' underlying liability coverage. If you need professional liability insurance, check with your insurance agent or a professional who specializes in insuring small businesses. Also, check with your professional or trade association(s) about liability insurance. You may be able to purchase it through one of these organizations, which can refer you to companies that insure members of your profession. Another source of information might be professional colleagues or people who own businesses similar to yours.

Financial Snapshot *Continued*   *Susan Kniser*

Susan met with her parents' insurance agent to help her evaluate the coverage provided by her employer and to have him recommend a program to make sure she had no gaps in her overall insurance coverage. Fortunately, her employer provided enough health, disability, and life insurance coverage to meet her immediate needs (although she's going to have to pay a large portion of her health insurance premium out of her own pocket). The family agent told Susan that she would have to buy an automobile insurance policy (required by law), and he encouraged her to purchase a

renters insurance policy, as well as a personal liability umbrella insurance policy.

"After the initial shock of learning about all the insurance I needed, I found out that I'm not going to be impoverished by insurance premiums. The agent reminded me that I needed to be aware of how my changing personal and financial life may affect my future insurance needs. Now that I feel that I have adequate protection at an affordable price, I have peace of mind that will allow me to concentrate on making a success of my new job."

Insurance

3

41

Insurance Evaluation *Checklist*

The following insurance checklist corresponds to the subsections in Chapter 3. Using checklists is a good way to ensure that you have attended to important insurance matters.

Insurance Evaluation

General Guidelines

Look for comprehensive policies and avoid narrowly defined coverage (e.g., cancer policies).
To reduce premiums, take the largest deductible you can afford.
Ask your agent to shop around for the best policy at the best price.

Life Insurance

Determine how much life insurance you need. One rule of thumb is that a worker with a spouse and two children should carry at least enough insurance to cover five to seven times his or her net annual income. (Add another year of income for each additional dependent.)
Determine whether term or cash value life insurance (or a combination) will best meet your needs. Term insurance buys the most protection per premium dollar over the short run, but cash value insurance can provide more flexibility and tax advantages. Often a combination of term and cash value is the best way to acquire life insurance protection.

Health Insurance

Review your health insurance policy to make sure you fully understand the extent of its coverage and its limitations.
Make sure *all* family members have adequate major medical insurance, including children away at school, parents, and adult children.
If you become unemployed, disabled, or divorced, take advantage of the provisions under COBRA to continue health care coverage.
If your employer does not offer health insurance coverage, or if you are self-employed, investigate the purchase of insurance on your own, preferably through an association, but, if necessary, on an individual basis.

Disability Insurance

Obtain and maintain sufficient disability insurance coverage to replace 60% to 70% of your work income. (Keep in mind that employer-provided disability benefits are taxable.)
Make sure you understand your disability insurance policy's features and limits, particularly your company's disability policy.
If you need to purchase a disability policy individually, compare several policies and evaluate carefully the various features they offer.

Automobile Insurance

Buy sufficient automobile insurance coverage in essential areas, but reduce or eliminate unnecessary coverage.
Look for ways to reduce your automobile insurance premiums.

(Continued on the next page)

Insurance Evaluation *Continued*

Insurance Evaluation

Homeowners and Renters Insurance

	Always maintain adequate homeowners or renters insurance coverage.
	Review your coverage at least every two years, and change it when necessary.
	Maintain replacement cost coverage on your home.
	Maintain replacement cost coverage on your personal possessions.
	If you have valuables, insure them separately with a floater or with an endorsement on your policy.
	Take a personal inventory of your household possessions, and keep that inventory up-to-date.

Umbrella Liability Insurance

	Protect yourself and your family from financially devastating lawsuits with umbrella liability insurance.
	Examine your umbrella policy to make sure that you understand its limits and that all family members are covered.
	If you are a self-employed professional or small-business owner, you probably need professional or business liability insurance.

Comments:

Insurance Coverage *Work Sheet*

Evaluate your insurance coverage status with the following work sheet. This will help you pinpoint weaker areas of coverage so that you can insure accordingly.

Insurance Coverage

Date:_____

Type of Insurance	Source of Coverage	Coverage Adequate	Coverage Not Necessary	Improved Coverage Needed	Coverage Needed but Not Yet Obtained
Life					
Health					
Disability					
Homeowners/Renters					
Automobile					
Umbrella liability					
Professional liability					

Comments:

Life Insurance Needs *Work Sheet*

Use the following work sheet to estimate your life insurance needs. If you enter amounts for each category of need, the resulting estimate should be viewed as a *maximum* amount of insurance that will meet all foreseeable needs of your survivors. **Note:** All amounts should be expressed in terms of current dollars.

Life Insurance Needs

Expenses

1. Final expenses (onetime expenses incurred by your death)

   a. Final illness (medical costs will probably exceed health insurance deductibles and coinsurance, so assume that you will have to fund at least those amounts) $.....................

   b. Burial/funeral costs   ....

   c. Probate costs (if unsure, assume 4% of assets passing through probate process)   ....

   d. Federal estate taxes (for most estates over $600,000 willed to someone other than spouse)   ....

   e. State inheritance taxes (varies by state)   ....

   f. Legal fees, estate administration   ....

   g. Other   ....

   h. Total final expenses $.....................

2. Outstanding debt (to be paid off at your death)

   a. Credit card/consumer debt   ....

   b. Car   ....

   c. Mortgage (if it's to be paid off at your death; otherwise, include payments in life income)   ....

   d. Other   ....

   e. Total outstanding debt $.....................

(Continued on the next page)

Life Insurance Needs *Continued*

Life Insurance Needs

3. Readjustment expenses (to cover the transition period of immediate crisis)

   a. Child care ....

   b. Additional homemaking help ....

   c. Vocational counseling/educational training (for a nonworking
      or underemployed spouse who expects to seek paid employment) ....

   d. Other ....

   e. Total readjustment expenses $.....................

4. Dependency expenses (until all children are self-supporting)

   a. Estimate your household's current annual expenditures ....

   b. To remove the deceased person's expenses, multiply this figure by:
      .70 for a surviving family of one
      .74 for a surviving family of two
      .78 for a surviving family of three
      .80 for a surviving family of four
      .82 for a surviving family of five

      $.................. (Line 4a) x .... (factor) = ...

   c. Deduct spouse's estimated annual income
      from employment (..................)

   d. Equals current annual expenses to be covered by currently
      owned assets and insurance ....

   e. To determine approximate total dependency expenses
      required, multiply by number of years until youngest child
      becomes self-supporting:

      .... (Line 4d) x .... (years) = ...

   f. If support for dependent parent(s) is to be provided,
      multiply annual support by the number of years such
      support is expected to continue:

      $.................. x .... (years) = ...

   g. Total dependency expenses (add Lines 4e and 4f) $.....................

(Continued on the next page)

Work Sheet

Insurance

3

Life Insurance Needs *Continued*

Life Insurance Needs

5. Education expenses

   a. Annual private school tuition in current dollars
      (if desired) ....

   b. Multiply by number of years and children left to attend:

      $.................... (Line 5a) x .... (years) = ...

   c. Annual college costs in current dollars ....

   d. Multiply by number of years and children left to attend:

      $.................... (Line 5c) x .... (years) = ...

   e. Total education expenses (add Lines 5b + 5d) $....................

6. Life income (for the surviving spouse after the children
   are all self-supporting)

   a. Annual amount desired (in current dollars) ....

   b. Deduct spouse's estimated annual income
      from employment   (....................)

   c. Equals annual expenses to be covered by currently
      owned assets and insurance   ....

   d. Multiply by number of years between when the youngest
      child becomes self-supporting and the surviving spouse
      begins receiving Social Security benefits and other
      retirement income, if any:

      $.................... (Line 6c) x .... (years) = $....................

7. Retirement income for surviving spouse

   a. Annual amount desired in current dollars
      (less Social Security and any pension income)   ....

   b. Multiply by number of years of life expectancy after
      retirement begins:

      $.................... (Line 7a) x .... (years) = ...

8. Total funds needed to cover expenses:
   (add lines 1h, 2e, 3e, 4g, 5e, 6d, 7b)   ....

(Continued on the next page)

Life Insurance Needs *Continued*

Life Insurance Needs

Assets currently available to support family

Proceeds from life insurance already owned $....................

Cash and savings ....

Equity in real estate (if survivors will sell) ....

Securities ....

IRA and Keogh plans ....

Employer savings plans ....

Lump-sum employer pension benefits ....

Other sources ....

9. Total assets ....

Additional life insurance required

10. Subtract available assets (Line 9) from total funds needed to cover expenses (Line 8). This shortfall represents the estimated amount that must be covered through life insurance. $....................

Work Sheet

Insurance

3

Life Insurance Needs *Work Sheet: Sample*

Sample for Married 40-year-old with $350,000 Estate

Use the following work sheet to estimate your life insurance needs. If you enter amounts for each category of need, the resulting estimate should be viewed as a *maximum* amount of insurance that will meet all foreseeable needs of your survivors. **Note:** All amounts should be expressed in terms of current dollars.

Life Insurance Needs

Expenses

1. Final expenses (onetime expenses incurred by your death)

   a. Final illness (medical costs will probably exceed health insurance deductibles and coinsurance, so assume that you will have to fund at least those amounts) $2,500

   b. Burial/funeral costs 2,500

   c. Probate costs (if unsure, assume 4% of assets passing through probate process) 14,000

   d. Federal estate taxes (for most estates over $600,000 willed to someone other than spouse) 0

   e. State inheritance taxes (varies by state) 7,000

   f. Legal fees, estate administration 2,000

   g. Other 1,000

   h. Total final expenses $29,000

2. Outstanding debt (to be paid off at your death)

   a. Credit card/consumer debt 800

   b. Car 4,300

   c. Mortgage (if it's to be paid off at your death; otherwise, include payments in life income) 0

   d. Other 6,700

   e. Total outstanding debt $11,800

(Continued on the next page)

Life Insurance Needs *Sample Continued*

3. Readjustment expenses (to cover the transition period of immediate crisis)

   a. Child care   1,200

   b. Additional homemaking help   400

   c. Vocational counseling/educational training (for a nonworking or underemployed spouse who expects to seek paid employment)   10,000

   d. Other   2,000

   e. Total readjustment expenses $13,600

4. Dependency expenses (until all children are self-supporting)

   a. Estimate your household's current annual expenditures   37,000

   b. To remove the deceased person's expenses, multiply this figure by:
       .70 for a surviving family of one
       .74 for a surviving family of two
       .78 for a surviving family of three
       .80 for a surviving family of four
       .82 for a surviving family of five

       $37,000 (Line 4a) x .78 (factor) =   28,860

   c. Deduct spouse's estimated annual income from employment   (18,000)

   d. Equals current annual expenses to be covered by currently owned assets and insurance   10,860

   e. To determine approximate total dependency expenses required, multiply by number of years until youngest child becomes self-supporting:

       $10,860 (Line 4d) x 14 (years) =   152,040

   f. If support for dependent parent(s) is to be provided, multiply annual support by the number of years such support is expected to continue:

       $0 x 0 (years) =   0

   g. Total dependency expenses (add Lines 4e and 4f) $152,040

(Continued on the next page)

Life Insurance Needs *Sample Continued*

Life Insurance Needs

5. Education expenses

   a. Annual private school tuition in current dollars
      (if desired)   0

   b. Multiply by number of years and children left to attend:

     $0 (Line 5a) x 0 (years) =   0

   c. Annual college costs in current dollars   12,000

   d. Multiply by number of years and children left to attend:

     $12,000 (Line 5c) x 8 (years) =   96,000

   e. Total education expenses (add Lines 5b + 5d) $96,000

6. Life income (for the surviving spouse after the children are all self-supporting)

   a. Annual amount desired (in current dollars)   25,000

   b. Deduct spouse's estimated annual income
      from employment   (18,000)

   c. Equals annual expenses to be covered by currently
      owned assets and insurance   7,000

   d. Multiply by number of years between when the youngest
      child becomes self-supporting and the surviving spouse
      begins receiving Social Security benefits and other
      retirement income, if any:

     $7,000 (Line 6c) x 11 (years) = $77,000

7. Retirement income for surviving spouse

   a. Annual amount desired in current dollars
      (less Social Security and any pension income)   6,000

   b. Multiply by number of years of life expectancy after
      retirement begins:

     $6,000 (Line 7a) x 25 (years) =   150,000

8. Total funds needed to cover expenses:
   (add lines 1h, 2e, 3e, 4g, 5e, 6d, 7b)   529,440

(Continued on the next page)

Insurance

3

Sample

Life Insurance Needs *Sample Continued*

Life Insurance Needs

Assets currently available to support family

Proceeds from life insurance already owned	$100,000
Cash and savings	50,000
Equity in real estate (if survivors will sell)	0
Securities	114,000
IRA and Keogh plans	46,000
Employer savings plans	10,000
Lump-sum employer pension benefits	80,000
Other sources	0
9. Total assets	400,000

Additional life insurance required

10. Subtract available assets (Line 9) from total funds needed to cover expenses (Line 8). This shortfall represents the estimated amount that must be covered through life insurance.	$129,440

Disability Income Needs *Work Sheet*

The following work sheet will help you determine how much disability insurance you need.

Disability Income Needs

Resources needed

1. Total annual family living expenses $...................

2. Subtract annual expenses which go away if you become disabled, such as taxes (disability benefits may be partly or fully tax free)*, work-related expenses, entertainment, and travel (...................)

3. Adjusted annual family living expenses (subtract Line 2 from Line 1) ....

Resources available

4. Annual income from savings and investments (dividends and interest) ....

5. Annual income from spouse's job ....

6. Disability benefits provided by employer's policy ....

7. Disability benefits provided by other disability policies currently owned ....

8. Total available resources (add lines 4, 5, 6, and 7) ....

9. Additional resources needed either from liquidating assets or additional disability insurance (subtract Line 8 from Line 3) $...................

*If you become disabled, very few expenses go away, but only benefits for which the insured paid the premium are tax free.

Disability Income Needs *Work Sheet*: *Sample*

The following work sheet will help you determine how much disability insurance you need.

Disability Income Needs

Resources needed

1. Total annual family living expenses	$37,500
2. Subtract annual expenses which go away if you become disabled, such as taxes (disability benefits may be partly or fully tax free)*, work-related expenses, entertainment, and travel	(9,500)
3. Adjusted annual family living expenses (subtract Line 2 from Line 1)	28,000

Resources available

4. Annual income from savings and investments (dividends and interest)	400
5. Annual income from spouse's job	15,000
6. Disability benefits provided by employer's policy	3,500
7. Disability benefits provided by other disability policies currently owned	0
8. Total available resources (add lines 4, 5, 6, and 7)	18,900
9. Additional resources needed either from liquidating assets or additional disability insurance (subtract Line 8 from Line 3)	$ 9,100

*If you become disabled, very few expenses go away, but only benefits for which the insured paid the premium are tax free.

Automobile Insurance Rate Comparison *Work Sheet*

Use this work sheet to compare automobile insurance premium quotations.

Auto Rate Comparison

	Amount of Coverage		Annual Premium Quotations	
Minimum coverage state requires for:		Name of Insurer:	....	....
Bodily injury liability	$...................		$...................	$...................
Property damage liability	....		....	....
Personal damage protection (no-fault states)	....		....	....
Uninsured motorist	....		....	....
		Subtotal:	$...................	$...................

	Amount of Coverage		Annual Premium Quotations	
Level of coverage desired for:				
Bodily injury liability	....		....	....
Property damage liability	....		....	....
Medical payments	....		....	....
Personal-injury protection (no-fault states)	....		....	....
Collision with:				
a. $100 deductible	....			
b. $250 deductible	....			
c. $500 deductible	....		....	....
d. $1,000 deductible	....			
Comprehensive with:				
a. No deductible	....			
b. $100 deductible	....			
c. $250 deductible	....		....	....
d. $500 deductible	....			
e. $1,000 deductible	....			
Uninsured motorist	....		....	....
		Subtotal:	$...................	$...................

(Continued on the next page)

Automobile Insurance Rate Comparison *Continued*

Auto Rate Comparison

	Amount of Coverage	**Annual Premium Quotations**	
Other coverage:			
Towing and labor	$....................	$....................	$....................
Rental car reimbursement	....	....	....
	Subtotal:	$....................	$....................
Other applicable charges:			
Membership fee	....	....	....
Surcharges	....	....	....
	Subtotal:	$....................	$....................
	Total annual premium:	$....................	$....................
	Less estimated dividends, if any:	(....................)	(....................)
	Net annual premium:	$....................	$....................

Comments/recommendations:

_____

_____

_____

_____

_____

_____

_____

_____

_____

_____

_____

_____

_____

_____

_____

_____

Work Sheet

Insurance

3

CHAPTER 4

Smart Investment Principles

This chapter teaches you everything you wanted to know about investments but were afraid to ask. In plain English, you'll learn to identify the kinds of investments that will help you meet your most important financial goals.

Smart Investment Principles

Questions

Why is inflation a major concern for investors?
What is dollar cost averaging?
How can I tell if real estate investing is right for me?
Is it important to invest in stocks?
Are bonds a good investment when interest rates are low?
What is a P/E ratio?
Are mutual funds a good idea for all investors?

Investing for a Secure Financial Future

In this chapter, you will learn about the many different types of investments—stocks, bonds, mutual funds, real estate, and more. You also will learn how to evaluate whether a potential investment makes sense for you.

The following five rules will help you become a better investor:

1. Know why you're investing. Everyone invests for different reasons, even if we all share one overall goal: achieving ultimate financial security. Some common investment goals also might include providing an emergency fund for unforeseen events, meeting major expenses—a first home, college education, a daughter's wedding—and, most importantly, saving for a comfortable retirement. You must be clear about your investment goals in order to achieve them.

2. Invest for growth. *Every* investor needs to invest some money for growth to offset the effect that inflation and taxes will have.

(Continued on page 60)

Financial Snapshot   *Nathan and Adelaide Newhart*

The birth of a second child—combined with a $25,000 inheritance—has jolted Nathan Newhart, age 38, and his wife Adelaide, age 35, into realizing that they need to get serious about investing. Most of this couple's $15,000 in savings is deposited in a low-yielding money market account, although Nathan did recently invest some money in a municipal bond fund. Neither Nathan, a service rep for a vending machine manufacturer, nor Adelaide, a restaurant manager, has ever taken the time to learn about the fundamentals of investing.

The $25,000 that Nathan inherited from his Uncle Damon, if properly invested, could be the cornerstone of a comfortable retirement fund, or could serve as a source of college tuition money. If the Newharts follow their usual investment pattern and put the inheritance money in certificates of deposit and savings bonds, inflation will steadily erode the value of their assets. Nathan and Adelaide are at a financial crossroads, and the choices they make now could have a major impact on their future financial security.

Bond An IOU issued by a government or corporation. It promises that the issuer, or borrower, will repay the principal to the lender (bond purchaser) at a specified future date, plus pay any interest over the life of the bond to its owner.

Bond yield The return earned on an investment. There are four types of yield: coupon yield, which is the interest rate stated and paid on the face value of the bond; current yield, which is based on the current market price of the bond; yield to call, which is based on the current yield and the difference between the purchase price of the bond and its call price (the price a company pays to redeem the bond prior to maturity); and yield to maturity, which is based on the current yield and the difference between the purchase price of the bond and the face value of the bond.

For example, if you own a $1,000 face value (coupon yield) 7% coupon bond with a 10-year maturity, you will receive $70 each year in interest payments. If that bond is currently selling at $920, the current yield (the coupon interest payment divided by the bond's current market price) would be 7.6%. The yield to maturity would be about 8.1%. Yield to maturity takes into account the coupon yield plus or minus the difference between the current value of the bond and the face value of the bond.

Diversification A principle that emphasizes the importance of investing in several different types of stocks and bonds, and allocating a percentage of the funds within each class. This guards against putting all of your investment dollars into a single type of investment and, by so doing, helps you counteract the effect of a decline in any one type of stock or bond, or in one particular investment class, such as common stocks.

Face value Value of a bond when issued and, usually, when it matures. Corporate bonds are usually issued with $1,000 face value; municipals with $5,000; Treasury bills with $10,000. Face value is also called par value.

Inflation An increase in the average price level of goods and services over time.

Mutual fund A corporation or trust whose only business is the investment of its shareholders' money, generally in common stocks, bonds, or money market instruments. It brings together the investable funds of many people with similar needs and objectives, with the hope of achieving a specific investment goal. It also endeavors to do a better job of investing, at a lower cost, than the individuals could actually do for themselves.

Portfolio An investor's combined holdings of stocks, bonds, real estate, and other investments.

Prospectus A document explaining a mutual fund's specific objective, what the fund invests in, how the fund will be managed, what the minimum investment amount is, and how you can purchase and redeem shares.

Stock A security that represents a portion of ownership in a corporation and that gives the owners (stockholders) a private interest in the assets and the earnings of the business. Ownership of stock also usually conveys the right to vote on matters of interest to the owners of the corporation.

Investments

4

3. Diversify across investments. Diversification is key to successful investing. No one investment category and no one industry has consistently outperformed all the others. When choosing particular areas of stocks, bonds, and mutual funds to invest in, don't bet too heavily on what's hot in the current market. Rather, consider what investment classes will continue to be attractive five and 10 years from now.

4. Diversify within investments. Diversifying among investment classes—holding a certain percentage in stocks, bonds, and mutual funds—is a good start to a successful investment portfolio. Within each category of investment, however, some are going to thrive, and others will not. The best way to protect yourself from the effect of a mediocre stock, bond, or mutual fund is to select more than one to invest in. You may want to hold an international stock mutual fund as well as a U.S. stock mutual fund to take advantage of investment opportunities both at home and abroad.

5. Take control over your investments. Perhaps the most important attribute of a successful investing program is to stay in touch with all your investments. Don't rely on someone else to watch over your portfolio and make all of your investment decisions. While professionals can make helpful suggestions, you also should be well enough informed to be able to make the final decision. (The Investment Management Action Plan at the end of the chapter will help you determine what you need to do to get your investments in order.)

It's easy to *not* plan ahead. For many young people, concern about funding a secure retirement does not compete with the costly and current realities of purchasing a new home and raising children. By the time they reach their 40s, thoughts of retirement start to set in—only to be pushed aside by the costs of college tuition or more concern with "buying" a more opulent life-style. Studies show that many people wait until they pass age 50 to focus on funding their retirement. That's unfortunate because, as the following chart illustrates, the sooner you start to save regularly and invest those savings wisely, the greater your chances of successfully meeting the financial challenges throughout your entire life.

The Importance of Investing Wisely				
Age When You Begin Investment Program	If you invest $2,000 per year at these average annual rates of return:			
	4%	6%	8%	10%
	At age 65 you will have accumulated:			
25	$190,000	$310,000	$518,000	$885,000
35	112,000	158,000	227,000	329,000
45	60,000	74,000	92,000	115,000
55	24,000	26,000	29,000	32,000

What percentage of your total income should be saved now? It depends on your current goals and how much money you will need to achieve them. For example, if saving for retirement is your objective, the chart above will give you an idea of how much you can accumulate by age 65 based on your current age. A careful analysis will determine how much you actually will need based on an estimate of retirement expenses and whether you work for a company that funds a pension plan for you.

The bottom line is, you should save at least 10% of your gross income. Given the common financial hurdles that most of us will have to overcome during life, like the erosive effects of inflation, and longer life expectancies, saving 15% to 20% of your income is preferable. Of course, those who prefer spending to saving will have another option: working three jobs to put their children through college, and flipping burgers at a fast-food joint when they're 75 in order to support their own "retirement." Do you really want to be in that position?

Inflation works against your savings. When considering how much money you will need to reach your financial goals, you must factor in the impact of inflation on the cost of living. For example, assuming that inflation averages 3.5% per year, your living expenses will double in about 20 years. If you anticipate needing the purchasing power of today's $30,000 in 20 years—for your child's college tuition or for your retirement—you will need, if living costs do double every 20 years, $60,000 at that time.

Therefore, your investment program should assure, over the long run, that your assets provide you with a rate of return that beats inflation. Assume, for example, that inflation for a given year is 4% and a certificate of deposit happens to have a 4% return for that year. On an inflation-adjusted basis, the CD just kept pace with inflation; it produced a zero inflation-adjusted return. On top of that, if the CD interest also was subject to income taxes, it actually lost ground to inflation after taxes were paid on the interest. If a stock mutual fund rose by 9% in a year when inflation was 4%, this investment beat inflation handily.

One of the advantages of owning stocks and stock mutual funds is that they have generally outperformed other types of investments when held for at least five to 10 years.

The following table shows how well stocks have fared in comparison with short-term interest-earning investments (as measured by U.S. Treasury bills) and long-term corporate bonds. These amounts have been adjusted for inflation.

Inflation-Adjusted Returns on a $10,000 Investment			
	Treasury Bills	Long-Term Corporate Bonds	Common Stocks	Inflation Rate
5 years from 1988 to 1992	$1,000	$ 4,700	$ 7,000	4.22%
10 years from 1983 to 1992	$3,500	$13,600	$20,700	3.81%
20 years from 1973 to 1992	$3,200	$ 8,500	$15,600	6.21%

Source: © *Stocks, Bonds, Bills, and Inflation 1993 Yearbook*™, Ibbotson Associates, Chicago (annually updates work by Roger G. Ibbotson and Rex A. Sinquefield). Used with permission. All rights reserved.

Note: Corporate bonds and stocks actually produced lower inflation-adjusted returns over the 20-year investment period than they did over the 10-year period. That's because the high inflation rates that prevailed from the mid-1970s through 1981 took their toll on the inflation-adjusted performance of all investments during that period.

Remember, the true test of a successful investment is how well it's able to keep ahead of inflation over many years.

> "The bottom line is, you should save at least 10% of your gross income."

4

An Investment Primer

Sorting out and understanding numerous investment alternatives is actually easier than you may think. Let's start by examining the three main categories of investments.

1. Interest-earning securities. These are divided into two components: bonds (fixed income) and cash equivalents (CDs and money market accounts). Fixed-income investments, including Treasury, municipal, and corporate bonds, are interest-earning securities with maturities greater than one year after their issue date. Backed by the "full faith and credit" of the federal government, Treasury bonds and notes are considered the safest bonds. Next in safety are municipal bonds. While they aren't guaranteed by Uncle Sam, they are backed by state and local governments or by specific revenue sources. And although cities and towns can default, or fail to pay their debts, they very rarely do. (Defaulting would seriously impair the issuer's credit rating.)

Least secure are corporate bonds. Why? Because these bonds are usually only backed by the company that issues them, their degree of safety is directly related to the company's health. If a firm goes bankrupt, the bonds can become worthless. Thus, bonds issued by financially strong blue-chip corporations are the safest type of corporate bond. To help investors evaluate the risk of corporate (and municipal) bonds, some companies, notably Standard & Poor's and Moody's, rate bond quality. Junk bonds are on the opposite side of the safety coin. They have lower ratings and are high-risk investments.

Cash equivalents are investments considered to be of such high liquidity and safety that they are virtually as good as cash. In addition to CDs and money market accounts, other cash equivalents are money market mutual funds and Treasury bills.

2. Stocks. Most people think of stocks as a synonym for investments. Yet, paradoxically, many Americans never take advantage of stock ownership because they consider them too risky. But they should because stocks can provide both regular income (in the form of dividends) and inflation-beating appreciation (increase in value over time).

3. Real estate. Owning real estate is perhaps the most complicated form of investing. Evaluating a property's potential for income, appreciation, and its tax ramifications is very difficult. On top of that is the need to monitor—and if you buy the properties yourself, manage—the property once it's purchased. Some people opt for passive real estate ownership through a limited partnership, which considerably simplifies the process of real estate investing. But it in no way safeguards your investment from real estate slumps. The easiest way to participate in the real estate market is to buy shares of real estate investment trusts (REITs), which are discussed later in this chapter, but returns may be far less than you could attain by buying individual properties.

All three investment categories will be discussed in greater detail later in this chapter.

> "…Develop a plan that will help guide you both in deciding on the types of investments to make and in reviewing your investments periodically."

Allocating Investments

Investing effectively is crucial to your financial success. Therefore, you need to develop a plan that will help guide you both in deciding on the types of investments to make and in reviewing your investments periodically. Periodically doesn't mean every day; otherwise, you'll become so concerned that you'll end up making investment changes too frequently. Rather, if you establish sensible criteria now, you will be able to invest wisely without needing to spend an inordinate amount of time worrying about your investments. The four steps to allocating your investments are:

Step 1: Decide how much of your money should be invested in stocks and how much in interest-earning securities (bonds and short-term securities).

Step 2: Once you know how much of your portfolio should be in each investment category, you need to determine how to purchase the securities you want. You can buy individual stocks and interest-earning securities yourself, or you can take advantage of professional management by investing in mutual funds. You may well want to use some combination of both approaches.

Step 3: For each investment category, determine what types of investments would be appropriate for your portfolio objectives and comfort level.

Step 4: Finally, you need to select and purchase the actual securities—such as a particular stock, bond, or mutual fund—that will work to achieve your investment goals.

Ideally, most portfolios should contain a balanced combination of the various types of investment vehicles discussed above, interest-earning investments (both cash equivalents and bonds), stocks, and, perhaps, real estate.

Once you have determined how to divide your portfolio, you can decide whether to directly—or indirectly—own your investments. Owning individual stocks or bonds is a form of direct investing, whereas buying stock or bond mutual funds is an increasingly popular form of indirect investing. Indirect investing means buying shares in a fund whose professional managers buy individual stock or bond issues for the fund investors.

Deciding how much of your hard-earned money to place in indirect as opposed to direct investments depends on several factors, including how much you have to invest and how much time you and/or your investment adviser want to devote to monitoring individual stock and bond investments. For purposes of illustration, assume that you want to maintain a 50%/50% split between total stock investments and total interest-earning security investments. A possible allocation might be as follows:

	25% in directly owned common stocks
	25% in stock mutual funds
Subtotal	50% in stock investments
	25% in directly owned, interest-earning investments
	25% in interest-earning mutual funds
Subtotal	50% in interest-earning investments
Total	100%

Once you have allocated your assets among directly and indirectly owned investments, you need to divide these investment categories further into specific industry, market, and/or fund categories. Directly owned, interest-earning investments might consist of short-term investments (money market accounts, certificates of deposit), municipal bonds, corporate bonds, and Treasury bonds. If you also decide to invest in interest-earning mutual funds, you might consider a Treasury bond fund and a municipal bond fund.

Finally, you will need to select specific investments within each of the industry or mutual fund categories that you have identified. (A detailed, step-by-step investment allocation plan appears later in this chapter.) One of the most important prerequisites for investment success is knowing to ask the right questions. Familiarizing yourself with the array of commonly available investments will help you ask the right questions so that you can become a more informed investor.

Interest-Earning Investments

All interest-earning investments share the following characteristics: they pay interest at specified intervals, and they pay you back the face value of your investment either on demand or when the security matures, depending upon the type of maturity you're investing in. A bond is an interest-earning investment. However, all interest-earning investments are not bonds.

Interest-earning investments can be broken down into two categories: cash equivalents and bonds (also known as fixed-income investments).

Cash Equivalents

Cash equivalents are short-term interest-earning securities that can be readily converted into cash with little or no change in principal value. In other words, you get your original investment back—no more and no less—when you sell, plus you receive interest along the way. Cash-equivalent investments include money market accounts (sold by banks), money market funds (sold by mutual fund companies), savings accounts, CDs, and Treasury bills. They provide stability of principal and offer interest rates that change periodically. (In contrast, bonds or fixed-income investments offer stable interest, but the principal can fluctuate.) The interest paid on cash-equivalent investments fluctuates when overall interest rates change. Hence, if interest rates decline—as they did in the early 1990s—investors who had a lot of money invested in cash equivalents end up suffering from declining interest income on these investments.

Because the interest rates on cash equivalents are generally close to the inflation rate for the same period, they are best viewed as a temporary parking place for your money while you are awaiting a more attractive investment opportunity.

Bonds

While the attention of the news media is usually focused on the stock market, bonds and bond mutual funds have been undergoing evolutionary changes that have made them both more complex and, at the same time, more attractive investments.

> "A bond is a certificate of debt or IOU issued by a government or corporation."

What is a bond? A bond is a certificate of debt or IOU issued by a government or corporation. It promises that the issuer, or borrower, will make payment at specified times.

Bonds are generally referred to as fixed-income investments because, in most cases, the interest rates they pay remain constant for the life of the bond. An investor who purchases a bond locks in a specific interest rate for as long as he or she owns the bond. It also means that an investor is exposed to an element of risk if interest rates should rise during this holding period.

The value of fixed-income investments moves in the opposite direction from changes in interest rates. Therefore, if interest rates rise, the value of your bond will decline, and vice versa. Some of the many available fixed-income investments include Treasury notes and bonds, U.S. savings bonds, mortgage-backed securities, municipal bonds, corporate bonds, and convertible bonds.

Treasury Securities

These securities are the means by which the U.S. government borrows money. Treasury bills, notes, and bonds are issued regularly by the Federal Reserve and are a popular investment for people who want very little risk. Since these are direct obligations of the U.S. government, the interest on Treasury bills, notes, and bonds is exempt from state income taxes.

Treasury bills are cash-equivalent debt instruments issued at various maturities; auctions of 90-day and 182-day bills take place weekly, and the Treasury also auctions 52-week bills once every four weeks. Treasury bills are issued in minimum denominations of $10,000, and subsequent purchases may be made at $5,000 increments. Treasury bills are sold at a discount from their face (maturity) value. The amount of the

discount is equal to the interest that will be paid at maturity. Therefore, upon maturity, the investor receives the face value of the Treasury bill. Treasury notes and bonds are fixed-income obligations that have longer terms and pay interest semiannually at a fixed interest rate. They are sold at face value.

An interesting subspecies of U.S. Treasury securities is the zero-coupon bond. These bonds pay no interest along the way. Instead, they are sold at a deep discount or at a price that is much lower than the maturity value of the bond. Since you don't get any interest during the holding period, your profit comes at maturity in the form of a large increase in the amount you receive. The *main advantage* to zero-coupon bonds is that you are guaranteed a set return at the original interest rate. Therefore, if interest rates decline, you don't have to worry about reinvesting interest income at a lower rate. This automatic compounding also avoids your having to decide on reinvesting the interest you would receive on a regular bond. One *main drawback* of zero-coupon bonds is that even though you are not receiving interest along the way, the IRS assumes that you are for tax purposes, so you have to pay income taxes on the imputed interest income. The upshot? These are good investments for retirement accounts such as IRAs and Keogh plans because taxes are deferred until you withdraw the income at a later date.

U.S. Savings Bonds

These are a popular way for savers to invest in government securities. Although they don't offer the highest rate of interest, savings bonds are a sound and comfortable way for investors to build up their savings. U.S. savings bonds also offer some tax advantages, as discussed later in this chapter.

Mortgage-Backed Securities

These securities have peculiar sounding names like Ginnie Mae, Fannie Mae, and Freddie Mac. These investments represent pools of mortgages backed by the specific government agency. Their relatively high yields have been attracting a lot of investor interest. They can be bought either individually or through a mutual fund, which offers a wider degree of diversification and security.

Municipal Bonds

Municipal bonds are used to finance long-term projects for cities, towns, villages, territories, and states. They are very popular investments because the interest they generate is free from federal taxation. Sometimes, if you purchase bonds of issuing authorities in your own state (or bonds of Puerto Rico and other U.S. territories), the interest is also exempt from state income taxes and, perhaps, local income taxes. These investments also can be purchased individually, or through a family of mutual funds.

Corporate Bonds

Corporations issue bonds to raise money just like the U.S. government and state governments. Due to changing economic conditions, some corporate bonds are no longer the safe haven for investors' money that they used to be. Too much borrowing and the sometimes rapidly deteriorating financial condition of corporations require careful selection and monitoring. Therefore, investors of corporate bonds are well advised to stick with highly rated bonds.

Convertible Bonds

These are corporate bonds that can be converted into stock at a predetermined price. They are more attractive to some investors than, say, regular bonds because they enable investors to gain from the appreciation of the underlying common stock. However, this conversion privilege usually means their yields are one or more percentage points below those of a straight bond.

Four Investment Risks You Need to Know About

Some people mistakenly think of bonds as staid, riskless investments. But like stock investing, bond investing isn't risk free. Four risks you should know about that affect the bond market are:

Interest Rate Risk

This is the risk that your investment's value will fluctuate with changes in the general level of interest rates. Because interest rates can fluctuate widely over the course of a year, price volatility is a factor that must be considered in planning and selecting fixed-income investments. Of course, when it comes to investing in a bond fund, such planning is left to experienced managers who are in touch with the day-to-day changes in the bond market and the overall economy.

In general, if interest rates rise, the market value of a bond declines. Conversely, if interest rates decline, the market value of a bond increases.

Purchasing Power Risk

This is the risk that a bond will lose purchasing power if inflation heats up. Because bonds have set interest rates and pay back the principal at a future date, they do not offer an inflation hedge.

Credit Risk

This is the risk of default by the bond issuer. In other words, it's the risk that you won't get your money back or the issuer won't make an interest payment. This is why corporate and municipal bonds are risk rated by rating agencies such as Standard & Poor's Corporation and Moody's Investors Services, Inc.

Note: Securities with a lower credit rating pay a higher rate of interest because investors generally require a higher incentive to take on the higher risk that the issuer will default.

Call Risk

This is the risk that a bond will be called, or bought back prior to maturity by the issuer on demand. This generally takes place after interest rates have declined substantially. Calling a bond then allows the issuer to reissue the bonds at a much lower interest rate. Investors in bonds that are called will then have to reinvest their money at lower interest rates.

Note: Some corporate and municipal bonds have call protection, which is a guarantee that a security can't be bought back by the issuer or they will not be called until a specific amount of time has elapsed. U.S. Treasury securities usually are not callable. A few bond issues are callable five years prior to maturity.

Interest-Earning Investment Strategies

The best time to purchase bonds (or bond mutual funds) is when you think interest rates are high and are unlikely to rise further and/or are likely to fall.

Fluctuating interest rates combined with the proliferation of many different kinds of bonds have discouraged many people from investing in these types of instruments. Instead, they are content with short-term securities such as money market funds. Yet, with a little effort, they can increase investment returns by taking advantage of the many bond investments that are available today.

The following nine tips will help you make savvy bond investments.

1. Seek expertise when necessary. Investments in bonds that you are unfamiliar with, perhaps foreign bonds, should definitely be made through a mutual fund with management specializing in these areas.

2. Keep an eye on price volatility. Since interest rates can fluctuate widely over the course of a year, price volatility is a factor that must be taken into account in planning and selecting bonds. Generally speaking, the longer the maturity date, the more volatile the price of that particular issue.

3. Ladder maturities. Laddering, or staggering, the maturities of bond investments is a tried and true strategy. Rather than investing in a single issue or in several issues with roughly the same maturity, you should opt for a variety of maturities—some short-term (less than three years), some intermediate-term (three to 10 years), and some long-term (10 to 30 years). That way, if there is a significant change in interest rates, you will have avoided placing a heavy, and perhaps incorrect, bet on a single maturity. Simply stated, laddering maturities reduces the risk in any bond portfolio. Don't forget to set some of the maturities to coincide with when you may need the money (for instance, to meet college tuition bills or to provide money during your retirement years).

If you invest in bond mutual funds, you also can follow a similar laddering strategy by spreading your money among money market and short-term bond funds, intermediate-term bond funds, and long-term bond funds.

4. Compare interest rates. Interest rates vary among types of bonds, both within the same investment category and between alternative categories. For example, if you shopped around a little, you might discover that the rate paid on CDs at your local bank is not as good as it might be. Over the past several years, interest rates on tax-exempt bonds have been very attractive compared with the after-tax returns on Treasury securities and corporate bonds.

5. Don't chase yield. While shopping for yield is a virtue, chasing yield is a sin. A bond investment that pays 10% interest when other bonds of the same type and maturities are at 6% is trying to tell you something. This probably is a junk bond (a high-yielding, highly risky type of bond that has a low, speculative credit rating) or similarly risky investment. Don't be fooled. Always remember, the higher the yield, the higher the risk.

6. Diversify. Unless you have only a very small amount of money to invest, don't concentrate your interest-earning investments in a single or very few securities. Select several different issues and several different categories of investments or mutual funds.

7. Keep maturities relatively short. Even though longer-maturity interest-earning investments usually have higher yields than shorter-maturity investments, many experts contend that there is usually not enough of a difference to justify the greater risks in concentrating on long-maturity bonds. Remember, the longer the maturity, the more the value of the bond will fluctuate in reaction to changes in interest rates.

8. Use mutual funds for investing in unusual bonds. If you want to invest in foreign bonds, chances are you won't have the time or ability to track the market as closely as a smart investor needs to do. By investing in a foreign bond mutual fund, you can diversify the bond portion of your portfolio and, at the same time, take advantage of the professional manager's foreign bond expertise.

9. Consider the tax effects. You may be able to increase your investment returns by carefully examining the tax effects of alternative interest-earning investments. While some are fully taxable, interest on Treasury securities is federally taxable but exempt from state taxes. Municipal bond interest is exempt from federal taxes and may be exempt from state taxes. It is important to keep in mind that the federally taxable securities should be purchased for your tax-deferred retirement accounts. Tax-favored investments like municipal bonds should be purchased for your personal investment account.

(Continued on page 71)

Savings bonds occupy territory between cash-equivalent and fixed-income investments. Unlike the other bonds described in this chapter, U.S. savings bonds are not fixed-income investments: they pay a variable interest rate, the amount of which is recalculated every six months. This interest rate is set at 85% of the benchmark five-year Treasury yield, with a 4% floor, which limits how far the bond yield can sink.

Series EE bonds sell for half their face or redemption value, which ranges from $50 to $10,000. The bonds must be held for at least five years to receive the minimum rate. Interest is subject to federal, but not to state and local taxes.

U.S. savings bonds offer several tax-deferral features. They are not subject to state and local taxes. Federal taxes on accrued interest can be deferred until you redeem your bonds or until your bonds reach maturity, whichever comes first. U.S. savings bonds have a variety of attractive features in addition to the Series EE tax deferral. For one thing, they may be used as a tax-free college savings vehicle. An exchange provision allows Series EE bonds to be converted into Series HH bonds in increments of $500.

Effective March 1, 1993, the guaranteed minimum rate on savings bonds was lowered to 4% from 6%. Series EE bonds issued on or after March 1 are subject to the new 4% minimum rate. Outstanding Series E and EE savings bonds and savings notes will retain their previously guaranteed minimum rates until the end of their original maturity periods or current extended maturity periods. (For example, for bonds purchased after November 1, 1986, the interest rate is 4.16% for the first six months, 4.27% for the first year, and then up 1/4% every six months until the

> "U.S. savings bonds are not fixed-income investments: they pay a variable interest rate, the amount of which is recalculated every six months."

fifth year, when it reaches 6%. For bonds purchased before November 1, 1986, this floor is set at 7.5%.) Similarly, Series HH savings bonds issued on or after March 1 will earn interest at a flat 4%, while outstanding Series H and HH bonds will retain their current interest rates until the end of their original maturity periods or current extended maturity periods.

The reduction in the guaranteed minimum rate was in response to the substantial decline in overall interest rates. The 6% minimum rate had become an above-market rate, spurring record sales of savings bonds, and calling the cost effectiveness of the savings bond program into question. The last change in the guaranteed minimum rate took place on November 1, 1986, when the minimum was reduced to 6% from 7.5%, in response to a sharp drop in market interest rates.

The market-based rate system and other basic features of Series EE bonds remain unchanged, assuring bond owners a competitive return under all market conditions. Series EE bonds held five years or longer earn the higher of the guaranteed minimum rate or the market-based rate.

(Continued on the next page)

Investments

4

The original maturity period for Series EE savings bonds issued on or after March 1, 1993, will be lengthened from 12 years to 18 years. The extended maturity will remain at 30 years. As a result, interest accruing at the guaranteed new minimum rate of 4% will double in 18 years (as opposed to 12 years when the rate was 6%).

No matter which bonds you own—EE or HH—you or your designated beneficiaries will be required to pay federal taxes on the face value amount when the bonds are redeemed or mature. (Note: Bonds from the old series—A, B, C, D, F, G, J, and K— no longer earn any interest and should be cashed in.) In addition, you will have to pay taxes on the interest paid on your HH bonds. However, if you redeem the bond and reissue it in the name of your child (the only way to legally give away a U.S. savings bond is to redeem it and reissue it in the name of your donee), and your child is under age 14, then the first $600 of investment income will not be taxed. The next $600 will be taxed—but at the child's rate—and any investment income over $1,200 will be taxed at the adult's (higher) rate.

If you own savings bonds, you may be headed for taxes on some of your bonds sooner than you think. For example, Series E bonds reach their final maturity after 40 years. If you elected to defer reporting the interest, the entire accrued interest becomes taxable in the 40th year, unless you exchange them for HH bonds. This exchange will allow you to defer reporting the interest until you redeem the HH bonds. A caveat: Series E bonds held for more than 40 years can't be exchanged for HH bonds. Moreover, many Series E and EE bonds have a 30-year maturity timeline. Series E bonds issued December 1965 through June 1980 mature from December 1995 to June 2010. Series EE bonds issued May 1967 to October 1970 mature from May 1997 to October 2000, and those EEs issued January 1980 and after start maturing in January 2010.

What is the advantage to the exchange provision that allows Series EE bond investors to convert the EE bonds into HH bonds? The conversion allows you to defer payment of taxes on the E or EE bonds' principal and accumulated interest amount. In other words, if you swap your Es and EEs for HHs, you don't have to report the accrued interest on the E or EE bonds to the IRS until you cash the HHs in. You will pay federal income taxes on the annual interest received from your Series HH bonds.

You can postpone the tax on your E or EE bonds' accrued interest for as long as 10 years or until you redeem the HH bonds— whichever comes first. After 10 years, there may be an extension period—typically 10 to 20 years—which will allow you to continue to defer reporting and paying taxes on the face value amount of your HH bonds.

Finally, while investors are guaranteed their principal back when the bond reaches maturity, they will probably incur stiff penalties by cashing in U.S. savings bonds before five years have elapsed.

> "If you own savings bonds, you may be headed for taxes on some of your bonds sooner than you think."

Purchasing Interest-Earning Investments

You can buy cash-equivalent or bond investments directly by buying individual securities through banks or stockbrokers, or indirectly through a mutual fund where, in essence, you buy a portion of a diversified portfolio of interest-earning securities. You need to evaluate how interest-earning investments fit into your overall investment portfolio (including your retirement accounts) and then decide the kinds of interest-earning securities that are most suitable. While interest-earning investments belong in every portfolio, the proportion of these investments in your total portfolio, as well as the type of investment vehicles, will depend on your particular financial situation and objectives.

Stocks

This section is designed to help you make an informed decision about stock investing. It will explore such areas as what stocks are, their advantages and risks, how you can tell if they're the right investment for you, and how you can select and purchase them.

The Stock Markets

Where are U.S. stocks traded? There are more than 10 active U.S. stock exchanges, but three major U.S. markets account for 99% of all stock trading: the New York Stock Exchange (NYSE), the American Stock Exchange (AMEX), and the National Association of Securities Dealers Automated Quotation (NASDAQ).

- **The NYSE** is the oldest and largest of the stock exchanges. Stocks of the largest U.S. companies are traded on the NYSE, together with those of many midsized companies. Examples of NYSE-listed stocks are Coca-Cola, General Motors, and IBM.

> "Stocks have consistently proven to be the best inflation-beating vehicle for long-term investors."

- **The AMEX** stocks are comprised mainly of smaller to midsized companies—in particular, a large number of oil and gas companies. Also, more foreign shares are traded on the AMEX than on any other U.S. exchange. Examples of AMEX-listed stocks are BIC, Hasbro, and Turner Broadcasting.

- **The NASDAQ** is a computerized system owned by the National Association of Securities Dealers. It has the second-largest dollar volume of trading (the NYSE is first). It provides brokers and dealers with price quotations from securities traded over the counter. Examples of stocks listed on the NASDAQ are Amgen, Lotus, and Microsoft.

Why is investing in stocks so important? If you are not investing in today's stock market, you risk falling short of realizing your financial goals. Why? Stocks have consistently proven to be the best inflation-beating vehicle for long-term investors. And if your investments aren't beating inflation, you're losing ground to the ever-increasing costs of living.

What Are the Risks?

There are risks to stock investing. For example, along with the opportunity of increasing stock prices, investors also must accept the risk that stock prices will decline. The risks (which can occur for a variety of reasons) include the following.

Individual Stock Price Fluctuations

Many new investors become too preoccupied with short-term fluctuations in the prices of stocks they own. Individual stock prices are always changing; however, there are ways to control price risk.

First, you can reduce risk by diversifying your holdings among several companies and industries. This includes owning stocks in larger, well-established corporations. While this can reduce portfolio volatility, the best way to protect yourself against unfavorable changes is to keep current on matters pertaining to the companies in which you've invested. Also, pay close attention to industry trends that may affect your companies. Unfortunately, even if a corporation's financial outlook does not change, the price of its stock can, and often does, fluctuate. Some causes of this fluctuation include intermittent transactions by buyers and sellers of the stock and investors' periodic preferences for different types of investments.

Stock Market Fluctuations

Everyone knows about the volatility of the stock market. Surprisingly, in only five of the years from 1970 to 1992 did overall common stock prices decline. Sometimes the yearly declines were substantial (almost 21% in 1974). Another way to look at it is that stock prices rose in 18 of the years from 1970 to 1992, including leaps of 37% in 1975, 32% in 1985, and 30% in 1991.

While you can't ignore price fluctuations, you shouldn't become preoccupied with them either, because they may simply be responding to overall market fluctuations. To the extent that price fluctuations are caused by market forces, your willingness to accept the risks associated with stock investing are likely to be rewarded with good, inflation-beating returns.

How Stocks Are Classified

There is a wide variety of common stock investments. Some pay dividends; others don't. Some have relatively stable prices; others are more volatile. Despite this variety, most common stocks can be classified into one of the following categories.

Growth Stocks

Investors buy growth stocks for capital appreciation. Because many companies have to finance their growth and may be involved in expensive research, most or all of their earnings are reinvested in the company for future expansion. Thus, growth stocks have the potential for increased market value, and they pay little in dividends. Therefore, prices of growth stocks are usually more volatile than those of other stocks.

Income Stocks

Income stocks are bought for current income because they tend to have a higher-than-average dividend yield. Companies whose stocks fall into this category are usually in fairly stable industries (for example, telecommunications and utilities), have strong finances, and pay out a substantial portion of their earnings in dividends. Many of the stocks are considered total return stocks because they offer the opportunity for both dividends and capital appreciation.

Blue-Chip Stocks

Blue-chip stocks are considered the highest quality of all common stocks because they are dominant companies that have the ability to pay steady dividends in both good and bad times. For example, all of the 30 stocks that compose the Dow Jones Industrial Average are blue-chip stocks. These companies hold dominant positions in industries that generally are not as vulnerable to cyclical market swings as in other industries.

Cyclical Stocks

Cyclical stocks are represented by companies whose earnings tend to fluctuate sharply with their business's cycles. When business conditions are good, a cyclical company's profitability is high and the price of its common stock rises; when conditions deteriorate, the company's sales, profits, and market price fall sharply. For example, when interest rates are high and business conditions slow down, the housing and steel industries suffer tremendously. The timing of ownership is crucial to a successful investment in cyclical stocks.

Defensive Stocks

In contrast to cyclical stocks, some companies are considered recession resistant. They sell products or provide services whose demand does not fluctuate with business cycles. Examples include food, cosmetics, and health care stocks.

Small Company Stocks

Small company stocks, also known as small cap stocks, are stocks of companies that typically have a total stock market value of less than $500 million. These stocks are usually traded on the over-the-counter market. Historically, small company stocks have outperformed larger company stocks—but they are more volatile because smaller companies usually have less stable and predictable earnings, and/or they may have insufficient assets to weather a business downturn.

Speculative Stocks

In a sense, all common stocks are speculative, since they offer a variable rather than a fixed return like a bond. But some stocks are more speculative than others. A speculative stock is subject to wider swings in share price—down as well as up—so it's riskier. For example, hot new issues, high-flying glamour stocks, and penny stocks are speculative stocks.

(Continued on page 75)

Investments

4

73

Stock Financial Indicators

When they evaluate a stock before purchase, successful investors scrutinize a variety of financial indicators. The following will help you do likewise.

• **Earnings per share.** This is a very popular indicator of a company's financial well-being, and it is determined by dividing a company's net income by the total number of common shares outstanding. A stock's price tends to keep pace with the growth or decline in its earnings. That's one reason why companies with steady growth in earnings per share are usually favored by both novice and professional investors.

• **P/E multiple.** The price/earnings multiple is determined by dividing the current market price of a stock by its earnings per share. For example, a stock whose earnings per share is $3 and whose stock price is $60 has a P/E multiple of 20 ($60/$3). The P/E multiple (also called the P/E ratio) is commonly used by investors who want to know how much they are paying for a company's earning power—and whether that price is reasonable or extravagant. But don't be horrified by what appears to be extravagance—it could be based upon severely depressed earnings or a particularly attractive stock. What may be more important to an investor is identifying sound companies trading at P/E multiples that are lower than the average P/E multiple for companies in the same industry. Theoretically, at least, a good company trading at a below-average P/E multiple should rise in value at a greater rate than its industry peers once the market discovers the company's real value.

• **Book value.** The difference between a company's assets and its liabilities, divided by the number of shares outstanding, will give you its book value per share. Investors use book value to help locate companies whose market price is attractive in relation to their book value. But looks can be deceiving, especially when it comes to book value. Many investors mistakenly assume that book value is synonymous with actual market value; in other words, the asset values on the company's balance sheet represent the current market value of the assets. Just because a company has an attractive book value per share in relation to its market value per share doesn't mean that it can't fall on hard times. Penn Central was a company with a book value per share of more than $60 just before it went bankrupt. Therefore, investors are always on the lookout for companies with asset values that are understated and are wary of companies with overstated asset values.

For example, take a semiconductor manufacturer that bought equipment only five years ago. That equipment is still on the books at a value of $8 million. However, if that company were to sell the equipment today, advances in the efficiency of the latest equipment may cause the actual cash value received to be a fraction of the $8 million book value.

(Continued on the next page)

Companies with undervalued assets are a real find for value investors. Some companies have assets that, because of the rules of accounting, are actually valued on their balance sheets at a fraction of what they're worth. One example of such a company is Woolworth. Its land and heavily depreciated buildings are thought to be worth far more than their book value. Oil companies also may be attractive to value investors since many own vast tracts of oil-rich land that are valued on their balance sheets at much less than they are thought to be worth.

• **Leverage.** Leverage relates to the amount of debt owed by a corporation in relation to the amount of its stockholders' equity. Highly leveraged companies have a higher proportion of debt compared with equity. Conservative investors tend to prefer companies with low leverage—in other words, with relatively low amounts of debt. More aggressive investors often prefer highly leveraged companies, because leverage may be advantageous for the common stockholders when the corporation's earnings are high—once interest is paid, shareholders share in the remainder of the earnings. Since debt interest must be paid before common stockholders are entitled to dividends, high leverage works against stockholders when earnings decline.

• **Return on equity (ROE).** ROE can be useful, particularly when comparing several companies within one industry. ROE measures the rate of return on investors' capital. To derive ROE, divide earnings per share by book value per share. For example, a company with earnings per share of $1.50 and a book value of $10 has an ROE of 15% ($1.50/$10). ROE measures how efficiently company management uses stockholders' equity. Value investors favor companies with above-average ROEs compared with companies with below-average ROEs in the same industry.

• **Dividend yield.** A company's dividend expressed as a percentage of the stock's current market value is known as its dividend yield. Investors seeking current dividend income prefer stocks with higher dividend yields (as long as the high yield is not caused by a severely depressed and declining stock price). Value investors look to dividend payment histories to determine strengths and weaknesses. Companies with long histories of consistent dividend payments, and preferably rising dividends, are favored by value investors.

Tips for Investing in Stocks

There are no guarantees for stock investment success, but there are many ideas that may prove to be helpful to you. Here are 10 of them.

1. Never buy stocks indiscriminately. Many investors buy stocks haphazardly simply because they have money to invest. This is a very bad practice; make investments only when you have a good reason to buy them.

Investments

4

2. Select a promising industry. At any given time, most industries in the economy are either on the upswing or the downswing. When choosing a stock, start by selecting a promising industry with a good future outlook. Then, look for a company within that industry whose prospects look the most promising.

3. Diversify. Try to own stocks in several different industries. The danger of too many eggs in one basket can't be overemphasized. However, overdiversification is also unwise. It's easier to keep track of five to 10 stocks than it is 25 stocks. You generally can achieve excellent diversification with about 10 well-chosen stocks.

4. Buy low and sell high. You don't necessarily have to be a contrarian to condition yourself to buy stock when a company's share price is down and sell it when the price is up. Stocks can gain when prices are low, and major selling opportunities come when the stock is hot (everybody wants to own it) and prices are high. This is the famous buy low, sell high rule; it's recommended that you use caution when following this or any other stock market strategy.

5. Stay abreast of market trends. Look at the general trend in the market. A stock that already has risen in value might be a good candidate for continued gains if the market is still rising. Conversely, a stock that does not respond to a general market rise might turn out to be a candidate for selling.

6. Use stop-loss orders to protect against loss. Potential losses can be effectively limited by using stop-loss orders, (they're not available on over-the-counter stocks), which fence in gains by restricting the effects of a market downturn on your stocks. Stop-loss orders also can be used to force you to sell. For example, say you buy a stock at $12 per share and it rises to $18 per share. You might put a stop-loss order in at $15 per share to lock in a gain. The risk of this strategy is that you might get left behind at $15 per share if the stock continues rising, but this may be less risky than a loss due to a sharp decline.

7. Buy value. Companies with strong finances (not too much debt) and solid earnings growth are consistently better long-run performers.

8. Buy low P/E /high dividend stocks. Many successful long-term investors use the investment strategy of purchasing common stocks of companies with relatively low price to earnings multiples and relatively high dividend yields. The logic behind this is that the stock price is depressed (a low P/E multiple), and hence, the stock is being purchased when no one else wants it. This is in itself a good strategy as long as the company has no major long-term problems. Moreover, when the stock price rises, the company probably will attempt to maintain its high dividend yield by raising its dividend. Investors, therefore, get the best of both worlds: rising stock price and higher dividend income.

9. Buy stocks in companies with strong dividend payment records. Consider stocks in companies that have a consistent history of paying generous dividends. In a bear market (in which stock prices have declined), these companies tend to decline less in price than companies that pay no dividend at all or pay dividends erratically, since investors are confident that the dividends will keep coming through thick and thin. Some companies have paid annual dividends for more than 100 years!

10. Finally, rely on your own experience and judgment. Often, looking for successful companies to invest in doesn't require that you go to Wall Street. Investment ideas can come from your own observations of how things are selling on Main Street. This common sense strategy (on Wall Street, it's known as real economics) has been used by some of the most successful investors and money managers for years. The next time you go to the mall, keep your eyes open for new investment opportunities.

Mutual Funds

A mutual fund is a professionally managed investment company comprised of a pool of investors' money used to purchase a diversified portfolio of stocks, bonds, money market instruments, or other securities. Each share in a mutual fund represents a small slice of the mutual fund's total portfolio.

The first open-end mutual fund started in 1924. However, it wasn't until the late 1970s, and particularly during the past decade, that mutual funds started to flourish. In fact, mutual funds grew from just over $100 billion in assets in 1980 to more than $1.6 trillion in assets by 1993. The result is that today there are more than 3,400 mutual funds to choose from compared with around 500 just a decade ago.

> "A mutual fund is a professionally managed investment company comprised of a pool of investors' money used to purchase a diversified portfolio of stocks, bonds, money market instruments, or other securities."

Why are mutual funds such a popular way to invest? There are several reasons, including the ease of investing in them. But one of the most important reasons may be their performance. The *average* stock mutual fund's annual rate of return over the past decade was almost 12%. In fact, many top-performing funds rewarded their investors with even greater returns.

What are other benefits associated with investing in mutual funds? Owning mutual funds is a low-cost way to diversify your investments, thereby reducing investment risk. Also, mutual funds are managed by experienced professionals who are responsible for monitoring and managing the stocks and/or bond holdings continuously. There are other benefits as well. You can add to your fund investments regularly and easily. Bookkeeping tasks, such as depositing dividend and interest checks and keeping track of securities transactions, are avoided. You have access to a number of convenient services, such as an option to automatically reinvest dividends and capital gains and automatic investments at regular intervals; and you can easily keep up-to-date on the performance of the funds you invest in since they're listed in the financial pages of the newspaper.

Of course, there are drawbacks. For one thing, like the securities they invest in, a stock or bond fund's asset value will fluctuate with changing market conditions. For another, the commission and fee structures of mutual funds can be confusing. The funds range from no-loads, which carry no sales commission and are sold directly to the public, to low-load funds, which have a commission of 1% to 3%, to load funds, which typically charge commissions of 4% to 8.5%. Some funds assess a charge if you redeem your fund shares within a specified period of time. Some funds also charge a sales distribution fee each year you hold the fund. (You always should find out about a fund's loads and fees before investing in it. See the section later in this chapter for more details on mutual fund fees.)

Mutual fund investors can't control the timing of capital gains taxes since it is the fund manager who makes the decisions about selling fund holdings. In contrast, if you held individual stocks or bonds, you could control the timing of capital gains recognition by simply selling or deferring the sale of a particular stock.

Mutual Fund Categories

Mutual funds vary in size, objective, and the type of investments they hold. As a result, knowing how and why they differ is important. First, there are three major fund categories:

1. Stock funds. A stock (or equity) mutual fund invests its money in stocks of individual companies, large and small, new and old, here and abroad.

2. Bond funds. A bond mutual fund invests its money in bonds of companies or governments that are as varied as those that stock funds invest in.

3. Money market funds. A money market fund invests its money in short-term financial instruments such as Treasury bills, and CDs.

Second, there are many different types of stock and bond funds, characterized both by the kind of securities the fund invests in, and by the fund's particular objective. The following list explains the most common types of stock and bond mutual funds.

Stock Funds

Maximum Capital Gains Funds. Also called aggressive growth funds, these attempt to achieve very high returns by investing in more speculative stocks, maximizing capital gains while generating little or no income from dividends. The potential for greater rewards is linked with increased volatility and greater risk in these funds.

Small Company Growth Funds. Also called emerging growth funds, these are a type of maximum capital gain fund specializing in stocks of promising small, emerging growth companies.

Long-Term Growth Funds. These seek capital gains from companies that have the potential for steady growth in earnings. Less volatile, and more consistent than maximum capital gains funds, growth funds aim to achieve a rate of growth that beats inflation.

Growth and Income Funds. These funds seek a more balanced stock portfolio that will achieve capital appreciation as well as current income from dividends. They are less risky than growth funds, because the dividend may offset at least some of the periodic losses in stock prices.

> "...The more specialized a fund becomes, the more risk it presents to the investor."

Equity-Income Funds. These generally invest most of their portfolio in dividend-paying stocks and the rest in convertible securities and bonds. Income funds may have capital growth as a secondary objective to providing current income.

International Stock Funds. These funds provide additional diversification to a portfolio. Most international funds invest throughout the world. Some invest only in one country or region. Global stock funds, however, differ only in that they also invest in U.S. securities.

Bond Funds

Within each bond fund category, there are usually several funds that specialize in investments of either short-term, intermediate-term, or long term duration. Bond funds pay monthly income. Except for funds that invest solely in government bonds, all bond funds have some degree of risk of default. However, the real risk of bond funds is that high inflation will outpace the returns and/or rising interest rates will reduce the principal value of the investment.

Corporate Bond Funds. These buy and trade bonds of corporations. There are two categories of corporate bond mutual funds: investment-grade corporate bond funds, which comprise high-quality corporate bonds and seek high income with limited credit risk, and high-yield (junk bond) bond funds, which offer potentially greater rewards with higher risk.

Government Bond Funds. Government bond funds own securities which are backed by the full faith and credit of the U.S. government. These funds offer total protection from bond default, although the value of government bonds will fluctuate with interest rates like all bonds and bond funds. One variety of government bond funds, government mortgage funds, holds mortgage-backed securities such as those issued by the Government National Mortgage Association (GNMA). Holders of mortgage funds receive both interest and a partial return of principal which may be reinvested.

Municipal Bond Funds. These provide investors with a means for tax-free income. Interest earned from bonds not issued in the investor's own state is fully taxable in his or her own state, so in order to produce maximum tax-free income, single-state funds have been developed. For example, a New York resident investor owning the New York muni fund will avoid state as well as federal taxes on the fund's interest income.

Convertible Bond Funds. These funds are bonds or preferred stock that can be exchanged for a fixed number of shares in the common stock of the issuing company. Convertible bond funds combine features of both stocks and bonds.

International Bond Funds. These typically invest primarily in high-quality foreign government or corporate bonds.

Specialized Stock and Bond Funds

Specialized funds offer mutual fund investors even more choices. However, the more specialized a fund becomes, the more risk it presents to the investor.

Balanced Funds. These funds maintain a balanced combination of common stocks, bonds, and perhaps preferred stocks. Balanced funds offer both income and growth because they hold both bonds and stocks. One of the advantages of balanced funds is the forced discipline that they impose on the fund manager. As stock prices rise, the fund manager is forced to sell stocks to bring the portfolio back into balance. Conversely, if stock prices decline, the fund manager will purchase more stock to bring the fund back to balance.

Specialized Industry Funds. Also known as sector funds, they invest only in the stocks of a single industry, such as biotechnology, waste management, utilities, health services, or energy. Sector funds, unlike traditional mutual funds, zero in on a particular area of the stock market. With sector funds, you lose the advantage of an already diversified portfolio because the fund concentrates in one industry.

Asset Allocation Funds. These invest in stock, bond, money market, real estate markets, and more so that any one market's losses may be offset by another's gain. In general, asset allocation funds are supposed to represent a one-stop fund for investors who want all the advantages of diversification in one account.

Precious Metal Funds. Often called gold funds, precious metal funds usually invest in stocks of gold-mining firms and other companies engaged in the business of precious metals. Some funds may actually purchase and store the metal itself.

Index Funds. These funds replicate the performance of all of the stocks in an index, for example, the Standard & Poor's 500. They simply duplicate a broad section of the market and are attractive to investors who want their investments to do the same. Usually the expenses of such a fund are very low in comparison with those of other stock funds.

Socially Responsible Funds. These limit their investments to companies considered to be socially responsible. For example, some funds do not invest in companies that manufacture defense-related or tobacco products.

Money Market Funds. These constitute the most widely held mutual fund category. Three main objectives of money market funds are preservation of capital, liquidity, and earning as high an income as can be achieved without sacrificing the first two objectives. Money market funds offer excellent liquidity: an investor need only write a check to transfer money. They provide liquidity because of the types of instruments they invest in, for example, Treasury bills and CDs. These funds are commonly used as a place to hold funds temporarily until new stock or bond investment opportunities arise. U.S. government money market funds and tax-exempt money market funds invest in short-term instruments of the U.S. government and states/municipalities, respectively. As with municipal bond funds, there are also some single-state tax-exempt money market funds.

Open-End Versus Closed-End Funds

Mutual funds also can be divided into the way they are organized and how their shares are priced.

Open-End Funds. Open-end funds can issue unlimited numbers of shares so that any investor who wants to purchase shares can do so. The value of open-end fund shares is based on the daily market value of the investments held by the fund. If the investments in the fund rise in value, the net asset value of the fund's shares rises, too, and vice versa. The net asset value (NAV) of a fund is the price of one share in the fund based on the total value of the fund's investments divided by the number of the fund's outstanding shares. It is calculated at the end of every trading day and is listed the following day in the financial section of most city newspapers as well as *The Wall Street Journal* and *Investor's Business Daily*.

Mutual Fund Loads, Fees, and Expenses

It's very important to understand and consider all commissions, annual expenses, and management fees *before* you invest in a fund.

• **Front-end load.** A load is an up-front sales commission charged and deducted from your initial investment amount. Load charges range as high as 8.5%, but most are in the 4% to 6% range. A subspecies of mutual funds is the low-load fund. These funds typically charge a fee of between 1% and 3%.

• **Back-end load.** More commonly known as redemption fees, back-end loads are taken from the net asset value of your shares when you sell them. The result is that your profit is dented, or your loss is increased.

• **Deferred loads (contingent deferred sales charges).** Some funds assess a charge if you redeem your shares before a specified time, often five years. In such instances, your initial investment amount is docked a percentage amount, and this percentage usually declines the longer you hold the fund. Deferred loads discourage investors from jumping out of the fund.

• **Reinvestment loads.** Some funds charge you for reinvested dividends and interest. But most don't.

• **12b-1 fees.** Some funds deduct the costs associated with advertising and marketing themselves directly from the fund's overall assets, rather than from management fees. The charge associated with such deductions is called a 12b-1. It typically amounts to one-fourth to one-half of 1%, but it can range as high as 1.25%.

• **Expense ratio.** Discussed in every fund's prospectus, the expense ratio expresses the cost of running a fund as a percentage of the fund's assets. A bond fund generally should have an expense ratio of less than 1%; a stock fund generally should have an expense ratio of no more than 1.25%. International funds may have considerably higher expense ratios (1.5% to 2%) because of the specialized nature of their investment activities. Index funds have expense ratios as low as .22%.

Closed-End Funds. Also known as publicly traded funds, closed-end funds have a fixed capital structure, just like that of an ordinary corporation, and have a fixed, limited number of shares outstanding. These shares are traded on the stock exchanges.

Closed-end funds have a net asset value, just as open funds do, but there's a twist: if the demand for the closed-end fund's shares is great, the price of the shares may trade above, or at a premium to, the NAV. Likewise, if demand for the shares declines, the shares may trade at a discount. If you buy a closed-end fund's shares at a discount, and then they later trade at an NAV premium, you will realize a gain, all other things being equal. But, just as with stock prices in general, it is impossible to predict if a closed-end fund's discount will narrow.

Mutual Fund Investment Strategies

Many investors are well served by investing a part of their money in several funds in different categories.

What Should You Look For in a Prospectus?

- How the fund has performed in the past
- How the fund is managed
- What the fund's objectives are
- What the minimum investment amount is
- What fees, if any, are associated with purchasing and operating the fund
- How you can purchase and redeem shares

> "A fund that consistently ranks above average *within its category* is probably a good choice as long as the fund itself invests in securities that you are comfortable with."

What should you be looking for? Long-term performance is an important criterion. Ideally, the fund should have been in existence at least five or, better yet, 10 years. That way, the organizations and periodicals that rate performance can evaluate the funds in both up and down markets. A fund that consistently ranks above average *within its category* is probably a good choice as long as the fund itself invests in securities that you are comfortable with. Ideally, it will rank above average over the past one, three, five, and 10 years.

How can you tell one fund from another? Each fund has a specific objective which dictates what that fund invests in, and how the fund will be managed. You find out about such details by reading the fund's prospectus, the document that describes the fund.

Why is a fund's objective so important? A fund's objective is its investment credo. It states the kinds of investments that will be made as well as specific strategies used by the fund manager. Since funds vary considerably in the amount of risk they take to achieve their objectives, you need to find a fund that matches your risk tolerance while working to achieve your financial objectives.

After you have decided on your portfolio allocation, the specific categories of investments within the stock and bond portions must be determined. Consider several things, including your investment objectives, current financial status, the current investment climate, and your familiarity with the various fund categories. The following table illustrates a typical mutual fund portfolio allocation, based upon a 50-50 split between stock and bond funds. Note that the stock fund portion of the portfolio includes aggressive funds, but it is heavily weighted in favor of more conservative funds. International stock funds also are included. The bond side of the portfolio is broadly diversified among a variety of interest-earning investment categories.

Sample Mutual Fund Portfolio Allocation

Investment category	Percent of Total Portfolio
Stock funds:	
Maximum capital gain	10%
Growth and income	20%
Small company	10%
International	10%
Subtotal: Stock funds	50%
Bond funds:	
Corporate bond	10%
Government bond	15%
Municipal bond	15%
Subtotal: Bond funds	40%
Money market funds	10%
Total Fund Portfolio:	100%

Once you have put together a mutual fund portfolio, evaluate it periodically both from the standpoint of the allocation of the total portfolio and individual fund performance. If you selected good funds in the beginning, you probably are better off holding on to them even if they disappoint you for a few months or quarters. However, a fund that consistently turns in results that are below average for its fund category is a candidate for replacement with a better performing fund. One rule of thumb: don't sell a fund unless it performs below its category average for two consecutive years.

Real Estate

Real estate is a great way for investors to accumulate substantial amounts of money. However, it is one of the most risky, complex, and time-consuming investment categories. Investors who are willing to devote the time to understand, locate, and manage investment real estate may well be handsomely rewarded for their efforts. The tax aspects of real estate ownership should be discussed with your tax advisor before investing in real estate properties.

Types of Real Estate Investments

There are many kinds of properties that fall under the investment real estate umbrella, but each fits into one of three broad categories: residential property, commercial property, and undeveloped land.

Residential Property

As an investment, residential rental property ideally produces a steady and predictable cash flow, which minimizes costs while the property (hopefully) increases in value. A residential rental property can be anything from a single-family or two-family house to a large multiunit apartment building. Location, condition, available utilities, and occupancy rate will all affect a property's value, as can local population movement and zoning changes.

> "If you have a relatively limited amount of money to invest in real estate, a single-family house is one way to get your foot in the door of real estate investing."

> "Real estate is a great way for investors to accumulate substantial amounts of money. However, it is one of the most risky, complex, and time-consuming investment categories."

The most important consideration in any real estate parcel is location. This truism is particularly crucial to residential real estate investing. Trying to find and invest in "turnaround neighborhoods" is best left to the professional.

Single-Family Homes. If you have a relatively limited amount of money to invest in real estate, a single-family house is one way to get your foot in the door of real estate investing. These units require a smaller amount of capital up-front than would a multifamily apartment, usually 20% to 30% of the total cost. Mortgage financing is generally available on satisfactory terms, and you may realize certain tax benefits from operating the property.

The potential for capital appreciation with single-family units varies. Such residences have provided attractive returns over the long term—10 years or more. But many short-term speculators in hot real estate markets for single-family homes have been badly burned.

The main problem with buying single-family residences for rental purposes is that it is difficult to locate properties that are priced low enough so that the rental income is sufficient to cover the mortgage payments and operating expenses.

Second Homes. Second homes, or vacation homes, are a popular form of real estate ownership because they can serve as both investment property and a place to get away from the normal, everyday living routine. Second home ownership provides some of the tax advantages of primary home ownership, plus economic advantages through its rent-producing potential.

Many people consider second homes to be investments because they have the potential to produce vacation and off-season rental income. The safest way to evaluate a second home's investment potential, however, is to make your decision assuming that it will generate *no* income. In other words, buy it purely for pleasure. If you are then able to realize some income on rentals, it will be an added bonus to the pleasure of owning a home away from home.

Condominiums. Condominiums are apartment units contained within larger multiunit buildings. Each unit is individually owned and controlled. Owners are free to mortgage their property as they wish, since all financing is done on an individual basis.

> "The safest way to evaluate a second home's investment potential is to make your decision assuming that it will generate *no* income."

Condominium living has become more popular in recent years as detached housing has become more expensive. While condominium units are generally cheaper than equivalent single-family homes, condominium ownership provides the same sort of tax advantages as does home ownership. Amenities and common areas like foyers, yards, and parking lots are generally owned by condominium owners' associations, which usually hire a building or site manager to maintain the common areas. Each unit is individually financed, so that if one owner defaults on his or her mortgage, the other residents need only assume the defaulting owner's share of operating expenses. Many first-time real estate investors purchase condominiums for rental purposes, only to end up subsidizing the renter because the rent is insufficient to cover the costs of owning the unit. Condominiums have a monthly maintenance fee that should be factored into their ownership.

Cooperatives. A cooperative, as opposed to a condominium, usually takes out a blanket mortgage on an entire building. Thus, if an owner defaults, the remaining tenants must assume the extra share of carrying costs. The reservations about condominium investing, noted above, apply to cooperatives as well. Nevertheless, condominiums or cooperatives may be viable investments in areas where rents can be increased significantly over time. In recent years, however, many areas of the country have been overbuilt with condos and co-ops, causing price declines in both rentals and property values.

Multifamily Homes and Apartment Buildings. There are greater opportunities for tax advantages and positive cash flow with multifamily apartments than with single-family structures. Included in this category are small two-, three-, and four-family homes that are often owner occupied. In fact, if you want to purchase your own home and get into the rental real estate game, you can accomplish both at the same time by buying a small apartment—a duplex or a triple-decker. Multifamily dwellings require a greater initial investment, but the cost per dwelling unit is lower. Multifamily units are relatively easy to finance for investors with sufficient resources to make the down payment, as lenders see the potential rental income as protection on their loans.

A major problem with large apartment units in some communities is the presence of rent control restrictions (either existing or potential). Other drawbacks include the possibility of overbuilding in a community, and the difficulty of selling the property quickly in the event the owner needs the money.

As with any other real estate, the property's location can make or break the investment; a prospective buyer should avoid areas of depreciating property values. Proximity to transportation, shopping, recreation, schools, and work is particularly important to the apartment dweller. If the physical condition of the property has been neglected, the costs of repair could boost expenses dramatically. Unexpected expenses such as re-roofing or replacing the electrical or heating systems may arise, so an investor who purchases an apartment building is well advised to have sufficient reserves to meet such contingencies.

Commercial Property

Office buildings, shopping centers, other retail property, and industrial real estate all offer investors with substantial resources an opportunity for significant gain, albeit at a significant risk. As the size of the property increases, however, buying and managing become more complicated, so you should already be experienced in real estate investing and be especially well informed about the specifics of the purchase. With the exception of very small, well-located, and fully occupied properties, commercial real estate is best left to the experts. But even they can experience trouble.

You may, however, want to consider making a commercial property investment via either a real estate limited partnership or a real estate investment trust. These indirect investment methods are discussed later on in this chapter, but the main areas of commercial real estate investment are briefly described below. If you are contemplating indirect investment in commercial properties, you should become familiar with the various categories of commercial property.

Office Buildings. Office buildings for investment may range from suburban office parks to central business district buildings. As with all real estate, location plays a critical role. With respect to office buildings in particular, occupancy rates are more unpredictable, and even a moderate amount of vacancies can be disastrous.

> "There are greater opportunities for tax advantages and positive cash flow with multifamily apartments than with single-family structures."

> ## "Raw land purchases often end up being poor investments."

Shopping Centers. These fall into five main categories: regional or superregional, community, neighborhood, discount, and specialty. Many of the smaller shopping center types are losing customers to superregional, mega shopping centers. Shopping centers can offer substantial returns, but like office buildings, this type of property has not fared well in weak economies. Also, older shopping centers are losing out to newly constructed ones.

Industrial Real Estate. Industrial property includes warehouses, wholesale and assembly sites, and manufacturing plants. While industrial property may be unfamiliar to the average investor, it can be an attractive investment. Industrial property ranges from industrial parks to miniwarehouse complexes (many of the latter are sold as limited partnerships). One great benefit to industrial real estate investments is that maintenance is usually minimal and tenant turnover is often lower than it is in office buildings.

Undeveloped Land

While undeveloped land might seem to be an ideal investment for a first-time real estate investor, it's been left for last because it is often the least appropriate investment. Why? Raw land purchases often end up being poor investments. For one thing, you will need deep pockets. Since undeveloped land doesn't generate any income, your money will be tied up for a long time. It's difficult to finance undeveloped land for more than a few years. In addition, successful land investors understand the current value and can anticipate the potential value for development of a given area. Investors also should be familiar with how regulatory and zoning issues affect, or may affect, a particular parcel of land. The importance of the regulatory environment can't be overemphasized. Legislation like the Federal Wetlands Act and several state-level laws, as well as environmental protection regulations, have made otherwise valuable land nearly worthless. Toxic waste is a nightmare, and the consumer should make sure that it's *not* associated with his or her dream house and the land it sits on.

Another cautionary note: large parcels of land that sell for peanuts usually spell t-r-o-u-b-l-e, not b-a-r-g-a-i-n. The price is probably cheap for a number of good reasons: lousy location, difficult access, bad drainage, etc. So if the land you want to purchase has more moose per square mile than people, don't expect to make any money on it. Land in particularly desirable areas, however, is always expensive to purchase but may, with some luck and a lot of skill, appreciate considerably in value.

Evaluating Potential Real Estate Investments

Suppose you come across a building that really appeals to you: it's in good condition, has some architectural character, and seems to be located in an up-and-coming neighborhood. While all these factors may incline you toward buying the property, they are meaningless until you know what it costs to operate the building and how much income it generates. Once you have these figures in hand—and have a good idea of the property's selling price—you can then determine whether buying it makes any sense.

The following yardsticks and formulas for evaluating real estate investments will help you make that decision.

Rent Multiplier

The simplest way to evaluate a property is to compare the price you'd have to pay for it with its current gross annual rental. Any property selling for much more than seven or eight times gross annual rental is likely to yield a negative cash flow; in other words, your rental income won't be sufficient to cover your mortgage and operating expenses, let alone make a profit. To determine the rent multiplier, which compares the total selling price with the current gross annual rental, use the following formula:

$$\text{Rent multiplier} = \frac{\text{Selling price}}{\text{Gross annual rental}}$$

For example, say the asking price of a duplex is $165,000 and it generates $15,000 in annual rent. The rent multiplier is calculated as follows:

$$\text{Rent multiplier} = \frac{\$165,000}{\$15,000} = 11$$

In other words, the property is selling for 11 times annual rental. As you read earlier, any property that is selling for much more than seven times the gross annual rental is probably not going to be a particularly good investment. Also remember that if you put a sizable cash down payment into the property to assure a positive cash flow, you're only fooling yourself because there's an opportunity cost associated with tying up a lot of cash that could otherwise be earning interest. You might be interested in knowing that professional real estate investors generally will not pay more than five to six times gross annual rental.

Similarly, if a real estate limited partnership pays more than seven times the gross annual rental to buy a property, the partnership is probably paying too much, unless it can reasonably expect a dramatic increase in the value of the property (for example, immediate condo conversion).

The Capitalization Rate

Calculating the capitalization rate, or cap rate as veteran real estate investors call it, is a more detailed method of evaluating a property. The cap rate is determined as follows:

$$\text{Capitalization rate} = \frac{\text{Net operating income}}{\text{Purchase price}}$$

A limited partnership investment in an apartment building requiring a total investment of $3.5 million has an estimated net operating income of $300,000. The cap rate is $300,000/ $3,500,000, or 8.6%. A cap rate of 8% or higher is considered desirable. Whether you are investing in real estate directly or through a limited partnership, make sure the amounts that go into the cap rate formula are realistic. The sum used for the total amount invested should include both the down payment and the borrowed money necessary to buy the property, while the net operating income is the total rental income (allowing for vacancies) less all the expenses except mortgage interest and principal.

Beware of a favorite trick called "bumping to market," which is used by real estate agents and general partners to make a deal look more attractive. "Bumping to market" is raising rent projections from what they actually are to what they ought to be according to a so-called market level. These are castle-in-the-sky projections.

Alternative Ways to Invest in Real Estate

Real estate investing can play an important role in a well-balanced investment portfolio for those investors who have the resources and the time available to research and, if necessary, manage real estate investments. Nevertheless, many people choose not to invest in real estate, and for good reasons— volatile prices and illiquidity chief among them. But if you are interested in real estate investing, here are four ways to do so.

> "Purchasing real estate yourself provides the greatest returns. But it takes a lot of hard work, and you have to have the right disposition to be a landlord."

Own It Yourself

Purchasing real estate yourself provides the greatest returns—and the greatest risks. Many people in this country have achieved their wealth through real estate investing. But it takes a lot of hard work, and you have to have the right disposition to be a landlord.

The best way to start out is to buy a small property, probably an apartment, to test the waters. You will find out in relatively short order whether you are cut out to be a landlord. If you get hooked, chances are that 10 years from now you'll own 10 buildings, and you'll be on your way to real estate riches. Along the way, however, don't overextend yourself. Remember, too much debt can be disastrous when the inevitable downturn occurs— vacancies rise and real estate prices drop.

Real Estate Limited Partnerships

Real estate limited partnerships are a way to pool money from a group of people to invest in larger properties.

Advantages to investment in real estate limited partnerships include:

- **Ease of buying in.** While direct ownership requires a complicated system of transfer, an investor in a limited partnership needs only to complete some documentation and send a check to the general partner. The partnership's prospectus gives you access to information necessary to make a reasonably quick decision.

- **Fixed cash requirements.** After you make the initial payment, you will not usually be responsible for financing any further cost overruns.

- **No management responsibility.** This is often a blessing to older investors. The general partner is responsible for finding tenants and arranging for maintenance, bookkeeping, tax reporting, and all other management duties.

- **Limited legal liability.** As a limited partner, your maximum legal liability is limited to the total amount you have invested in the partnership, so your other assets are not at risk.

- **Smaller initial investment.** In most deals, you need to invest as little as $5,000 (less if you invest through an IRA or other retirement plan) to receive the benefits of a large real estate project.

- **Lower overall risk.** Diversification and professional management can make limited partnership investments less risky than direct ownership.

There are also disadvantages to investing in real estate limited partnerships. These include:

- **Less control.** A limited partner has no say in the management of the property, nor can he or she dictate when or to whom the property is sold.

- **Lower overall return.** This is due to fees and commissions paid to set up the partnership, to operate the property, and upon liquidation of the partnership.

- **Limited tax-saving opportunities.** Under current tax rules, tax shelter opportunities for limited partnerships have been either severely restricted or eliminated altogether.

- **Illiquidity.** Because there is little demand for existing limited partnership investment units, if they can be sold at all they will likely sell for far less than the original investment. This could be a major drawback for anyone who may need to sell the investment on short notice to provide income or who wants to remove illiquid investments from his or her estate.

Because of the many problems experienced by real estate limited partnerships in the 1980s, investors should be very cautious when contemplating these investments, particularly in areas where real estate conditions remain weak.

> "REIT shares allow you to participate in the real estate market without the hassle of management and without the problem of illiquidity."

Real Estate Investment Trusts

A real estate investment trust (REIT) is a corporation that invests in real estate or mortgages. REIT shares trade on the major stock exchanges, so they provide excellent liquidity. They allow you to participate in the real estate market without the hassle of management and without the problem of illiquidity. Capital gains realized through the trust go directly to the shareholders, and the diversified portfolio minimizes risks. The ability to sell REIT shares on the stock market provides greater liquidity than other real estate investments.

REITs, like mutual funds, bring the advantages of centralized, professional management to individual investors. Since they are subject to strict regulations, they tend to be well managed.

But before you conclude that REITs are the best thing since sliced bread, you need to know that REIT share prices suffer in bad real estate markets just as much as limited partnerships or directly owned investments. Many REITs invest in major commercial properties, and overbuilt real estate markets have adversely affected leasing environments.

Nonetheless, if you want to play the real estate market, the REIT route may still be the best and easiest one to take. For one thing, REITs have traditionally provided a rich dividend yield. Real estate investments are renowned for their extreme boom/bust cycles, and it's at the perceived bottom of a cycle that experienced real estate professionals jump in and reap extraordinary returns. The REIT vehicle was legislated into existence specifically to enable the smaller investor to participate in such gains. If you want to take the plunge, look for REITs that specialize in apartments or cater to the elderly.

Real Estate "Rich" Companies

There is one final way by which you can invest in real estate. Consider purchasing stock in companies with substantial real estate holdings. Investment professionals often point to large paper companies, and some retailers that own a lot of their outlets, as attractive "real estate rich" companies. By investing in these companies, you can possibly gain some of the benefits of owning real estate while skipping the hassles of direct real estate ownership, or the risks of limited partnerships.

Real Estate Investment Strategies

The following four suggestions may help you make better real estate investments and avoid costly mistakes.

1. Know what to avoid. Knowing what to avoid is one way to investment success. The following is a list of real estate investments to avoid.

- Many highly touted real estate limited partnerships.
- No-money-down real estate come-ons.
- Cheap land deals.
- Foreign land or property.
- Uninspected property.

2. Buy what you know. Consider purchasing parcels that are close to your home. Since real estate is so closely tied to local economies, your best chances for investment success are tied to your knowledge of the locale in which you live. Those who are familiar with the real estate market in their local community enjoy a significant advantage over those who try to purchase real estate in an unfamiliar locale.

3. Consider investing in distressed properties. Distressed properties are always available, and some regions of the country have more than their fair share. You may be attracted to the appealing notion of obtaining a property at a foreclosure auction or through the Resolution Trust Corporation (RTC), which is charged with disposing of the foreclosed properties of defunct savings and loans. But remember, both methods of acquiring property are fraught with peril. Even though extensive investigation of each property is required before bidding commences, most auctions disallow the time it takes to do a thorough job, selling the property "as is," without contingencies for inspection and without warranty. Moreover, foreclosed properties sold at auction are often in very poor condition. There also may be liens on the property or clouds in the title. You'll need an attorney to scrutinize it. Finally, dealing with the RTC can be a time-consuming, bureaucratic nightmare. (A local real estate broker may be able to assist you—for a fee.)

4. Consider real estate limited partnerships. The deals are structured much more sensibly than they were prior to 1986; however, most deals rely on price appreciation—not something that can be guaranteed anymore.

Despite the negatives, real estate investing can be very profitable. Some professional investors emphasize that down markets present unprecedented opportunities for investing in real estate. But remember, this is the kind of opportunity that only experienced real estate investors can exploit. More often than not, it is the new investor who is exploited.

Investment Allocation Overview

Investing effectively is crucial to your ultimate financial well-being. It's now time to illustrate the four-step process that was described under Allocating Investments in the beginning of this chapter. That way, you can develop your own plan to help guide you in both deciding upon the types of investments to make and in reviewing your investments periodically. Remember, "periodically" doesn't mean every day; otherwise, you'll become so concerned that you're likely to make investment changes too frequently. Rather, if you establish some sensible criteria now, you will be able to invest wisely without spending an inordinate amount of time worrying about your investments.

The following Investment Allocation diagram will serve as the basis for the subsequent investment illustrations.

Investment Allocation			
	Investment Category		
Method of ownership		Interest-	
	Stock	Earning	Real Estate
Direct Ownership			
Indirect Ownership (Mutual Fund/ Partnership)			

The following example shows how an appropriate investment portfolio can be put together.

EXAMPLE: Over the past few years, Josh and Laura Wineland have managed to set aside $25,000, which is now in a money market account. Having just read this chapter, they are ready to invest their money more sensibly.

Step 1: They decide that, while they may want to invest in real estate sometime in the future, they don't have enough money yet, and therefore should restrict their investments to stocks and interest-earning securities. They decide that 60% of their $25,000 ($15,000) should be invested in stocks, and 40% ($10,000) in interest-earning securities.

Note: Most pension funds invest about 60% of their funds in stocks.

Step 1: Deciding on Proportion to Be Invested in Each Category

Method of ownership	Investment Category		
	Stock	Interest-Earning	Real Estate
Direct Ownership	60% ($15,000)	40% ($10,000)	0%
Indirect Ownership (Mutual Fund/ Partnership)			

Step 2: Because their portfolio currently isn't very large, they plan to begin investing most of their money in mutual funds. Nevertheless, they want to become familiar with direct investing as well, so, as indicated below, they are going to invest $5,000 in stocks and $3,000 in directly owned interest-earning investments.

Step 2: Deciding How Much to Invest Directly and Indirectly

Method of ownership	Investment Category	
	Stock	Interest-Earning
Direct Ownership	$5,000	$3,000
Indirect Ownership (Mutual Fund/ Partnership)	$10,000	$7,000
Grand total	$15,000	$10,000

Step 3: Josh and Laura next need to decide on the kinds of securities they will purchase within each of the four categories. After some deliberation, they decide upon the investments that are indicated below.

Step 3: Deciding on Appropriate Kinds of Investments

Method of ownership	Investment Category			
	Stock		Interest-Earning	
Direct Ownership	High-quality growth stock	$ 2,500		
	Blue-chip stock	2,500	Certificate of deposit	$ 3,000
	Total	$ 5,000	Total	$ 3,000
Indirect Ownership (Mutual Fund/ Partnership)	Maximum capital gains fund	$ 3,000		
	Growth and income fund	5,000	Government securities fund	$ 4,000
	International stock fund	2,000	Corporate bond fund	3,000
	Total	$10,000	Total	$ 7,000
	Grand total	$15,000		$10,000

Step 4: Now Josh and Laura need to select specific investments for each of the categories that they have decided to invest in. They, as well as you, will have to do that on their own, or with the help of their investment adviser. Whichever route you take, you will be in a better position to make the most suitable decisions, now that you know what your investment options are.

This chapter has covered a lot of investment ground—from designating types of available investment alternatives to selecting appropriate investments. No matter what the size of your current investments, you can apply the principles of this chapter to their—and your—advantage.

The following illustrations will take you from a $1,000 portfolio to a $100,000 portfolio. All of the illustrations assume that the investor wants to maintain an allocation of 50% stock investments and 50% interest-earning investments, which is a conservative but common allocation.

The $1,000 Portfolio

Most everyone starts at zero (or less). There's no reason why you shouldn't begin to develop good habits by investing your $1,000 much like a pension manager handles a multibillion-dollar portfolio. The rules are the same.

You can start out by putting $500 into a growth and income stock mutual fund and $500 into a government securities fund. Incidentally, there are many good mutual funds that have investment minimums of $500 or less. Alternatively, you could invest the $1,000 in a balanced mutual fund, which consists of both stock and interest-earning securities. The $1,000 portfolio is presented below.

Sample $1,000 Portfolio

Method of ownership	Investment Category	
	Stock	Interest-Earning
Direct Ownership		
Indirect Ownership (Mutual fund)	Growth and income fund $500	Government securities fund $500

The $10,000 Portfolio

When you have $10,000 to invest, you can begin to expand your investment horizons somewhat, although you will still probably want to restrict your holdings to mutual funds and, perhaps, a CD. While you aren't quite at a level where direct investments make sense, there are many mutual funds that will help you meet your investment objectives.

As the following table shows, you can divide your portfolio among several mutual funds, and the funds will provide diversification as well as professional management of your hard-earned savings.

Sample $10,000 Portfolio

Method of ownership	Investment Category	
	Stock	Interest-Earning
Direct Ownership		
Indirect Ownership (Mutual fund)	Aggressive growth fund $2,000 Growth and income fund 3,000 Total $5,000	Government securities fund $3,000 Corporate bond fund 2,000 Total $5,000

The $100,000 Portfolio

Once your portfolio exceeds $20,000 or so, you can begin to make directly owned investments in stock and interest-earning securities. The following table shows how a $100,000 portfolio might be structured so that $25,000 is invested in each of the four boxes, thereby maintaining a 50%/50% split between total stock investments and total interest-earning investments. The directly owned stocks box includes $5,000 in each of five high-quality stocks. Most of the dividend-paying companies that you would want to invest in have dividend reinvestment programs.

The larger portfolio allows you to invest in a wider range of securities. Note that the stock mutual funds component now includes investments in an international fund and a small company fund.

Method of ownership	**Sample $100,000 Portfolio** Investment Category				
	Stock		Interest-Earning		
Direct Ownership	$5,000 in each of five high-quality blue-chip stocks and growth stocks		CD	$ 5,000	
			Municipal bonds	10,000	
			Corporate bonds	10,000	
	Total	$25,000	Total	$25,000	
Indirect Ownership (Mutual fund)	Aggressive growth fund	$ 5,000	Government securities fund	$10,000	
	Growth and income fund	10,000	Municipal bond fund	10,000	
	International fund	5,000			
	Small company fund	5,000	Corporate bond fund	5,000	
	Total	$25,000	Total	$25,000	

The Investment Summary Work Sheet at the end of the chapter will help you take an inventory of your existing investment portfolio, while the Asset Allocation Work Sheet (also at the end of the chapter) will help you develop the right portfolio structure for your investments.

Gradual Investment

One stone remains unturned in the all-important asset allocation process, and it is a crucial one. Many investors, once they get serious about allocating their investments appropriately, find that they have to make a major reallocation of their investments. For example, if you have been investing in conservative money market accounts and are now convinced that you need to invest in stocks and bonds, the crucial issue is how fast should you do it? Additionally, if you have recently received a cash windfall, say an inheritance, how fast should you invest it? If you invest it all tomorrow, the risk, of course, is that you make a major investment in stocks just before the market declines or a major investment in bonds just before interest rates shoot up.

All too often, investors become so wary of a possible loss amidst uncertain market conditions that they end up investing very conservatively—too conservatively. One way to reduce the risk of ill-timed investing is to devise a plan of gradual investment of your money rather than taking the chance of investing a significant portion of your money at a stock market high and/or an interest rate low.

Gradual investment of your money is, in essence, a form of dollar cost averaging which is widely and successfully used for investing in individual stocks or mutual funds. The following table shows how you might devise an investment timetable over the next two years. This allows for a gradual investment of the available money rather than an immediate commitment. (For the sake of illustration, assume that you eventually want an allocation of 50% stocks and 50% interest-earning securities. Also assume that you would like your distribution to be fully invested within two years.)

Gradual Investing Timetable

Investment Category	Percent of Total Investment		
	Now	Within Next 12 Months	From 12 to 24 Months
Stocks	15%	30%	50%
Fixed Income	25	35	40
Cash Equivalent	60	35	10
Total	100%	100%	100%

As the timetable indicates, a large portion of the money initially sits on the sidelines in low-yielding cash-equivalent investments, e.g., money market funds, short-term CDs, Treasury bills. Alternatively, if you are willing to accept some interest rate risk during the course of your investment program, you could use short-term bonds or short-term bond funds in lieu of much of the cash-equivalent allocation which will probably enable you to get a somewhat better yield.

Within the first 12 months of the investment program, your stock exposure is increased from 15% to 30% and fixed-income exposure from 25% to 35%. The third column shows a fully invested allocation which would be achieved within a two-year period.

Gradual deployment of investments makes a lot of sense, particularly when you think stock prices are high and/or interest rates are low. Certainly, opportunities may be missed by following such a timetable, but costly mistakes also may be avoided.

"Gradual deployment of investments makes a lot of sense, particularly when you think stock prices are high and/or interest rates are low."

Two Smart Ways to Add to Your Investments

• **Automatic investing.** Most leading mutual fund companies and brokerages allow you to invest automatically. You specify a fixed amount to be withdrawn at regular intervals from your bank checking account and put into your investment account. It's a great way to begin and to stick with a regular investing program.

• **Dollar cost averaging.** One of the best ways to add to your investments slowly but steadily is to use dollar cost averaging— investing a fixed amount in a particular stock issue or mutual fund account on a regular basis. The trick is to stay with your schedule regardless of whether the stock price goes up or down. Because you're investing a fixed amount at fixed intervals, your dollars buy fewer shares when the stock price is high and more when it is low. As a result, the average purchase price is lower than the average market price over the same period of time.

The following table illustrates the benefit of dollar cost averaging.

	Amount Invested	Price	Number of Shares Purchased
1st period	$ 4,000	$13⅝	300
2nd period	4,000	8	500
3rd period	4,000	6⅝	600
4th period	4,000	8	500
5th period	4,000	20	200
	$20,000		2,100

Total amount invested over 5 periods: $20,000
Number of shares purchased: 2,100
Average market price: $11.20
Average cost: $9.52

This chapter opened with a look at one couple—Nathan and Adelaide Newhart—who had some modest savings, and who had just received a small inheritance. Of their savings, $12,000 was in cash-equivalent investments, and $3,000 had been recently transferred into a municipal bond fund. Including the inheritance money, the Newharts had $40,000 in assets.

Nathan and Adelaide spent several months discussing what to do with their money, but couldn't come to a satisfactory conclusion. Adelaide's father had lost a good-sized portion of his retirement savings speculating in the stock market, so she was afraid of stocks. Nathan was pleased with the performance of his new municipal bond fund, and for a while leaned toward putting all the money into the fund. Only the financial difficulties that were plaguing the state government deterred Nathan from pursuing this course of action.

It wasn't until Nathan attended a financial planning seminar sponsored by his company that he realized that investing wisely is not a black art. In fact, he learned that it wasn't even that difficult. The seminar speaker explained how smaller investors could enjoy the same professional money management that Nathan had imagined was available only to the rich, simply by investing in mutual funds. The key, Nathan was told, was to determine how much money you ought to have in stocks, how much in bonds, and how much in cash equivalents (very little, he learned). Once an asset allocation had been determined, the speaker explained, all you had to do was to select the appropriate mutual funds—either on your own or with the help of an investment professional.

The speaker further explained that no one, no matter how conservative, should forgo stocks: the most conservative portfolio should have at least 30% in stocks, while the most aggressive ought never to be more than 70% in stocks (in the seminar leader's opinion). Whatever the portfolio allocation, the speaker said, diversification was very important. (Fortunately, Nathan never followed up on his original idea of putting all his assets into a municipal bond fund.) Finally, Nathan learned that there are literally thousands of stock and bond funds from which to choose, and that these funds are categorized by investment strategy.

For the two weeks following the seminar, Nathan and Adelaide read everything they could about mutual fund investing. They developed a sensible portfolio allocation, choosing to invest half of their assets in stocks and half in bonds. When they finally narrowed their fund choices down to a short list of funds with good long-term records, they deployed their money gradually over the next six months. To be assured that they had a solid investment portfolio that would allow them to meet their long-term investment objectives, they decided to seek the help of a Certified Financial Planner to get a second opinion on the work they had done themselves.

Investment Management Action Plan *Work Sheet*

Investment Management Action Plan

Current Status		
Needs Action	**OK or Not Applicable**	
		1. Summarize all of your investments, including any retirement plan investments that you manage.
		2. Determine how your investments are allocated, in total, among the three investment categories: stock, interest-earning, and real estate.
		3. Plan how you are going to re-deploy your investments to achieve a more appropriate allocation.
		4. Begin, if you haven't already, to save at regular intervals to build up your investment portfolio.
		5. If your income is likely to fluctuate, adjust your saving and investing to assure that sufficient resources will be available to meet living expenses.
		6. Spend some time learning about investments and the current investment climate.
		7. Periodically review the status of your portfolio.
		8. Coordinate your investing with other areas of financial planning, particularly taxes and estate planning, but don't let the desire to save on taxes dominate your investing.
		9. Recognize that a buy-and-hold strategy is almost always the most beneficial way to manage a personal portfolio.
		10. Keep in mind that mutual funds, preferably no-load funds, should play a role in every portfolio.
		11. While real estate is often a sound long-term investment, never invest in a property that violates general guidelines outlined in this chapter.
		12. Select and control your investment advisers carefully.
		13. Above all, be consistent in carrying out your investment objectives.

Comments:

Investment Summary *Work Sheet*

Use this work sheet to facilitate the often-laborious process of summarizing your investment portfolio.

Date at which market values are indicated:_____

Investment Summary

Description	Number of Shares or Face Value	Date Acquired	Original Cost	Current Market Value	Estimated Annual Interest or Dividend
1. Cash-equivalent investments: Money market funds and accounts			$	$	$
Savings accounts					
CDs					
Other cash-equivalent investments					
Total cash-equivalent investments			$	$	$

(Continued on the next page)

Investment Summary *Work Sheet Continued*

Investment Summary

Description	Number of Shares or Face Value	Date Acquired	Original Cost	Current Market Value	Estimated Annual Interest or Dividend
2. Fixed-income investments: U.S. government securities			$	$	$
U.S. government securities funds					
Mortgage-backed securities					
Mortgage-backed securities funds					
Corporate bonds					
Corporate bond funds					
Municipal bonds					
Municipal bond funds					
Other fixed-income investments					
Total fixed-income investments			$	$	$

(Continued on the next page)

Work Sheet

Investments

4

Investment Summary *Work Sheet Continued*

Investment Summary

Description	Number of Shares or Face Value	Date Acquired	Original Cost	Current Market Value	Estimated Annual Interest or Dividend
3. Equity investments: Common stock in publicly traded companies			$	$	$
Stock mutual funds					
Precious metals and precious metal funds					
Other equity investments					
Total equity investments			$	$	$

(Continued on the next page)

Investments

4 *Work Sheet*

Investment Summary *Work Sheet Continued*

Investment Summary

Description	Description	Date Acquired	Original Cost	Current Market Value	Estimated Annual Interest or Dividend
4. Real estate investments: Undeveloped land			$	$	$
Directly owned, income-producing real estate					
Real estate limited partnerships					
Total real estate investments			$	$	$
5. Interests in privately held businesses:			$	$	$
Total interests in privately held businesses			$	$	$
Grand total investments			$	$	$

Work Sheet

Investments

4

Asset Allocation *Work Sheet*

This work sheet allows you to view the percentage allocation of your total portfolio versus your desired, or target, allocation. Transfer the current market value totals for each investment category from the Investment Summary into the first column below. Then calculate the percent of your total investment portfolio in each category. Compare these percentages with your desired portfolio allocation, which can be entered in the right column. This analysis should be prepared at least annually.

Date at which market values are indicated:_____

Asset Allocation

| Investment Category | Current Market Value | | | Percent of Portfolio | Target Percent of Portfolio |
	Personal Investments	Retirement Plan Investments*	Total		
Stock	$	$	$	%	%
Interest-earning investments					
Real estate					
Grand total	$	$	$	%	%

Comments:

*List all retirement plan investments in which you control the investment allocations, including IRA and 401(k) plans.

Investment Allocation Planner *Work Sheet*

It's now time for you to plan how you should allocate your investments just as has been done in the chapter. If you don't yet have any investments, you can still plan for the day when you will, because that day (hopefully) won't be far off.

Allocation Planner

Method of ownership	Investment Category		
	Stock	Interest-Earning	Real Estate
Direct ownership			
Indirect Ownership (Mutual Fund/Partnership)			

Comments:

Investment "To Do" List:

CHAPTER 5

Income Tax Planning

Tax planning can be easy, efficient, and rewarding—all it takes is a little know-how. This chapter provides the income tax planning strategies and reporting basics you'll need to improve your bottom line when tax time comes.

Income Tax Planning

Are there any deductions that an average income earner can take?
How can I tell if my home office qualifies for a deduction?
What resources can I get to help me prepare my returns?
Are tax-free investments right for me?
When do capital gains taxes have to be paid?
What is AGI?

Becoming Tax Savvy

Finding sensible ways to save on taxes is a great way to cut expenses. Every taxpayer can benefit from learning ways to cut his or her taxes. Yet, many people pay more taxes than they have to—even though they dislike paying them. They do this in spite of another fact—the law has consistently upheld the American right to pay only the minimum legal tax. In the often quoted words of Judge Learned Hand, "Over and over again, courts have said that there is nothing sinister in so arranging one's affairs as to keep taxes as low as possible. Everybody does so, rich or poor; and all do right, for nobody owes any public duty to pay more tax than the law demands; taxes are enforced exactions, not voluntary contributions."

The other side of this tax-saving coin is that many tax-saving strategies simply aren't worth the effort, and some may even end up costing you more. In other words, simply because there are legal ways to reduce your tax bill doesn't mean that each and every option will be of benefit to your particular situation. Wise tax planning is knowing when *not* to undertake tax-saving strategies and in knowing which tax strategies to actually use.

Perhaps the most important thing to remember about tax planning is that it is an important part of total personal financial planning. But keep in mind that it is just one part. Even though any investment or financial decision should include an evaluation of its tax ramifications, none should be made solely or even primarily on that basis alone.

Financial Snapshot — *Tom Collins*

At age 53, Tom Collins remains a bachelor—by choice. Tom faces two last major financial hurdles: paying off the mortgage on his condo before he retires, and adding to his retirement savings. Tom's job, while secure, doesn't provide much of a chance for dramatically increasing his income, but that fact hasn't stopped him from devising a smart alternative—moonlighting—in order to boost his retirement funding. Tom also would like to use a portion of this extra income to pay off his condo mortgage.

However, just when he is at the stage in his life where he can finally begin to save some extra money, Tom is suddenly faced with substantially higher taxes.

Now he is getting concerned about the bite that taxes take out of his income. Are there ways to reduce the tax bite so that he can increase his savings and retirement-oriented investing? What are they, and how helpful are they?

> "Every taxpayer can benefit from learning ways to cut his or her taxes."

Income Tax Saving Strategies

Tax planning consists of much more than simply taking advantage of every possible deduction. Rather, it consists of developing a coherent, long-term strategy to reduce taxes over the coming years. Tax planning is a year-round process, not just to be used between Christmas and New Year's. One of the best things about multiyear tax planning is that you eventually learn to avoid past mistakes. One of the most common mistakes people make is to become "tax driven" rather than "tax aware." "Tax driven" describes one who wishes to reduce taxes at any cost. "Tax aware" suggests that a taxpayer is knowledgeable about the tax ramifications of a particular action. However, you are far better off making financial decisions on the basis of economic merits of the investments being considered.

Using Capital Gains Tax Laws to Your Advantage

Creating a sound investment portfolio requires dealing with the capital gains tax effectively. In spite of all the tax legislation over the past decade that eliminated most tax-saving strategies, stock investments remain one of the last, great tax shelters. So it pays to understand how stock investments are taxed.

Stock investors make money by receiving cash dividends and by selling stocks at a gain. Uncle Sam gets his piece of your good fortune just as he does with interest income and employment or retirement income. The following is a brief description of how your stock investments are taxed.

> "One of the most common mistakes people make is to become 'tax driven' rather than 'tax aware.'"

Cash Dividends

Most dividends that are paid to stockholders in cash are taxable. Sometimes, a company (i.e., a utility) will pay out a nontaxable return of capital. You won't have to pay taxes on this return of capital, but you are required to reduce the cost basis of the stock by the amount of the nontaxable distribution.

Stock Dividends

If you receive additional shares of company stock as a dividend, it is generally not taxed. Similarly, additional shares received as a result of a stock split are generally not taxable; however, the per share cost basis of the stock will be reduced pro rata.

Unrealized Capital Gains

Unrealized capital gains—in other words, gains on stock that you still hold—are not subject to income taxes. This is a major tax advantage, and many investors have accumulated considerable wealth by buying and holding stocks. The value of their stocks rises over the years, and yet they haven't paid one cent in capital gains tax. Since rising stock prices often mean rising dividends as well, long-term stock investors can have the best of both worlds—a steadily rising source of income and an appreciating, untaxed stock portfolio.

Realized Capital Gains

When a stock is sold at a gain—in other words, at a price that is higher than its cost basis—the amount of the gain is subject to federal income tax at capital gains rates. Currently, these rates are the same as ordinary income tax rates, but they do not exceed a rate of 28%. Therefore, investors in a higher tax bracket will pay tax on capital gains at a rate that is lower than their marginal income tax rate. Since unrealized gains are not taxed, stock investors have complete control over the timing of when they will pay their taxes on capital gains.

Realized Capital Losses

Not all stock investments are winners. Inevitably, some will have to be sold at a loss. Fortunately, realized capital losses can be used to offset realized capital gains—which can often be a smart move. In addition to offsetting capital gains, up to $3,000 of excess capital losses may be used each year to offset other taxable income. While this is a small consolation to the misfortune of taking capital losses, at least you are saving some income taxes from going on a one-way trip to Washington. Any net realized capital losses in excess of $3,000 may be carried forward indefinitely to future tax years to reduce future taxable income.

32 Useful—and Free—IRS Publications

These publications, which are available free from the IRS, can help you establish a tax-wise library which, in turn, can help you to clarify some common income tax concerns. To order these publications (as well as any tax forms that you might need), call the IRS at 1-800-TAX FORM (1-800-829-3676).

Publication

Number	Title
1	Your Rights as a Taxpayer
17	Your Federal Income Tax
54	Tax Guide for U.S. Citizens and Resident Aliens Abroad
334	Tax Guide for Small Business
448	Federal Estate and Gift Taxes
501	Exemptions, Standard Deduction, and Filing Information
502	Medical and Dental Expenses
503	Child and Dependent Care Expenses
504	Tax Information for Divorced or Separated Individuals
505	Tax Withholding and Estimated Tax
508	Educational Expenses
520	Scholarships and Fellowships
521	Moving Expenses
523	Tax Information on Selling Your Home
525	Taxable and Nontaxable Income
526	Charitable Contributions
527	Residential Rental Property (Including Rental of Vacation Homes)
529	Miscellaneous Deductions
530	Tax Information for Homeowners (Including Owners of Condominiums and Cooperative Apartments)
533	Self-Employment Tax
535	Business Expenses
550	Investment Income and Expenses
552	Recordkeeping for Individuals and a List of Tax Publications
559	Tax Information for Survivors, Executors, and Administrators
560	Retirement Plans for the Self-Employed
564	Mutual Fund Distributions
571	Tax-Sheltered Annuity Programs for Employees of Public Schools and Certain Tax-Exempt Organizations
575	Pension and Annuity Income
587	Business Use of Your Home
590	Individual Retirement Arrangements (IRAs)
909	Alternative Minimum Tax for Individuals
910	Guide to Free Tax Services

The Role of Tax-Exempt Investments

Many investors can benefit from investing in municipal securities, although they may not realize it. Here's a quick rule of thumb: consider investing in tax-free securities if your taxable income is expected to place you in the 28% federal tax bracket or higher.

Why invest in tax-free securities and tax-free mutual funds? With few exceptions, interest earned on municipal investments is exempt from all federal income taxes and, in many instances, from state and local taxes.

Although there have been numerous changes in the tax laws over the past decade, one thing has remained constant: federal and state taxes continue to take a sizable bite out of investment income. Higher taxes are causing many investors to consider the benefits of investing in municipal bonds. This section will help you understand municipal securities and will help you determine if tax-free investing should become a part of your investment program.

What Are Municipal Securities?

Municipal securities—often referred to as munis—are debt obligations issued by state and local governments and governmental agencies, such as a highway department, an airport authority, a school district, even a sewer commission. Debt obligations are interest-paying IOUs that raise money for a variety of state or local government purposes. Since state and local governments issue debt obligations for a variety of reasons, investors can choose from among different types of municipal securities. Keep the following points in mind when investing in munis.

> "Higher taxes are causing many investors to consider the benefits of investing in municipal bonds."

Interest. Most municipal securities' interest is exempt from federal income taxes. Some securities that finance private ventures are taxable to all investors, and others may be taxable if you are subject to the alternative minimum tax (AMT).

The interest on most municipals issued by state agencies is exempt from federal, state, and local taxes as long as the investor is a resident of the state that issues the bonds. For example, if you reside in California, interest on municipal securities issued by the state of California or by California municipalities would be exempt from both federal and state income taxes.

Interest on municipal securities issued by U.S. territories (the Territory of Guam and the Commonwealth of Puerto Rico, for example) is exempt from both federal and state income taxes.

Risk. One risk of owning either individual municipal bonds or shares in a municipal bond fund is that if interest rates rise, the value of the securities may decline. This is known as interest rate risk. If interest rates decline, the value of the municipal bonds or the share price of a municipal bond fund investment may increase.

Capital Gains Taxes. Capital gains that may be realized when a municipal security is sold will be subject to federal and most state capital gains taxes. Sometimes a bond fund manager may sell some securities at a gain. These realized capital gains are taxable to the fund shareholders, who may have to pay a capital gains tax even though they haven't yet sold their shares in the fund.

Why Invest in Municipals?

Many people shy away from municipal securities because their yields are usually lower than those of other types of interest-earning securities like Treasury and corporate bonds. But the yields on tax-free municipals and taxable securities are comparable only after you have factored in the taxes that would have to be paid on taxable securities. In other words, it's what you get to keep after taxes have been paid that's most important.

Taxable Equivalent Yield. The taxable equivalent yield enables you to compare the interest that you receive on a tax-free investment with the interest on a taxable investment. Here's how it's calculated:

$$\text{Taxable Equivalent Yield} = \frac{\text{Interest rate on a tax-free security}}{(1 - \text{Tax rate})}$$

EXAMPLE: Gary and Sarah Williams are in the 28% federal income tax bracket. They're considering purchasing either a tax-free investment paying 6% interest or a Treasury bond paying interest of 7.5%. Research done by the Williamses has revealed that the relative risk and term of both investments are comparable to each other. In order to accurately compare the yields, they must first compute the taxable equivalent yield on the municipal bond, as follows.

First, convert their income tax bracket to its decimal equivalent:

28% becomes .28

Second, apply the above formula:

$$\text{Taxable Equivalent Yield} = \frac{6\%}{(1 - .28)} = \frac{6\%}{.72} = 8.33\%$$

Conclusion: The taxable equivalent yield of the tax-free security is 8.33% compared with 7.5% for the Treasury bond. While the tax-free investment has a lower yield, after taxes have been factored in, it has a higher after-tax yield than a taxable security.

Double Tax-Free Securities. Investors who hold municipal securities of issuers located within their own state get a double benefit: interest on these bonds or notes is free from both federal and state taxes.

To compare a taxable investment with an investment whose income is free of both federal and state taxes, multiply the yield you can receive on a double tax-free security by the following multiplier that applies to both your federal and state tax rates on interest income. For example, a 7% federal and state tax-free yield would be the equivalent of a 10.2% fully taxable yield for an investor in the 28% federal income tax bracket whose state rate on interest income is 5% (multiplier = 1.46). By multiplying the 7% yield times 1.46 (the multiplier), you will get 10.2%. Use the table on the next page to compare a taxable bond with a bond that is free of both federal and state taxes.

Multiplier Based On Your Income Tax Bracket*					
	15% bracket	28% bracket	31% bracket	36% bracket	39.6% bracket
Tax Rate For Your State					
2%	1.20	1.42	1.48	1.59	1.69
3	1.21	1.43	1.49	1.61	1.71
4	1.23	1.45	1.51	1.63	1.72
5	1.24	1.46	1.53	1.64	1.74
6	1.25	1.48	1.54	1.66	1.76
7	1.27	1.49	1.56	1.68	1.78
8	1.28	1.51	1.58	1.70	1.80
9	1.29	1.53	1.59	1.72	1.82
10	1.31	1.54	1.61	1.74	1.84
11	1.32	1.56	1.68	1.76	1.86
12	1.34	1.58	1.70	1.78	1.88
20% of Federal Tax Liability	1.21	1.47	1.61	1.68	1.80
25% of Federal Tax Liability	1.22	1.49	1.63	1.72	1.84

* The multipliers only apply to interest, not total returns (interest plus capital gains).

Question: How much would an investor have to earn on a taxable investment to equal a 6% yield on an investment that is both federal and state tax free? The investor is in the 28% federal and 5% state income tax brackets.

Answer: 8.76% (6% x 1.46).

How to Invest for Tax-Free Income

1. Buy your own municipal securities.
You can buy and sell municipal securities through a broker. For starters, you will need at least $5,000 to invest in a single bond. You also will need considerably more money to purchase and maintain a well-diversified muni portfolio. Just like with other directly owned securities, you need to monitor your holdings because interest rate conditions change, and the financial strength of municipal issuers also can change, particularly in times of fiscal austerity. Because there are literally tens of thousands of different municipal issues, the current price of a particular tax-free security that you might own will probably not be listed in the newspaper. Information about the financial strength of a particular municipality is also not easy to come by. Therefore, maintaining your own portfolio of municipal securities is often both expensive and time consuming. Likewise, you will only receive interest income on a semiannual basis.

2. Invest in tax-free mutual funds.
Municipal bond mutual funds are an excellent vehicle for both new and experienced investors seeking tax-free income.

• Municipal bond funds are an increasingly popular and easy way for investors to earn tax-free income.

• Municipal bond funds provide investors with monthly tax-free income in an investment that is professionally managed and provides ready access to your money, if needed.

• Interest earned from bonds not issued in the investor's own state is fully taxable in his or her own state. In order to produce maximum tax-free income, single-state funds are available that hold bonds of issuers of only one state.

(For more on the advantages of mutual fund investing, see Chapter 4.)

Tax-Deferred Investments

The IRS looks favorably upon working people who set aside money for retirement via 401(k) plans, 403(b) plans, IRAs, etc., by allowing such savings to grow free of taxes until the money is withdrawn. In many instances, the money that you originally contribute to these plans is not currently subject to federal income tax. (See Chapter 6 for details.) Anyone with earned income should consider establishing an individual retirement account (IRA); anyone with income from self-employment also should consider contributing to a self-employed retirement account such as a Keogh or simplified employee pension (SEP) plan, and anyone whose employer offers a 401(k) plan or thrift plan should be sure to participate to the maximum extent.

> "... Anyone whose employer offers a 401(k) plan or thrift plan should be sure to participate to the maximum extent."

Nine Easy Ways to Save on Taxes in the 1990s

1. Keep good tax records. Improving your tax record-keeping system will help prevent you from paying more taxes than necessary. Keep a notebook handy to record miscellaneous tax-deductible expenses. This will enable you to have a reliable record of possible tax deductions.

2. Request IRS Publication 17. Call or write the IRS to request a copy of IRS Publication 17—Your Federal Income Tax. This booklet can help you gather information for your annual tax return. Each new tax year, several excellent tax preparation guides also are available in most bookstores.

3. Make a charitable donation of stock that has appreciated in value rather than giving cash. If you donate to a charity stock held over one year that has appreciated in value, you get a deduction for the current market value of the stock—thereby avoiding any capital gains tax.

4. Keep a record of all cash charitable contributions you make. Most people guesstimate their charitable cash contributions when tax time rolls around. But the IRS will disallow these if tangible proof does not exist. Therefore, keep a record of all your cash contributions or, better yet, write a check.

5. Donate unneeded clothing and other personal items to recognized charities. If you have usable clothing, furniture, or other personal property, donate it to a recognized charity. You can take a tax deduction for the donated items' fair market value by obtaining a receipt from that charity.

6. File returns separately (rather than jointly) if it will result in lower taxes. Sometimes married taxpayers will end up paying less in taxes if they file separate returns rather than a joint return.

7. If the IRS owes you a refund, send in your tax return early. Sending your tax return ahead of time, especially if you're going to get some money back, allows you to reinvest your money sooner.

8. If you owe the IRS money, don't send in your tax return early. As long as you have paid enough tax during the year to avoid a penalty, there's no reason to file your tax return early if you owe money to the IRS. Keep your money working for you until it's due.

9. Amend your return if you overpaid taxes the previous year and are entitled to a refund. But don't wait—there's a time limit of two years.

Income Tax Deductions

Finding a new tax deduction is like finding a forgotten $10 bill in last season's coat pocket.

Do you know what deductions the average taxpayer takes? The IRS recently released a detailed breakdown on the deductions claimed by taxpayers in different income brackets on their 1990 tax returns, which is the latest year for which statistics are available. The following table shows averages based upon those figures.

What Kind of Deductions Does the Average Taxpayer Take?

Adjusted Gross Income	$30-$40K	$40-$50K	$50-$75K	$75-$100K
Charitable contributions	$1,213	$1,315	$1,665	$2,122
Medical expense deductions	3,137	3,612	4,002	6,003
State and local taxes	2,447	3,015	4,049	5,888
Interest paid deductions	5,011	5,667	6,595	8,847
Deductible IRA contributions*	1,424	1,200	1,639	1,872
Keogh contributions	3,268	3,454	4,586	6,590
Miscellaneous deductions subject to 2% floor**	2,396	2,524	2,977	3,861
Fully deductible miscellaneous expenses	2,166	2,053	1,993	3,087
Income tax (before credits)	3,738	5,138	8,054	13,658

* This category does not include IRA contributions of spouses of those eligible to deduct IRA contributions.

** This category includes expenses subject to the 2% of adjusted gross income floor, such as unreimbursed employee business expenses. Figures are deductions net of the 2% floor.

Note: This chart is based on 1990 returns.

Important: Even a taxpayer whose deductions are less than these averages can be audited. However, taxpayers should not pass up claiming extraordinary deductions just because they are above the average.

Here are some of the most common deductions.

Homeowners Expenses

Some homeowners expenses—mortgage interest and property taxes—are tax deductible. You also can deduct points you pay when you take out a mortgage. If you refinance, you generally can't deduct all the points in one year—they must be spread out over the term of the mortgage. Also, if you refinance, any interest prepayment penalties are deductible.

Moving Expenses

You may be eligible for moving expense deductions if you are moving because you are changing jobs—or are being transferred to a new location by your employer. One caveat: the IRS requires that to qualify for the deduction, your new work location must be more than 35 miles from your old home.

Business and Job-Related Expenses

How job-related expenses are treated on your tax return depends on whether they are reimbursed by your employer. All reimbursed employee business expenses are deductible from your gross income. But since the reimbursed amount is part of your gross income, the deduction is essentially cancelled out. Unreimbursed employee business expenses, including car expenses and travel, are claimed as miscellaneous itemized deductions.

Miscellaneous itemized deductions generally must exceed 2% of your adjusted gross income (AGI) before the deduction is allowed. As a result, many people find that none of their unreimbursed expenses help reduce their taxable income. To find out if your expenses qualify, add up all of your miscellaneous itemized deductions. If they exceed 2% of your AGI, you can claim the excess as a deduction.

> "You can deduct points you pay when you take out a mortgage."

Travel Expenses

Deductible travel expenses generally consist of transportation costs incurred while away from home on business. Your tax home is either (1) your regular place of business; (2) if you have several places of business, the principal one; or (3) your residence. If you are temporarily assigned to another locale as part of your job, you may generally deduct travel expenses while temporarily employed away from home.

With respect to local transportation, you are entitled to deduct as a business expense local transportation costs incurred in traveling (1) from your principal place of business to another location where business-related activities occur, and (2) between one place where business-related activities occur and another such place.

Automobile Expenses

If you use your automobile in connection with your business or occupation, you may be able to deduct part or all of your car expenses using either a standard mileage rate or the actual cost. The standard mileage rate is certainly more straightforward to use, and you also can deduct parking fees and tolls incurred during business use on top of the standard mileage rate. Nevertheless, the actual cost method will usually give you a greater tax deduction. You must keep thorough records of all car-related operation and costs to substantiate your deductions. Automobile expenses also may be deductible when incurred in connection with charitable activities and when seeking medical care.

Meals, Entertainment, and Gifts

It is often hard to determine whether the cost of a business meal, entertainment, or gift is tax deductible. As a rule, you can deduct 50% (effective January 1, 1994) of the cost of these items, although the burden is on you to prove that the meal, gift, or entertainment expense was truly business related. Business gifts in excess of $25 per donee per year are not deductible.

Home Office Deduction

In 1993, the Supreme Court ruled in favor of the IRS's position regarding home offices which determines whether a home office deduction is allowable.

The IRS rule requires taxpayers to prove that their home is their principal place of business when claiming a deduction. The key term here is *principal* place of business. In the Supreme Court's judgment, just because work done in the home office is essential to your business, it won't necessarily qualify you for a deduction.

The case concerned a Virginia anesthesiologist who practiced at several hospitals but had no office in any of them. Instead, he used a spare bedroom in his home as his office for storing and working on patient records. According to the case, the doctor spent 35 hours in various hospitals, and 15 hours in his home office. The Supreme Court concluded that the doctor's home office was not his principal place of business and therefore denied the deduction.

Many people who have been claiming the home office deduction are affected by this ruling, but the IRS has said it won't revisit past tax returns where the deduction was allowable under the old rules.

> "The IRS rule requires taxpayers to prove that their home is their principal place of business when claiming a deduction."

Under this new interpretation, if you provide most of your services outside the home, you probably will not qualify for a home office deduction. If, however, you do all or most of your work in your home—say you're a free-lance writer, or you regularly see your patients, clients, or customers in your home office—then you still may qualify.

Be sure to keep meticulous records of home office use. Failure to do so will likely bring a rejection from the IRS of your hoped-for deduction.

To be deductible, a home office must be an area used exclusively for business, and it must generate income. These are in addition to the criteria established above by the latest Supreme Court ruling.

Commonly Overlooked Tax Deductions

The following items *may* be tax deductible, although a lot of taxpayers don't realize it. Be careful, however, because many of these items are deductible only under certain circumstances. For example, they are deductible only if they are associated with business activities. To find out more, check one of the many income tax preparation guides or the applicable IRS publications.

- Accounting fees for tax preparation services and IRS audits
- Appreciation on property donated to a charity
- Business gifts of $25 or less per recipient
- Casualty loss
- Cellular telephones
- Cleaning and laundering services when traveling
- Clerical costs to assist in looking for a new job in current occupation
- Commission on sale of property
- Depreciation of home computer
- Dues to labor union
- Employee educational expenses
- Employee's moving expenses, including those related to house hunting, selling your old home, or settling an unexpired lease, and travel
- Employment agency fees
- Fees for a safe-deposit box to hold investment papers
- Foreign taxes paid
- Gambling losses to the extent of gambling gains
- IRA trustee's administrative fees billed separately
- Out-of-pocket expenses relating to charitable activities, including standard mileage deduction
- Passport fee for business trip
- Penalty for early withdrawal on savings
- Points on home mortgage and certain refinancing
- Self-employment tax
- State personal property taxes on cars
- Theft losses
- Trade or business tools with life of one year or less
- Tuition fees for medical care
- Uniforms and work clothes not suitable as ordinary apparel
- Worthless stock or securities

Commonly Overlooked Medical Expense Deductions

You can deduct out-of-pocket medical expenses that exceed 7.5% of your adjusted gross income (AGI). Medical expenses also include dental and drug expenses. If there is any likelihood that your medical expenses should exceed the 7.5% of AGI threshold, you should tally them up in November or early December. If you're over the threshold, try to pay as many medical expenses as you can before year-end so that you can take maximum advantage of the deduction. You may even be able to prepay some medical procedures that will be performed in the next year. Frequently overlooked medical expense deductions are:

- Alcoholism and drug abuse treatment
- Childbirth preparation classes (for the mother, not for the coach)
- Contact lenses
- Contraceptives, if bought with a prescription
- Health insurance costs for self-employed persons
- Lead paint removal
- Meal and lodging expenses incurred en route to medical treatment
- Medical examination required by employer
- Medically prescribed items
- Mileage (transportation)
- Orthopedic shoes
- Parking fees and tolls
- Prescribed diet foods
- Special diet foods
- Special equipment for the disabled or handicapped

> "You can deduct out-of-pocket medical expenses that exceed 7.5% of your adjusted gross income (AGI)."

Year-End Tax Planning

The following are some strategic year-end moves to make in order to minimize your tax bill.

1. If you make estimated state income tax payments, rather than paying the last installment in January pay it in late December so that it can be deducted on the current federal return this year. Make sure your tax savings will exceed the amount of interest lost by paying early, however.

2. Give vent to your charitable impulses. Don't forget that donations of such items as old clothing, furniture, and books are deductible at fair market value. Donations of appreciated stock are often better than cash, since in addition to your income tax deduction, you can avoid paying tax on any capital gain if you sold the item.

3. Make sure your withheld and estimated taxes will equal or exceed either last year's tax bill or 90% of what you'll owe for the current year. (Some taxpayers may have to pay in even more to avoid a penalty.) If you think you'll come up short, there may still be time to compensate by increasing the taxes withheld from your salary at the end of the year.

Financial Snapshot *Continued:* **Tom Collins**

Tom Collins was concerned about the conflict in his financial life between the need to set aside more money for retirement and the higher portion of his income that was going to taxes. But he found several ways to minimize his tax bite so that he could increase his savings for retirement.

• He organized his tax records, which enables him to take more deductions than he had in the past. "I used to be afraid to guess at deductions, but with my tax files and appointment book which I carry all the time, I make note of *everything* I spend or do that may result in a tax deduction. It's like putting several hundred dollars in my pocket, and I no longer dread the prospect of an IRS audit."

• With these savings, he is accelerating the repayment of his mortgage so that he'll be mortgage free by the time he retires. "The taxes I save on mortgage interest are really peanuts compared with the interest I'll save by paying off my mortgage early."

• He's increasing his participation in his company's 401(k) plan, and he has set up a tax-advantaged simplified employee pension (SEP) plan for his moonlighting income.

• Finally, Tom has invested some of his personal savings in tax-exempt bonds and tax-exempt bond mutual funds. Not only is he saving taxes, but he's actually earning a higher after-tax return than he was in CDs.

Tax Planning Action *Checklist*

Tax Planning

Current Status		
Needs Action	**OK or Not Applicable**	
		1. Familiarize yourself with the many available ways to reduce taxes.
		2. Coordinate your income tax planning with other important personal financial planning areas, including investments and retirement planning.
		3. Don't lose sight of the role of old-fashioned tax-advantaged investments like tax-exempt bonds and buying and holding stock and real estate.
		4. Maintain complete and well-organized income tax records throughout the year. Your tax record keeping should be coordinated with your personal record-keeping system.
		5. Effective income tax planning is both a year-round process and a multiyear process. Spend some time after tax season—with your advisor, if applicable—planning your income tax strategies over the next five years.

Comments:

Tax-Free Investing Yield Calculation *Work Sheet*

Tax-Free Investing Yield Calculation

To determine the **after-tax yield** on each interest-earning investment you're considering:

Interest rate on the investment	%
Times (1 – tax rate paid on the investment*)	x
Equals **after-tax yield**	= %

* The tax rate paid on the investment depends on the type of security:

Type of Investment	Tax Rate Paid on Investment
Corporate and mortgage-backed securities:	Combine both your federal and state tax rates
Treasury securities:	Federal income tax rate
Out-of-state municipal securities:	State income tax rate
In-state municipal securities:	Exempt from both federal and state income taxes

Example: Say you're in the 31% federal and 6% state income tax brackets. You're considering investing in one of four securities: a corporate bond yielding 8%, a Treasury bond yielding 7%, an out-of-state municipal bond yielding 6%, and an in-state municipal bond yielding 5%. Which pays the most **after-tax** interest income?

	Corporate bond	Treasury bond	Out-of-state municipal bond	In-state municipal bond
Interest Rate on the Investments	8%	7%	6%	5%
x (1 – Tax rate paid on the investment)	x .63	x .69	x .94	x 1.0
= **After-tax yield**	5.0%	4.8%	5.6%	5.0%

Conclusion: In this example, the out-of-state municipal bond has the highest after-tax yield. Therefore, it pays the most after-tax interest income.

Year-End Tax Planning *Checklist*

Tax Planning

1. Consider making year-end charitable contributions of personal property such as clothing and furniture.

2. Consider making a contribution of appreciated securities to avoid paying capital gains tax (but be wary of possible adverse alternative minimum tax (AMT) consequences).

3. Consider bunching miscellaneous expenses, including professional dues, tax preparation fees, and unreimbursed employee business expenses, into the current year so that the total exceeds 2% of adjusted gross income (AGI).

4. If the 2% threshold will not be exceeded even through bunching, consider postponing as many of these expenses as possible until next year.

5. If enough money has not been withheld to meet the current year's tax liability, consider increasing the amount withheld from pay late in the year.

6. Make the maximum possible deductible individual retirement account contribution.

7. Increase participation in employer's 401(k) plan.

8. If there is any income from self-employment, consider opening a Keogh account on or before December 31 to shelter up to 20% of net earnings from self-employment.

9. If taxable income is nearing the 33% bracket, consider deferring income, to the extent permissible, until the succeeding year.

10. Consider paying the last installment of estimated state income tax payments in December rather than in January.

11. Determine AMT liability and shift itemized deductions that are treated as exclusion items for AMT purposes into years in which no AMT liability will be incurred. These include personal interest, state and local taxes, and most miscellaneous itemized deductions.

12. Determine whether medical expenses are likely to exceed the 7.5% of AGI hurdle. If so, bunch them in current year. If not, defer them.

13. Consider realizing capital losses to offset capital gains and investment interest or vice versa if you currently have net capital losses in excess of $3,000.

(Continued on the next page)

Year-End Tax Planning *Checklist Continued*

Tax Planning

14. Use installment sales method to defer capital gain recognition, particularly if it is likely that you will be in a lower tax bracket in later years.

15. If a change in filing status is expected in the succeeding year, defer current income and accelerate deductions if the change in status will lower tax rates. If higher rates are expected, reverse the strategy.

Comments/recommendations:

Planning for Financial Freedom in Retirement

Everything you do during your working years— from saving regularly to maintaining adequate insurance coverage, to investing wisely—should be directed toward your most important objective: a financially secure retirement. This chapter will help you on your way to achieving this objective.

Planning for Financial Freedom in Retirement

Questions

How old should I be before I start saving for my retirement?
Won't Social Security cover at least half of my retirement living expenses?
How can I estimate my current retirement saving's progress?
How much money will I need to have saved in order to retire comfortably?
What are the best retirement-oriented investments for me?
Are annuities appropriate for a retiree and in pre-retirement planning?

Retirement Realities

Many people neglect to plan for their retirement and end up either working beyond their desired retirement age or living a financially crimped retirement life-style. Overlooking the importance of planning for your own retirement is playing with fire, as the Retirement Facts show.

The ultimate goal of all the financial planning you do throughout your working years, including saving regularly, investing your savings wisely, and insuring against the unforeseen, is to be financially secure by the time you retire. Yet, despite the fact that all of us want to retire someday, planning for a comfortable retirement is often neglected. That's unfortunate because, of the so-called three legs of the retirement stool—pension, Social Security, and personal savings—the first two legs are wobbly at best. That leaves personal savings as the main source for

(Continued on page 128)

Retirement Facts

• According to a recent Employee Benefit Research Institute (EBRI) poll, 28% of the respondents age 55 or older had not yet begun to save for their retirement.

• Only 31% of workers age 55 or older who are currently working are receiving, have received, or expect to receive a private- or public-sector pension.

• Of those over age 55 who are retired or not currently working, 47% are receiving, have received, or expect to receive a private- or public-sector pension.

• According to the American Bankruptcy Institute, the percentage of the average American's paycheck that is consumed by monthly bills has risen from 62% in 1983 to more than 83% today.

Financial Snapshot · *Barry and Hannah Flynn*

Barry and Hannah Flynn are baby boomers who are approaching age 50. They, like most of their peers, are becoming increasingly concerned about their retirement prospects. "Our youngest child is a junior in college, and we're almost finished with college tuition bills," notes Hannah, "so it's time to really concentrate on retirement." Like many soon-to-be empty nesters, the Flynns feel like they've just passed one financial hurdle (raising children) and now have to concentrate on their retirement. Barry observes, "With all the child rearing and tuition bills, it almost seems like Hannah and I are starting from scratch. But we have equity in the house, some investments, and some IRAs. I know we've got to do more, and it's time to get started."

Key Words

Annuity A formal contract, usually issued by an insurance company, that guarantees a fixed or variable payment to the annuitant (the purchaser of the annuity) at some future time.

Deferred annuity Typically used to accumulate *retirement savings*. The money you invest can grow, tax deferred, in order to create a sizable nest egg. You can purchase a deferred annuity with a single sum or by making periodic payments.

Defined benefit pension plan A retirement plan that is structured to provide a certain, predetermined annual retirement benefit. Usually a formula is included in an employee benefit handbook.

Defined contribution pension plan A retirement plan under which each participant shares in the contributions to the plan. Today, the most popular defined contribution plan is a 401(k) plan.

401(k) plan A plan that allows an employee to contribute pretax dollars to a company investment program, which is invested in stocks, bonds, or money market instruments; also known as a salary reduction plan.

403(b) plan A special type of salary reduction retirement savings plan—also known as a tax-sheltered annuity—that is available only to employees of educational institutions and other qualifying nonprofit organizations.

Future dollars The number of dollars needed at some future date to provide the equivalent purchasing power of today's $1.

Income annuity An annuity that provides *retirement income*. In exchange for a lump-sum payment or payments, the annuitant receives periodic, usually monthly, income. The basic types of income annuities are deferred and immediate.

Individual retirement account (IRA) Tax-deferred retirement account that anyone with earned income can contribute to. Not everyone can deduct IRA contributions, but even a nondeductible IRA can still play an important role as a retirement savings vehicle, because dividends, interest, and/or capital gains earned on the IRA money is not taxed until it's withdrawn.

Keogh plan A formal arrangement in which the owner or owners of an unincorporated business (a sole proprietorship or a partnership) provide tax-deferred retirement benefits to the owners or partners and their eligible employees, if any.

Mandatory distribution rule A rule requiring that IRA and other retirement plan withdrawals must begin by April 1 following the year you turn age 70-1/2. Minimum withdrawals must be made each year, taking into account life expectancy or, if a beneficiary has been designated, your joint life expectancies.

Retirement-oriented investment plans Investment plans designed to provide income when the investor retires. Deposits to these plans may be tax deductible, and all such plans provide tax-deferred buildup of investment income until withdrawn. Examples include 401(k) plans, IRAs, and tax-sheltered annuity plans.

Rollover A tax-advantaged transfer of your assets from one IRA to another or a transfer of your company plan's lump-sum distribution to an IRA.

Simplified employee pension (SEP) plan A retirement savings plan frequently used by self-employed people and small businesses. Instead of maintaining a separate pension plan as is required with a Keogh, SEP contributions are deposited into an IRA.

funding a secure retirement for the majority of people. That is why, no matter what your income, achieving a secure retirement requires many years of planning.

The Retirement Landscape

Retiring comfortably is tougher now than it used to be. Several factors have changed the retirement landscape, and you should keep them in mind when you plan for your own retirement. These factors are as follows.

Longevity

Today, a person who reaches age 65 should plan on living another 25 years, and many will live well beyond age 90. Therefore, a person who wants to retire at age 65 will typically work for 35 to 45 years, during which time he or she will have to accumulate a retirement fund that is large enough to last 25 years or more.

Inflation

Inflation is firmly entrenched in our economy. Inflation makes it more difficult to accumulate resources in advance of retirement and makes it harder to maintain an adequate living standard over the course of a long retirement. Even at moderate rates of inflation, many retirees will see their cost of living double or triple during their retirement years.

Increased Reliance on Personal Savings

Fiscal pressures on the government and employers mean that working people will have to rely less on Social Security and company pension plans and more on personal savings and investments to assure an adequate retirement income.

Ambitious Retirement Expectations

Today, many people expect to retire without affecting their accustomed life-style. In contrast, previous generations expected to scale back when they retired. Your expectations will, in part, dictate the amount of savings you will need to accumulate. Compounding the problem of overambitious retirement expectations is an increase in forced early retirements. (See the discussion later in this chapter.)

> "Despite the fact that all of us want to retire someday, planning for a comfortable retirement is often neglected."

Early Retirement

Many people look forward to being able to retire early. Some are forced to do so. Since doing so requires much planning, both groups have their financial planning work cut out for them. For one thing, early retirees face a potential double whammy: they have fewer years to accumulate sufficient resources to fund a longer period of retirement. As a result, personal savings and investments play an even more important role for the early retiree.

The above caveats notwithstanding, it is possible to retire comfortably, but you *must* plan ahead.

Four Steps to Successful Retirement Planning

Recognizing what it takes to accumulate the necessary resources for retirement is a first step. The earlier you take this step and begin planning for retirement, the better your chances are of being able to get where you want to go.

The time to start planning for retirement is *now*. This chapter will first discuss four steps critical to planning for retirement.

1. Estimate how much income you will need during retirement. If you are many years from retirement, estimating your income requirements at retirement age may be of little concern to you now. But you should pay some attention to your retirement aspirations. After all, it's likely that you will spend more than one-third of your life retired. If you are nearing retirement age, you must begin to think about your retirement life-style in detail.

Once you have an idea of how and where you want to live when you retire, you can then estimate your expenses, first in *current dollars* and then in *future, inflated dollars*. Here's a helpful rule-of-thumb: to maintain the same standard of living in retirement that you enjoy today, you will probably need annual retirement income of approximately 75% of the amount you currently spend.

If you are under age 50, make some well-thought-out approximations of your expenses if you were to retire today. If you're within 10 to 15 years of retirement, you should prepare a detailed retirement living expense budget as soon as possible. Doing so will reveal that some costs decline, including work-related expenses and income taxes (but not dramatically). Social Security withholding taxes may drop to zero unless you work part time. However, other costs will increase, including health care (be sure to provide for health insurance) and, if you are so inclined, travel.

One of the biggest mistakes that people make in planning for retirement is either ignoring or underestimating the effects of inflation. Even though it is much lower now than it was during the double-digit years of 1979 to 1981, inflation still erodes your purchasing power. Many retirees, in particular, see their purchasing power diminished by inflation since much of their income may be either fixed (such as coming from retirement annuities) or may lag, or fall behind, inflation (derived from Social Security). When projecting your retirement expenses, consider inflation from now until you retire, and then factor in inflation for all of your retirement years.

> "The time to start planning for retirement is *now*."

Even though projecting inflation is a tricky business, it can and must be done. When making financial projections, many experts recommend assuming a future annual inflation rate of around 4% to 5%. The average annual inflation rate during the 1980s, including the high rates of the early 1980s, was 4.7%. In the early 1990s, it was closer to 3.5%.

Just what are the effects of an inflation rate of 4.5%? Assume that you will need $30,000 of annual income in today's dollars per year (including taxes) in addition to Social Security and pension benefits to live comfortably when you retire. Also assume that you're 50 years old and expect to retire at age 65. To offset the toll inflation takes, in 15 years' time you will need much more than $30,000 to have the same purchasing power as $30,000 of income today. How much more? Assuming an inflation rate of 4.5%, you would need almost $60,000 of income at age 65 to enjoy the same life-style that $30,000 buys today.

2. Figure out how much you will need to accumulate in order to fund a comfortable retirement. Once you estimate how much annual income you will need at retirement, you then need to forecast how much to accumulate personally (in addition to estimated Social Security and pension benefits) to provide that income (plus inflation) throughout your retirement. Before making the actual calculations, two important matters must be accounted for: life expectancy and inflation during your retirement years.

In the previous example, we discovered that an income of $60,000 would be needed 15 years hence to enjoy the same purchasing power that $30,000 provides today. But that's only part of the inflation equation. Unfortunately, inflation doesn't go away when you retire. By the time the example's 50-year-old reaches age 75, about $90,000 (at a 4.5% inflation rate) will be needed to have the same purchasing power that $30,000 buys today.

3. Review your progress in meeting your retirement needs. To start taking stock of your progress, tally up the assets that you currently have available that will be used for retirement purposes. (See the end of this chapter for a three-part work sheet that will help you determine your actual progress.) All of your savings (except those that are earmarked for specific nonretirement-related purposes like the down payment on a home or educating your children) will eventually be channeled to support you during retirement.

Two caveats: (1) Don't include the value of your home in your retirement-related assets unless you plan to sell the house and downsize or become a renter when you retire. (2) Don't include the value of your personal property (automobiles, furniture, etc.). Even if you have a collectible sports coupe, chances are it won't be worth much when it comes time to sell it—if you ever want to sell it.

When reviewing the state of your current retirement planning efforts, don't neglect housing costs. As part of your retirement planning, you should probably strive to be mortgage free by the time you retire. If you can be mortgage free or have a very low mortgage by the time you retire, your living expenses will be considerably lower than if you remain tied to a large mortgage or rent payment.

> "To maintain the same standard of living in retirement that you enjoy today, you will probably need annual retirement income of approximately 75% of the amount you currently spend."

4. Close the gap between the resources you now have and the resources you will need for retirement. Figuring how much savings you need to be able to retire comfortably often leads to the realization that you don't yet have enough money to meet your retirement income needs. Take corrective action. You can use the investment strategies discussed in Chapter 4 to help you increase your assets. You also can increase your participation in tax-deferred retirement-oriented investments.

Early Retirement

Early retirement—whether you choose it or it's forced upon you—is increasingly common. More than one-half of the workers eligible to collect Social Security retirement benefits begin collecting before age 65. That is because turning the dream (or necessity) of early retirement into a reality is a formidable financial challenge. If you would like to retire early, or if your company is making you an early retirement offer that you can't refuse, you need to take a hard look at how you will be able to meet your current living expenses when you retire, and also 10, 20, and 30 or more years thereafter.

It *is* possible to retire early and retire well, but you need to be certain that your long-term financial security is assured. If you have accumulated sufficient personal resources, your projections may indeed show that you can afford to retire early. However, it may be well worth the expense of hiring a financial planner or an accountant to help you make absolutely certain that your early retirement income and expense projections are reasonable and attainable.

Planning a Successful Early Retirement

If you are contemplating early retirement, there are two rules of thumb to help you gauge the viability of your plan. First, if you would have to rely on Social Security benefits to meet living expenses before age 65, you may not be able to afford an early retirement. Second, if a significant amount of your retirement income is going to be a fixed amount per month or year—in the form of an annuity, for example—and once you are retired you will not be able to save a generous portion of it to help fund increased future living costs, you may not be able to afford an early retirement.

Who can afford to retire early? Two common characteristics of people who make a successful go of early retirement are planning and sacrifice. This is how they do it:

• **They plan early.** Successful early retirement usually takes *decades* of planning. Many successful early retirees began planning for their dream in their 20s and 30s. They worked for companies with generous pension plans and avoided hopping jobs so that they could accrue substantial pension benefits. Some couples made the decision not to have children so they wouldn't incur the expenses of raising them. Many lived in cities and towns with low costs of living (housing costs, property taxes, etc.).

• **They sacrifice during and after their working years.** Most people have trouble saving 10% of their salary; however, successful early retirees realize that they need to save a minimum of 10% to 20% of their income during their working years. They are experts at living well below their means. They often live in inexpensive housing and keep living expenses low. Those who own homes pay off mortgages as soon as they can, and no later than when they plan to retire.

Even though they have spent many working years living modestly, successful early retirees cut back even further when they retire. They realize how much money they will have to continue saving to make ends meet 30 or 40 years later. Some go as far as to relocate to low-cost areas of the country or even to low-cost foreign countries.

"Two common characteristics of people who make a successful go of early retirement are planning and sacrifice."

Early Retirement Incentive Plans

Your company may tempt you or even force you to take early retirement. Some early retirement incentive plans sound particularly appealing, especially if times are tough and you feel that there are no guarantees that you'll be able to keep your job if you don't accept the offer. These plans *are* compelling, but some offer far less than meets the eye. The decision-making process is often made all the more difficult by the limited amount of time—often only a month or so—that you will have to evaluate the offer. That's scarcely enough time to weigh all the financial repercussions of this major financial decision. For this reason, it's advisable to hire a professional to evaluate the components of the plan in the context of your needs and resources.

Even a beefed-up early retirement pension is likely to be considerably smaller than the pension you could expect if you continued to work until age 65. That's because your pension is probably based on the average of what you earned in the last few years you worked. Even if the early retirement incentive plan adds bonus years of employment and bonus years to your age as input to the pension formula, it won't be able to make up the difference between your average salary for the last five years and your presumably higher average salary for the last five years if you had continued working.

The crucial issue is not how the early retirement package compares with the normal retirement options, but whether the package is sufficient to meet your retirement income needs. To answer that question, you will have to project your retirement income and expenses, just as you would if you were intending to retire at age 65.

Another issue that often takes early retirees by surprise is the emotional impact of their newly acquired freedom. Deciding where you will live, and, perhaps more importantly, what you will do, may seem easy. But many early retirees find, for example, that golfing or playing tennis for weeks in a row leads to boredom.

Planning in advance for the psychological impact of retiring is obviously a personal matter. Nevertheless, the happiest retirees tend to be those who wanted to retire in order to pursue another interest or hobby. Be sure that you have at least one thing you want to do on an ongoing basis so that the natural loss of esteem resulting from severing your relationship with your work place—the place wherein you developed your professional sense of self—does not become a problem for you.

Inflation's Toll on Early Retirees

If you aspire to early retirement, inflation—whose toll can knock your savings for an unprofitable loop—is even more of an issue in determining whether your pension and savings are sufficient to support you, than if you retired at age 65. This is because you will be spending for more years in retirement, and therefore, you will be more heavily affected by inflation. The following table shows how much more inflation severely affects early retirees. It shows how much living expenses will increase between retirement and the time you reach age 80.

Effects of Inflation on Early Retirees

Retirement Age	If Your Living Expenses When You Retire Are $40,000, Your Living Expenses at Age 80 Will Be*
65	$72,000
60	$88,000
55	$107,000

* Assuming a 4% annual inflation rate.

As the table (assuming a 4% inflation rate) shows, people who retire at normal retirement age would experience an 80% increase in living expenses by the time they reach age 80. Those who retired at age 60 would experience a 120% increase. Those who retired at age 55 would experience a 170% increase in the cost of living by the time they reach age 80.

Commonly Overlooked Costs of Early Retirement

Knowing some of the commonly overlooked costs of early retirement may help you plan to meet them or prompt you to reconsider retiring early.

Health Insurance

Unless you're taking an early retirement package that extends your company health insurance coverage until age 65, you'll need to factor in high health insurance premiums for an individually purchased policy until you become eligible for Medicare at age 65.

Unreliability of Part-Time Employment

Many early retirees count on working part time to supplement their retirement income. Part-time employment answers the two most frequent complaints of early retirees: too much time and too little money. But don't count on this option. Good part-time jobs that are financially and emotionally rewarding may not be as available as you may think.

Reduced Social Security Retirement Benefits

You can begin receiving your Social Security retirement benefits as early as age 62, but your benefits will be reduced if you do. Not only are the monthly checks lower, but the future dollar increases also are proportionally lower because they are calculated from a lower initial benefit amount.

While it still may be appropriate to begin drawing Social Security benefits early, one rule of thumb is that if your projections show that you must begin drawing Social Security benefits early to help meet basic living expenses, you probably can't afford to retire early.

Effects on Other Benefits

Any funds that you have set aside to supplement your retirement pension through individual retirement accounts (IRAs), Keogh and/or simplified employee pension (SEP) plans, 401(k) plans, or deferred annuities may be affected by your early retirement decision. Not only will you have contributed to the plans for fewer years when you retire, you probably also will begin making withdrawals sooner. Withdrawing funds from tax-advantaged accounts prior to age 59-1/2 may subject you to penalties. You should consult with a tax advisor.

Social Security

The myth that Social Security can satisfy all your retirement income needs must be dispelled. In fact, as your only retirement resource, Social Security would barely keep you over the poverty level. The hard truth is that Social Security benefits will probably support you in a moderate life-style for about one week in each month. Assuming that you want to live comfortably the other three weeks of each month, you will need other income sources—pension plans and personal investments. Nevertheless, as part of a comprehensive retirement portfolio, Social Security is a basic building block of guaranteed income. Social Security benefits have an important feature that is lacking in most retirement annuities: they are indexed for inflation. Although these benefits may lag the rate at which your living expenses are rising, the inflation adjustment is none-theless crucial.

Social Security Basics

Social Security benefits are not paid out automatically; *you* must initiate the monthly payment process yourself. If you don't, you won't receive a penny from the Social Security Administration (SSA).

You must apply in person or by phone, but all the follow-up can be done through the mail. No matter which initiation and follow-up options you use, you'll need to keep either photocopies of documents sent or accurate phone records—including the date, time, and individual you spoke with—so that, in the event of a foul-up, you'll have a complete record.

Unless you are receiving disability benefits, you should file a claim with your local SSA office *at least three months before you would like your retirement benefits to begin.*

> "The hard truth is that Social Security benefits will probably support you in a moderate life-style for about one week in each month."

Your Benefit Amount

The amount of your benefit is based on your earnings averaged over most of your working career using a formula that places the greatest emphasis on wages in your most recent years of work. Other important benefit notes:

- Higher lifetime earnings result in higher benefits.

- If you have some years of no earnings or low earnings, your benefit amount may be lower than if you had worked steadily.

- Your benefit amount is also determined by the age at which you start receiving benefits.

- The earlier you start collecting retirement benefits, the smaller the size of your monthly payments for life.

- Once you start receiving benefits, the amount will be adjusted subsequently to account for inflation.

Social Security currently uses age 65 as the normal retirement age. However, this age will slowly be increased, until it reaches age 67 in the year 2027. For every month you retire before you reach age 65, your benefits will be reduced by five-ninths of 1%—this translates to a sizable 20% reduction if you retire at age 62. A later retirement *increases* your benefits by 4% each year your retirement is postponed until age 70. This delayed retirement credit of 4% will gradually be increased from now through 2008 to a level of 8% per year—even though you can continue to draw a normal salary during those years.

After the year 2007, if you postpone retirement for five years beyond age 66, which will then be the normal retirement age, your Social Security benefits will increase *40%* (8% x 5 years). However, increasing the benefit by delaying the Social Security also reduces the number of years the benefits will be paid and may not be beneficial unless you live a very long time.

"It's a very good idea to have an ample cash reserve— for emergency use only. What constitutes 'ample'? Typically six months of living expenses."

Retirement-Oriented Plans and Investments

You should become familiar with the following summary of plans and investment vehicles that are designed to help you accumulate enough money for a secure retirement. Each of these plans has special benefits, yet some are more advantageous than others. For example, pension plans where your employer makes all contributions cost you nothing. Other pension plans may consist of your employer making partial contributions, with you making up the difference. Next are retirement-oriented plans where you make tax-deductible contributions, followed by plans or investments which include contributions that are not tax deductible, but whose income is tax deferred until retirement.

Before you put all your savings into retirement-oriented plans, remember that money invested in them is generally going to be tied up at least until you reach age 59-1/2 unless (1) you retire; (2) you die; (3) you become disabled; (4) you leave or lose your job; (5) your plan is terminated, and no successor plan is established; or (6) you demonstrate extreme need.

You need to ensure that you will have ready access to some cash reserves should the need arise. Therefore, you should keep some investments outside of your retirement plans (so that you don't have to dip into your retirement funds for unrelated needs). Also, it's a very good idea to have an ample cash reserve—for emergency use only. What constitutes "ample"? Typically six months of living expenses. Otherwise, you may end up having to sell your tax-advantaged investments (and remember, you could be penalized for this) at an inopportune time.

Employer-Sponsored Plans

The following plans are either wholly or partially subsidized by the employer.

Pension Plans

The extent to which a pension plan can contribute to meeting your retirement income needs can vary from zero (more than half of the nation's private-sector employees are not covered by pension plans) to a considerable amount. Thousands of companies are scaling back their pension plans or eliminating them altogether, and shifting to the individual the burden of accumulating retirement funds. Those who are fortunate enough to work for an institution that still has a pension plan may retire with a pension that goes a long way toward covering their retirement needs. If you are in this position, it's important that you examine the benefit projections provided by your employer to determine just how generous your plan truly is.

Although each company's pension plan is somewhat different, all plans share certain features. Most pension plans are formal, written plans; they have defined rights, benefits, and eligibility standards and use predetermined formulas to calculate your benefits. The reason for all this formality is self-interest. Federal regulations, largely promulgated by ERISA (Employee Retirement Income Security Act), require company pension plans to conform to certain rules in order for your employer's contributions to the plan to be tax deductible.

There are two basic types of pension plans: *defined benefit* and *defined contribution plans*.

"Most pension plans are formal, written plans; they have defined rights, benefits, and eligibility standards and use predetermined formulas to calculate your benefits."

Defined Benefit Plans

With this type of plan, the benefits you receive at retirement are determined in advance, although contributions made to the retirement fund are not. Defined benefit plans concentrate on the benefits to be received by you (the retiree). This allows you to budget your income accordingly—expecting a specific amount of benefits no matter how well or badly the pension investments perform.

From both sides of the equation—your employer's and your own—defined benefit plans create a certain amount of risk. How so? Your employer is responsible for delivering your specified pension benefits upon your retirement. It's conceivable that employers who suffer severe financial difficulties may not be able to provide all of the projected benefits to you.

For many years, this type of plan used to be the most common private pension plan. With a defined benefit plan, you receive a fixed amount of money based on your years of service, salary level, and other factors. The amount you receive is your vested interest in the plan. It often requires seven years of service for an employee to become fully (100%) vested.

Defined Contribution Plans

With this type of plan, your employer makes a certain contribution to the pension fund each and every year. Contributions are based on salary and years of service. At retirement, you receive a pension benefit or lump-sum payment based on whatever happens to be in the fund at the time. This type of plan is usually very advantageous if you have a long working life, and if your employer contributes enough to build up a substantial retirement fund. Contributions into defined contribution plans are limited, but benefits out of the plan are unlimited. With defined benefit plans, contributions are not limited, but benefits are. The most popular type of defined contribution plan today is a 401(k) plan. Other types include employee thrift and savings plans, and 403(b) plans. Each is discussed here.

• **Employee thrift and savings plans.** These usually require after-tax contributions, which are either wholly or partially matched by the employer's contributions. Even though there are no immediate tax benefits, you get something for nothing (your employer's contribution), and your savings will benefit from accumulating tax deferred.

• **401(k) plans.** When you participate in a 401(k), your employer diverts a fixed portion of your pretax salary into a company-sponsored investment plan. There are two immediate advantages to this: your overall taxable income is reduced, and you've started investing in your own future. While 401(k) plans have long been available to employees of large corporations, they are becoming more popular with smaller companies. Many employers also match part of each employee's contribution to 401(k) plans.

401(k) plans are easy to join and convenient to use. Most importantly, direct withdrawal from your paycheck makes it more likely that you will invest—rather than spend—the money you need to be socking away for retirement.

401(k) plans save federal income taxes in two ways. First, earnings placed into a 401(k) are deducted from your gross pay, so the more you put into your plan, the more income taxes you save each year you contribute. Because money in this plan is deferred compensation, it doesn't appear on your W-2 form and thereby avoids federal income tax, until the time the money is distributed. Also, depending upon where you reside, your 401(k) contribution may escape state and local income taxes. The second tax benefit is that earnings from the plan are not currently taxed until you begin making withdrawals. Dividends, interest, and capital gains aren't taxed until withdrawal.

You have to choose how to invest your 401(k) investments. Depending upon your employer, you may be able to choose from among a limited number of mutual funds, or you may be able to invest your money in a wide variety of investment vehicles, such as an array of mutual funds and a guaranteed investment (or guaranteed income) contract (GIC). But over the long run, a mix of stock and bond mutual funds will usually provide a superior return. Perhaps a split of 45% in stock funds, 45% in bond funds, and 10% in a GIC would be suitable.

Note: Investment percentages should be determined in conjunction with reviewing your whole portfolio of investments, not just plan assets.

You also have the right to switch the instruments in which your 401(k) is invested up to four times per year. But you can only switch into those accounts that are preset by your employer. These rules regarding shifting are specific to your company's plan. Be sure to contact your employee benefits department to find out what they are.

There is also a mandatory distribution rule. Benefits accruing from 1987 or later are subject to a mandatory distribution rule which takes effect when you reach age 70-1/2. The rules that govern 401(k) mandatory distribution are, with a few exceptions, the same as those that govern IRA mandatory distributions.

401(k) Plans—A Powerful Retirement Planning Tool

Unfortunately for some high income earners, the IRS has put a cap on the amount of money that can be put into a 401(k) plan. As of 1993, the maximum salary reduction allowed was $8,994. Even so, this is a very powerful retirement planning tool that should not be ignored.

For example, let's assume you could make a contribution of $4,000 per year to a 401(k) plan for the next 15 years until you retire. Let's also assume that your employer matches just 25%, or makes an additional contribution of $1,000 per year to your account. If $5,000 was invested in a stock mutual fund that compounded at just 10% per year for the next 15 years, your tax-deferred account would grow to a whopping $175,000 by retirement.

You could then withdraw income at a rate of 8% per year, or $14,000, to use as part of your retirement income along with Social Security payments and personal savings. Assuming this account continued to grow at 10% per year, and if you were only withdrawing at a rate of 8%, the money would never run out. You can readily tell that the sooner you begin to take advantage of and accumulate funds in this type of account, the more money you'll have available to use at retirement.

- **403(b) plans.** In many ways, a 403(b) plan is the nonprofit sector's answer to the 401(k) plan. 403(b)s—also known as tax-sheltered annuities—are a special type of salary reduction retirement savings plan. They are available only to employees of educational institutions and other specified nonprofit organizations.

Some institutions offering 403(b) plans make available to their employees several plans from which to choose. To find out what your organization offers, simply contact your employee benefits or personnel office and request the appropriate literature.

If you want to participate in a 403(b), you must agree to have your employer automatically reduce part of your current salary and transfer the money into a 403(b) account. As with a 401(k) plan, you generally have several options as to how you can invest your 403(b) funds. Since your paycheck will be reduced by the amount of money taken out of your salary, your minimum tax liability will decrease. Meanwhile, the funds invested in your 403(b) will generate dividends, interest, and capital gains totally free of taxes until you begin making withdrawals during retirement.

Before you can participate in a 403(b) plan, you have to sign a contribution agreement that tells your employer how much of your salary to withhold. You can initiate your 403(b) plan at any time during the year. However, once you have chosen a date and signed the agreement with your employer, you may not be able to alter the agreement—except to terminate the remaining payments due for that year.

After you've signed your 403(b) contribution agreement, the next step is to decide how to invest the funds. Employers who offer 403(b) plans generally provide participants with several investment alternatives.

> "If you want to participate in a 403(b), you must agree to have your employer automatically reduce part of your current salary."

In addition to your employer's automatic diversion of a portion of each paycheck into the plan, you can make voluntary additional plan payments—up to certain limits. The three limitations that affect your plan are as follows:

1. Elective deferral limitation. Ordinarily, your annual voluntary contributions to a 403(b) cannot exceed $9,500. If you are already making contributions to a SEP or to a 401(k), you may find that the amount of voluntary 403(b) contributions you can make may be lower than the usual maximum. Specifically, the more you contribute to a SEP or 401(k) plan, the less you will be allowed to voluntarily contribute to your 403(b) plan.

Special rule: If you have been working for your current employer for more than 15 years *and* your previous contributions to tax-sheltered annuities with your current employer did not exceed $5,000 per year, you can now make annual contributions of $12,500. However, you can make these larger $12,500 contributions for only five years; after that, you must comply with the standard $9,500 ceiling.

2. Annual limitation. The sum of your total annual voluntary contributions cannot exceed 20% of your reduced salary—the salary remaining after the contribution amount has been deducted from it—in any given year. While 20% would be nice to set aside, most of us can't afford that amount. Try 10% to 15%, or whatever you can afford. The important thing is to take advantage of tax-deferred accumulation and participate.

3. Overall limitation. Finally, the law limits the total amount you can invest in a 403(b) plan based on a variety of factors, including your employment history and your use of other retirement plans. Check with your employee benefits administrator to see how the overall limitation rules may affect your participation in a 403(b) plan.

As with a 401(k) plan, a mandatory distribution rule affects a 403(b) plan. Benefits accruing from 1987 or later are subject to a mandatory distribution rule which takes effect when you reach age 70-1/2. The rules that govern 403(b) mandatory distribution are, with a few exceptions, the same as those that govern IRA mandatory distributions.

Vesting, Rollovers, and Your Defined Benefit or Contribution Plan

Vesting is the rate at which your pension contributions to your pension account become permanently available to you. To understand how vesting works and when it occurs, you should read the provisions of your employer's pension documents very carefully. This document must be made available to all employees.

Vesting is also affected by a break in your service for an extended period because of illness, an accident, or personal reasons. Although ERISA strictly regulates this aspect of pension plans, you can lose all nonvested benefits accrued to a certain point if you are unable to work for a long time. For this reason, it's very important to understand your employer's policy on breaks in service.

Should you terminate your employment with a company and receive the vested benefits, they must be put into a rollover IRA within 60 days, or otherwise they will be regarded as taxable income for that year. If not rolled over, they may be subject to a 10% penalty tax for distributions if received before you reach age 59-1/2.

Current vesting schedules for most plans require five-year "cliff" vesting (100% vesting upon completion of five years of service) or an alternative, seven-year, graduated vesting schedule (20% after three years of service and 20% for each year thereafter).

Sometimes, if you leave a company, you may opt to keep your vested pension benefits in the company plan until you reach retirement age, at which time you can then draw a small pension. Whether to let the money sit there or roll it over into an IRA is entirely up to you. If you are confident that you can manage your own accounts, the IRA alternative is probably better. If not, keep the money in the company pension plan. Whatever you do, don't withdraw the money for your own use. Younger people, in particular, are inclined to view what may be a relatively small amount of money as unimportant for their retirement. The result is that they end up spending the money that should remain earmarked for their retirement. Not only are they heavily taxed and penalized, they also sacrifice some resources that may be important to their retirement.

> "Vesting is the rate at which your pension contributions to your pension account become permanently available to you."

The decision to roll or not to roll over your company pension benefits is a little less clear if you are laid off. If you think you might be out of work for a long time, you may need to use these retirement benefits to meet living expenses—but you should do so only as a last resort.

Note: Chronic job hoppers, even if they dutifully roll over whatever pension benefits they receive, usually end up with far less pension income than those who remain with one employer. Most large institution pension plans favor those employees who have many years of service.

Self-Employed Retirement Plans

If you have any income from either full- or part-time self-employment, you are eligible to set up your own retirement plan. Two types of plans to consider are Keogh plans and simplified employee pension (SEP) plans.

Keogh Plans

A Keogh plan is a formal arrangement in which the owner or owners of an unincorporated business (a sole proprietorship or a partnership) establish a program to provide tax-deferred retirement benefits to the owners or partners and their eligible employees, if any.

- **Important deadline.** Keoghs must be established by December 31 of the tax year when you want to begin taking the deduction. However, you can delay making the contribution until your tax return is filed (including extensions) in the succeeding year. If you miss the deadline, you can set up a SEP.

Keoghs are generally set up as defined contribution plans. They can be structured to allow you to contribute, and deduct, up to 25% of your net income from self-employment up to a maximum of $30,000.

- **Keogh accounts and IRAs.** If you have a Keogh plan, you can also open, or continue to contribute to an IRA (see below). Therefore, in addition to the regular tax-deductible Keogh contribution, you can contribute up to $2,000 over and above this amount to your IRA. Whether you can deduct the amount contributed to the IRA is based on certain limitations (see below).

Workers can still contribute to a Keogh after age 70-1/2. However, they also must begin taking distributions based on life expectancy after April 1, following the year in which age 70-1/2 is reached.

Simplified Employee Pension Plans (SEPs)

These are retirement savings vehicles frequently used by self-employed people and small businesses. Instead of maintaining a separate pension plan as is required with a Keogh, SEP contributions are deposited into your IRA.

- **Important deadline.** You may establish a SEP *after* the end of the tax year in which you want to begin taking the deduction as long as it is funded before your tax return filing deadline, plus extensions.

The SEP has tax advantages similar to those of regular qualified retirement plans. Employer contributions to SEPs are tax deductible up to a designated limit. The deductible employer contribution is generally 15% of your compensation (subject to certain maximum limits), but flexibility allows your employer to set up a percentage less than 15%. The same percentage must apply to all employees. Employer contributions are not subject to FICA or Federal Unemployment Tax Act (FUTA) tax withholdings, although state income tax usually has to be paid on the contribution.

How much can you contribute to a SEP? Generally, you may contribute 15% of your gross self-employment income, subject to maximum annual limits. You also can make an IRA contribution in addition to your SEP contribution, subject to the deductible limits.

As with Keogh plans, if you set up a SEP plan, it must be offered to all employees. As with a Keogh, you can still contribute to a SEP after age 70-1/2, but you also must begin taking distributions.

Individual Retirement Accounts (IRAs)

Anyone who has earned income can contribute to an IRA and enjoy the benefits of tax deferral. Unfortunately, not everyone can deduct IRA contributions. However, nondeductibility is not a good reason to forgo making IRA contributions. Even a nondeductible IRA due to its tax-deferral benefits can still play an important role as a retirement savings vehicle.

Opening an IRA is as easy as calling or visiting your local bank, brokerage house, mutual fund company, or insurance company and asking for an IRA application form. There are two types of IRA contributions: tax deductible and tax deferred.

> ## "There are two types of IRA contributions: tax deductible and tax deferred."

You need to designate a beneficiary when you open an IRA: your spouse, estate, another person, or a group of people. Designating beneficiaries is an important matter that is often not given sufficient attention. The rules and choices governing the receipt of IRA funds by the beneficiary in the case of the IRA owner's death are important, as they can significantly affect the beneficiary's tax liability.

Tax-Deductible IRAs

If neither you nor your spouse is an active participant in a qualified retirement plan, you may make tax-deductible IRA contributions regardless of your income level. Remember, the money invested in your IRA must come from earned income. An exception to the active-participant rule allows some low- and middle-income people to make contributions to IRAs even if they or their spouses are active participants in a qualified plan. For instance, single people with adjusted gross incomes of $25,000 or less can take full advantage of the IRA deduction. Married individuals filing a joint return who have an AGI of less than $40,000, and married individuals filing separate returns if a spouse has an AGI of less than $10,000, also may be able to deduct IRA contributions.

For a married person filing a separate return for any taxable year, the IRA deduction will be either reduced or eliminated if his or her spouse is an active participant in another employer-maintained retirement plan. This rule does not apply to married people who file separately and who live apart from their spouses during the entire tax year.

Partial deductibility is afforded single people who are active participants and whose adjusted gross income (AGI) is between $25,000 and $35,000. For active married participants who file joint returns, the applicable AGI is between $40,000 and $50,000. This rule also holds true for married individuals filing separate returns if one spouse has an AGI below $10,000. For every $5 that your AGI increases above the applicable dollar amount, your maximum IRA deduction is reduced by $1.

Nondeductible—But Tax-Deferred—IRAs

If you are an active participant in a qualified plan and therefore may not be eligible to make even partially deductible IRA contributions, you may be able to make designated nondeductible contributions (DNCs). Tax on the earnings of these DNCs is deferred until withdrawn. Your DNC cannot exceed the lesser of $2,000 ($2,250 in the case of a spousal IRA) or 100% of the compensation over the amount allowable as deductible for IRA contributions. Thus, a single taxpayer who is permitted a $900 deductible IRA contribution may contribute an additional $1,100 in nondeductible contributions. IRS Form 8606 is required of taxpayers who make nondeductible IRA contributions. (See the chart on the next page.)

Can You Take An IRA Deduction?

This chart sums up whether you can take a full deduction, a partial deduction, or no deduction.

IRA Deduction

If Your Modified AGI* is:		If You Are Covered by a Retirement Plan at Work and Your Filing Status is:			If You Are Not Covered by a Retirement Plan at Work and Your Filing Status is:			
At Least	But Less Than	• **Single** • **Head of Household**	• **Married Filing Jointly** (even if your spouse *is not* covered by a plan at work) • **Qualifying Widow(er)**	**Married Filing Separately****	**Married Filing Jointly** (and your spouse *is* covered by a plan at work)	• **Single** • **Head of Household**	• **Married Filing Jointly or Separately** (and your spouse *is not* covered by a plan at work) • **Qualifying Widow(er)**	**Married Filing Separately** (even if your spouse *is* covered by a plan at work)***
		You Can Take	You Can Take	You Can Take	You Can Take	You Can Take	You Can Take	You Can Take
$0.01	$10,000.00	Full deduction	Full deduction	Partial deduction	Full deduction	Full deduction	Full deduction	Full deduction
$10,000.00	$25,000.01	Full deduction	Full deduction	No deduction	Full deduction			
$25,000.01	$35,000.00	Partial deduction	Full deduction	No deduction	Full deduction			
$35,000.00	$40,000.01	No deduction	Full deduction	No deduction	Full deduction			
$40,000.01	$50,000.00	No deduction	Partial deduction	No deduction	Partial deduction			
$50,000.00 or over		No deduction	No deduction	No deduction	No deduction			

*Modified AGI (adjusted gross income) is: (1) for Form 1040A—the amount on line 14 increased by any excluded Series EE bond interest shown on Form 8815, Exclusion of Interest from Series EE U.S. Savings Bonds Issued after 1989, or (2) for Form 1040—the amount on line 31, figured without taking into account any IRA deduction or any foreign earned income exclusion and foreign housing exclusion (deduction), or any Series EE bond interest exclusion from Form 8815.

**If you *did not* live with your spouse *at any time* during the year, your filing status is considered, for this purpose, as Single (therefore, your IRA deduction is determined under the "Single" column).

***You are entitled to the full deduction *only* if you *did not* live with your spouse *at any time* during the year. If you *did* live with your spouse during the year, you are, for this purpose, treated as though you are covered by a retirement plan at work (therefore, your IRA deduction is determined under the "Married Filing Separately" column in the "If You Are Covered by a Retirement Plan..." section of the chart).

When Is the Best Time to Make IRA Contributions?

Although the IRA contribution can be deferred until April 15 of the following year, investors realize a substantial increase in the return on their IRA investment if their deposit is made at the beginning of the tax year.

Why? This allows the earnings on the contribution up to an extra 16-1/2 months to accumulate tax free. For example, if an IRA contribution for 1993 was made on January 2, 1993, rather than on April 14, 1994, the money can grow and compound tax deferred for an extra 16-1/2 months.

Using this approach, annual contributions of $2,000 with a 10% rate of return over a 20-year period would grow to $16,000 more than if the contributions were made 16-1/2 months later. In addition, by making the IRA payment early in the year, interest or dividend income that would otherwise be taxed in that year will be automatically tax sheltered. However, it may be advantageous for you to wait until after the end of the year, if you are unsure whether IRA contributions will be deductible or if your financial situation precludes your making the contribution earlier.

Once you reach age 70-1/2, you cannot continue to contribute to your IRA. If you have a younger spouse, you *can* make contributions to his or her account.

The deadline for opening or contributing to the previous year's IRA is April 15 (tax day) of the following year. If you send your tax return to the IRS early, however, the contribution does not have to be made before the return is sent. An extension for filing a tax return no longer allows an extension to contribute to an IRA beyond April 15.

When you open an IRA, you direct where your money will be invested. Your options may include one or more of the following: certificates of deposit, U.S. government securities, money market funds, stocks and bonds, mutual funds, corporate bonds, zero-coupon securities, unit investment trusts, limited partnerships, options (for self-directed IRAs only), and U.S. gold and silver coins. A custodian must hold these investments.

Despite this flexibility, IRAs should be managed very carefully. Some people mistakenly think that because their IRA money is earmarked for retirement, it should be invested very conservatively. Hence, a lot of IRA money languishes in money market accounts, CDs, and low-yield securities when it should be invested in securities that offer the opportunity for capital appreciation as well as income. Remember that retirement security means the ability to keep up with inflation.

Pension Plan Rollovers

When you want to transfer funds from an existing IRA directly into a new IRA, you sign a transfer form authorizing the new custodian to request funds from the old custodian, who then transfers them to the new IRA. You may make as many direct transfers as you want. The key to a transfer is never to take possession of the funds yourself.

If you are eligible to receive a distribution (or partial distribution) from a qualified retirement plan or tax-sheltered annuity, you may elect a direct rollover into an IRA to postpone the payment of taxes.

You must make a direct tax-free rollover of funds from an employer or self-employed pension to an IRA; otherwise, you will be subject to income tax withholding on the funds you receive from your employer. Anyone who is entitled to receive vested pension benefits prior to age 59-1/2 should either roll them into an IRA, or, if taking another job, might be able to roll them into the new employer pension plan.

Under a new law which took effect in January 1993, you must notify your current employer of where you wish to transfer these funds before they are actually paid out, to avoid 20% withholding. If you take direct receipt of the funds, 20% will be automatically withheld and sent to the government for tax purposes.

For example, if you are entitled to $50,000 from your current pension plan and the check is mailed directly to you, $10,000 will be withheld by your employer and sent to the government. Even though the check you receive will be for only $40,000, this does not preclude you from setting up a rollover IRA for the entire $50,000 amount. But you must come up with the extra $10,000 out of your own pocket to fund the account. You also have only 60 days to decide on where to roll over your distribution and to contribute the $10,000. (You can apply for a refund of the $10,000 later.)

To avoid this problem, you should decide on the new IRA custodian beforehand and instruct your employer to send the funds directly to it. In our example, the entire $50,000 would go to the new IRA custodian. Even though this new law puts pressure on the recipient to decide much faster, you avoid withholding on the funds.

Workers with well-funded retirement plans need to be cautioned against making oversize withdrawals. Otherwise, they could well incur a special 15% tax whose existence is almost unknown outside the IRS offices. The Internal Revenue Code penalizes pension payouts that exceed $150,000 in any calendar year by levying an additional 15% tax *over and above* the normal income tax. Ironically, unless you are careful, you could be penalized for planning too well for your retirement years.

> "You must make a direct tax-free rollover of funds from an employer or self-employed pension to an IRA; otherwise, you will be subject to income tax withholding on the funds you receive from your employer."

Fortunately, the law provides an escape hatch of sorts: retirees who opt to take a lump-sum payout—instead of a series of annual payouts—don't have to pay the 15% surtax on the first $750,000 of funds withdrawn from a retirement plan. If you have two plans, a company plan and an IRA, you can take advantage of both exemption allowances at once. The increased exemption limit must be used in conjunction with the company retirement plan. However, taxpayers must stick to the $150,000 limit for IRAs. Thus, you could withdraw $750,000 from a company plan and $150,000 from an IRA during the same calendar year and avoid paying the surtax. Timing is everything, though—the $750,000 exemption can be used only once, and in most cases, the taxpayer must be over age 59-1/2. Finally, to take advantage of the exemption, the taxpayer must elect to use five- or 10-year income averaging in calculating how much *income* tax is owed on the payout.

Other strategies are available for avoiding the onerous tax. In cases where retiring employees can spread plan payouts over several years, receiving the money in installments of $150,000 or less may be the most straightforward means of avoiding the 15% surcharge. As with any matter that involves taxes, it pays to plan ahead when devising a payout schedule. Whatever form the payout schedule takes, payouts do have to begin by age 70-1/2.

Note: You should contact an experienced professional who is knowledgeable about these special laws to help with your particular situation.

> "You *must* begin IRA withdrawals by April 1 following the year you turn age 70-1/2."

Withholding

Federal income tax will be withheld from IRA distributions unless you instruct a direct transfer of your rollover to a new custodian as described previously.

If you receive a distribution from your IRA, you will receive Form 1099-R, Distributions From Pensions, Annuities, IRAs, Insurance Contracts, etc., or a similar statement. IRA distributions are shown in Boxes 1 and 2 of Form 1099-R. A number or letter code in Box 7 tells you what type of distribution you received from your IRA.

Withdrawal

Withdrawing money from your IRA can be a complicated proposition—especially if you want to avoid a penalty tax. The following information simplifies the process.

If you are younger than age 59-1/2, there will be a 10% penalty tax to pay on early withdrawals. The 10% penalty does *not* apply to distributions payable to a beneficiary upon the death of an IRA owner or payable to his or her estate. Also, if the before-age-59-1/2 distribution is an annuity over your life expectancy or the joint life expectancy of you and the beneficiary, the distribution is not penalized. The rules are complicated, so chances are you will need expert assistance if you're going to avoid penalties in early withdrawal.

• **When you may begin to withdraw.** You may begin withdrawing from your IRA at age 59-1/2, or earlier if you fit one or more of the exceptions noted above. If part of a premature distribution is tax free because it is an allocation of nondeductible contributions, the 10% penalty applies only to the taxable portion of the distribution.

• **When you must begin to withdraw.**
You *must* begin IRA withdrawals by April 1 following the year you turn age 70-1/2. (Failure to make minimum withdrawals can subject your funds to a 50% penalty from the IRS on the difference between the amount you should have received and the amount you did receive.) Minimum withdrawals must be made each year, taking into account your life expectancy or, if you've designated a beneficiary, your joint life expectancies.

Computing Minimum Withdrawals

To compute the minimum withdrawals that are required for IRA owners older than age 70-1/2, follow these three steps.

1. Determine the account balances in all of your IRAs as of the previous December 31.

2. Find out your life expectancy or the joint life expectancies of you and your beneficiary. The IRS provides life expectancy tables (request IRS publication number 590, Individual Retirement Arrangements (IRAs)), which provide the fraction used to compute the minimum amount that must be withdrawn from an IRA. Special rules apply to non-spousal beneficiaries.

3. Calculate the minimum amount you must withdraw. This is done by dividing the amount of money in your IRAs found in step one by the life expectancy factor found in step two. For example, a single woman, age 70, with a 15-year life expectancy would take out one-fifteenth of her IRA savings upon reaching age 70-1/2. The next year, she would take out one-fourteenth of the remainder, and so on. Alternative methods are also available.

One of the advantages of following the minimum withdrawal schedule is that the funds left in the IRA continue to accumulate tax free. The following table shows how much this can actually increase the funds that will be received during your retirement. The table calculates total withdrawals of $67,314 over 19 years. (The table assumes that the withdrawals will commence by the time you reach age 70-1/2.) If you took this IRA in a lump sum, you would receive $25,000 in the first year; if, instead, the money is withdrawn in installments and the withdrawal schedule is refigured each year by a changing life expectancy, the accumulation is greater. For the highest accumulation, it is best to take out the smallest amount possible while allowing for your financial needs. The table assumes 10% interest on an account with minimum withdrawals:

Year	Beginning Year Balance	Fraction	Minimum Withdrawal Amount
1	$25,000	1/19	$1,315
2	26,052	1/18	1,447
3	27,065	1/17	1,592
4	28,021	1/16	1,751
5	28,896	1/15	1,926
10	31,025	1/10	3,102
15	24,983	1/5	4,996
19	7,315	remainder	7,315

If your IRAs are spread among more than one account, the minimum withdrawal schedule will be the same for each, but you may decide from which accounts the withdrawals will be taken. Note that the table above is only a minimum schedule and that after age 59-1/2 withdrawals can be as large as you desire. If in any year a withdrawal is larger than the minimum, then your remaining minimum withdrawals will be reduced.

IRA Withdrawal Options

Lump-Sum Withdrawal. Some people may prefer taking the whole IRA in one lump sum. One reason to do this is that it eliminates any risk of the penalty for falling below the minimum withdrawal schedule. However, the money withdrawn will be currently taxed and what's left should be reinvested in non-IRAs, which will be subject to tax on capital gains, dividends, and interest (except municipal bond interest).

IRA Annuity. Retirees may use their IRAs to purchase an annuity. Buying an annuity that begins regular payments by age 70-1/2 satisfies the IRS's withdrawal rules. Like an annuity, it can be purchased for your life expectancy or jointly for the combined life expectancies of you and your spouse or other beneficiary. One advantage of this option is that it guarantees payments for your lifetime or, in the case of a joint annuity, for the lifetime of both you and your beneficiary. There also may be a provision in the annuity that provides for payments to heirs. Details about annuities appear below.

Income Annuities

There are two basic types of income annuities: a deferred or an immediate annuity.

Both deferred and immediate annuities may be purchased as either fixed or variable investments. A fixed annuity provides a fixed rate of return based upon (1) the amount invested, and, with respect to income that pays benefits over your lifetime, (2) your age. In contrast, a self-directed variable annuity provides a variable rate of return based upon the performance of the investment instruments (usually a range of mutual fund portfolios) that you select.

Many people assume that a fixed annuity is the more secure investment. That assumption is usually the result of confusing reliability with security. It is crucial that you do not make the same mistake.

Deferred Annuity

A deferred annuity is typically used to accumulate *retirement savings*. The money you invest can grow, tax deferred, in order to create a sizable nest egg. You can purchase a deferred annuity with a single sum or by making periodic payments. If the annuitant dies, the beneficiary receives the total amount of dollars you invested in the annuity even if the value of the mutual fund portfolio in which the annuity is invested has declined. (If the value of the mutual fund has increased—a much more likely long-term result—the beneficiary receives the increased amount.)

> "There are two basic types of income annuities: a deferred or an immediate annuity."

Immediate Annuity

An immediate annuity, as the name implies, is used to provide *retirement income* immediately. It starts with your investment of a lump sum (you purchase an immediate annuity with a single payment), and begins generating periodic, usually monthly, income payments within a short period of time. An immediate annuity is often used by a new retiree to provide a reliable source of retirement income.

• **Fixed annuities** are reliable in that they guarantee you a specified interest rate for a specified period of time, often one year. In the case of deferred fixed annuities, this rate is usually guaranteed for one, two, or three years, or other specified period. After the specified period (you need to be sure you understand what happens after the guaranteed rate period expires), your interest rate will change in accordance with prevailing interest rates in the marketplace. However, there is often a minimum guaranteed rate per contract, often 4%.

A fixed-rate annuity may provide you with a reliable and predictable accumulation or monthly benefit, but when you factor in inflation, the purchasing power of the fixed return diminishes. Over many years, the purchasing power can diminish considerably.

• **Self-directed variable annuities** are designed to protect your money from the diminishing purchasing power effects of inflation. The performance of a self-directed variable annuity investment is based not on a fixed interest rate, but on the performance of a portfolio of mutual funds (called separate accounts) that *you* select. What's the purpose? To provide you the opportunity for a return that far exceeds the return you could get out of a fixed annuity contract. Moreover, unlike an IRA, 401(k), or other tax-deferred investments, there is *no limit* as to how much you can invest in a self-directed fixed or variable annuity.

> "Fixed annuities are reliable in that they guarantee you a specified interest rate for a specified period of time, often one year."

Annuity Settlement Options

Straight-Life Annuities. Straight-life annuities make payments to the annuitant until death do you part. A straight-life annuity is a win-or-lose deal. You can win by living longer than the insurance company figures you will live, or you can lose by dying earlier than the company estimates. (Heirs get nothing under these arrangements.) Remember that insurance companies have a great deal of experience in working with mortality tables.

Joint-and-Survivor Annuities. Joint-and-survivor annuities deal with the risk of loss by guaranteeing that neither you (the annuitant) nor your spouse will outlive the income. Payments will continue to your spouse even after you die, should you die first, although the survivor will be paid smaller installments than both of you received previously. Also, because the annuity is intended for a longer period of time, the regular payment to both spouses will be smaller than with a straight-life annuity.

In the vast majority of situations, couples are well advised to take joint-and-survivor annuities to protect the surviving spouse. In other words, don't simply waive a joint-and-survivor annuity in your pension plan by buying an insurance policy. While this may work in some instances, be sure to understand the pitfalls before making such a significant and irreversible commitment.

Life Annuities With Certain Installments.
Life annuities with certain installments
provide a way of overcoming the risks of
straight-life annuities. They resemble straight-
life annuities in that they guarantee regular
payments until death. In addition, a certain
number of payments are guaranteed: if death
occurs before a specified number of years
has elapsed, the balance of the guaranteed
payments will be paid to your survivors.
Most commonly, the guaranteed payments
are for a period of 10 years, which is usually
shorter than the expected life expectancy at
retirement. Thus, premature death results
in a smaller monetary loss for the family
with this type of annuity than with a straight-
life annuity. But the periodic annuity payment is less as well.

Refund Annuities. Refund annuities
alleviate some of the risk inherent in straight-
life annuities by guaranteeing that the retiree
or his or her survivors will receive back as
much money as was originally paid into the
purchase. Therefore, if the retiree dies pre-
maturely, the balance will be paid to his or
her beneficiaries. This balance can be paid
either in one lump sum (a cash-refund annuity)
or in regular installments (an installment-
refund annuity).

Note: It is important not to misunderstand the
meaning of the term "refund." Refund does not mean
that the money originally paid can be returned at any
time, but only upon the annuitant's death. There is
still a risk of loss in this annuity, as money is tied up
in the annuity and may not be used for personal investing to create more income. Both refund annuities and
life annuities with certain installments offer lower
annuity payments than straight-life annuities do.

The Role of Self-Directed Variable Annuities in Your Retirement Portfolio

Think of your self-directed variable annuity
as an all-weather investment. How so? The
fact that your investment is diversified in a
portfolio of mutual funds provides you with
the opportunity to outperform not only fixed
annuities, but other types of investments
such as bonds and money market funds.
Effectively matching your investment needs
to the right mutual fund portfolio is crucial
to your ultimate financial well-being. First,
you need to understand what portfolio
options are available. Then you need to
select the right one for you.

Choosing Between a Lump Sum and an Annuity

While some pension plans require you to
take a monthly annuity payment at retirement,
your plan may allow you the option of taking
a lump-sum payout. There may be some
advantage to taking a lump sum, but this
option must be considered carefully.

Most annuities offer monthly payments
which are not adjusted for inflation. However,
if you are confident that you or your investment adviser can invest the lump-sum amount
more profitably, then this option may be a
much better choice. You'll probably be able
to generate more income than with the
annuity and, at the same time, beat inflation.

But you must consider the drawbacks to
taking a lump sum. For example, if you or
your spouse should incur substantial uninsured medical expenses (i.e., a long-term
nursing home stay), subject to the claims of
creditors or the mismanagement of money,
your lump-sum retirement fund may be
jeopardized. In the worst instances, this
could seriously erode or altogether wipe out
your pension resources. This eventuality
must be weighed carefully in deciding on
the lump-sum option as opposed to an
annuity. Once more, money that is in an
annuity is usually protected from these
adverse occurrences.

What is the solution? Perhaps a partial lump-sum settlement and partial annuity may be a desirable compromise (if allowed by your employer). Be sure to examine all the annuity options available to you. Payout rates on income annuities vary widely. Shop around for the company that offers the most attractive terms. If you take a lump sum, you have some homework to do as well. You may be able to take advantage of forward averaging to reduce the tax impact of the distribution, or, you can postpone paying taxes on the distribution by rolling it over into an IRA. Only when you begin withdrawing money from the IRA will taxes become due.

If you are fortunate enough to expect a large annual income from your retirement plans or you expect to take a large lump-sum distribution, you should speak with an income tax or financial planning professional about your potential exposure to the onerous 15% surtax on so-called excess distributions from retirement plans discussed earlier.

> ## "Payout rates on income annuities vary widely."

Set Your Retirement Watch According to This Financial Freedom Timetable

Actually, the sooner you begin to invest in a personal savings program, the greater your chances are of achieving financial security by the time you retire. You can't count on Social Security for all your retirement needs. Since there is no guarantee you will build up a fortune in a company-sponsored pension plan, it's imperative that you invest regularly and wisely to achieve the secure retirement you want.

The following Financial Freedom Timetable will help you synchronize your investments with your retirement goals.

Financial Freedom Timetable

It's never too early to plan for retirement. To prepare for a financially comfortable retirement, you need to take action throughout your working years. The following timetable describes important steps to take at various ages.

During All Working Years

1. Be sure you have adequate cash reserves for emergencies. (A minimum of six months' living expenses is best.)
2. Make sure you always have adequate and continuous insurance coverage including medical, life, disability, property, casualty, and liability (auto, home, and umbrella).
3. Consider the ramifications on future pension benefits of any contemplated job change. Job hopping can curtail pension benefits severely.
4. Roll over any vested pension benefits received as a result of a job change into an IRA or other tax-deferred retirement plan.
5. Make certain that you are doing a thorough tax planning job so that you maximize your after-tax income.

Before Age 40

1. Contribute regularly to an IRA or other retirement-earmarked savings fund, as well as to a 401(k) or 403(b) plan if available.
2. Purchase a home so that by the time you retire your housing costs will be under control.
3. Discuss the fine points of the pension plan with your company's benefits officer.
4. Write a will.

Ages 40-49

1. Periodically check with Social Security by requesting and filing Form SSA-7004. You will receive a Personal Earnings and Benefit Estimate Statement to verify that your wages are being properly credited to your account and to prepare retirement income projections.
2. Analyze personal assets, and work out a plan for funding an adequate retirement income.
3. Actively manage your IRA and other retirement funds with appropriate emphasis on capital-gains-oriented investments.
4. Write a will, and review it every three years or when moving to another state. Discuss other estate planning techniques with an experienced estate planning attorney.

Ages 50-59

1. Periodically request your Social Security Personal Earnings and Benefit Estimate Statement.
2. Regularly review your status with your company's pension plan.
3. Revise your retirement income and expense projections, taking inflation into consideration.
4. Confirm the beneficiary designations on life insurance policies.
5. Join the American Association of Retired Persons (AARP) to take advantage of the information that it offers. The address is:
   AARP
   601 E Street N.W.
   Washington, DC 20049
   (202) 434-2277

Ages 60-64

1. If you are contemplating an early retirement, discuss the advantages and disadvantages with your employer's personnel officer and the local Social Security office.
2. Collect the documents necessary to process Social Security benefits. These include both spouses' Social Security cards, proof of both spouses' ages, marriage certificate, and a copy of your latest income tax withholding statement (W-2).
3. Before taking any major actions, such as selling a house, weigh the merits of waiting until age 55 when many special breaks are available to the elderly or retired.
4. Determine the status and duration of ongoing financial commitments such as mortgages and loans.
5. Prepare detailed cash flow projections from estimated year of retirement until age 90, taking inflation into consideration.
6. Practice living for a month under the planned retirement income.
7. Consider different retirement locations. If a location other than the current home is chosen, try living there for a while before making the move. For example, check out income tax rates.
8. Determine what activities will keep you active in retirement. Develop interests, hobbies, and a support network of friends.

Right Before Retirement

1. Establish what your retirement income will be, and estimate as closely as possible what your retirement costs of living will be.
2. Have your employer's personnel officer determine exactly what your pension benefits will be, what company or bank will send the pension, and when the first check (or lump-sum distribution) will arrive; what can be done about accumulated vacation time; whether there are any special annuity benefits; and whether supplemental medical or hospital insurance is available.
3. Register with the Social Security Administration at least three months before retirement.
4. Inquire about possible entitlements to partial pensions from past jobs.
5. Consider long-term care insurance and a Medicare Supplemental policy if you are eligible for Medicare (at age 65).

Common Retirement Planning Mistakes

- Failing to participate in retirement savings plans.

- Neglecting to prepare retirement income and expense projections during the working years.

- Expecting that Social Security will provide adequate retirement income needs.

- Accepting an early retirement incentive offer without thoroughly analyzing its financial consequences.

- Failing to consider the toll inflation takes on retirement savings.

- Failing to take out the required IRA minimum withdrawals after age 70-1/2.

Financial Snapshot *Continued*   *Barry and Hannah Flynn*

With the help of their Certified Financial Planner, Barry and Hannah have, in her words, "taken several positive steps in the direction of securing a comfortable retirement. For one thing, we're both contributing to IRAs, and Barry has just started contributing to a 401(k) plan with his employer—my employer doesn't offer one. Thanks to our planner's help, we've started to prepare retirement income and expense projections so that we will have a better idea of how much we will need to set aside."

Barry adds, "We're going to check with Hannah's and my employee benefits people and Social Security to verify our expected retirement income, and we're reading literature on various investment options."

While the Flynns admit they have their work cut out for them, Hannah looks on the bright side. "We're finally getting a handle on what we will need to be able to retire when we want to, and in the style that we want. It certainly beats worrying every day about our retirement outlook."

Retirement Planning *Work Sheet*

Use this three-part work sheet to forecast the amount of retirement income you will require and to estimate the amount of savings you will have to accumulate to meet your retirement income needs.

I. Retirement Expense Forecaster

This section helps you approximate the amount of annual retirement income that will allow you to maintain your pre-retirement standard of living. First, the approximate income necessary to maintain your current living standard in current dollars is calculated. Then, by reference to future value tables and by using the assumed rate of inflation, you can project this amount to your estimated retirement date.

Current gross annual income[1] $...................

Minus amount of annual savings[2]   (...................)

  Subtotal (the amount you spend currently)   ....

Multiplied by 75%[3]   x .75

Equals approximate annual cost (in current dollars) of maintaining
  your current standard of living if you were retiring this year $...................

Multiplied by inflation factor
  (Refer to inflation factor table below)[4]   x...................

Equals approximate annual cost (in future dollars) of maintaining
  your current standard of living when you retire $...................

Inflation Factor Table

Number of Years Until Retirement	Factor
5	1.2
10	1.6
15	1.9
20	2.4
25	3.0
30	3.7
35	4.7
40	5.8

Explanations:

[1] "Current gross annual income" includes all income from all sources.

[2] "Annual savings" includes, in addition to the usual sources of savings, reinvested dividends and capital gains, and any contributions to retirement plans that are taken from your annual income.

[3] The 75% multiplier is a general rule of thumb that says, in essence, that a retiree can maintain his/her pre-retirement standard of living by spending roughly 75% of his/her pre-retirement income. Of course, individual circumstances may dictate a higher or lower percentage. Ideally, you should prepare a retirement budget that details expected expenses. You may find a multiplier less than 75% in some circumstances (for example, low housing costs due to paid-off mortgage) or, in other circumstances, a higher multiplier (for example, extensive travel plans).

[4] In order to project retirement expenses to retirement age, current dollar living expenses must be multiplied by a factor to account for inflationary increases. The inflation factor table can be used for that purpose.

(Continued on the next page)

Retirement Planning *Work Sheet Continued*

This section can be used to forecast pension and Social Security benefits at retirement age and then to approximate the aggregate amount of savings/investments that will be needed by retirement age to cover any shortfall between Social Security/pension benefits and your total income needs.

II. Retirement Resources Forecaster

	Current Dollars	Times Inflation Factor[1]	Future (Retirement Age) Dollars
1. Estimated annual living expenses at retirement age (From Part I)			$..................
2. Annual pension income (projection at retirement age available from employer)[2]	$.................. x	.... =	....
3. Plus annual Social Security benefits (projection at retirement age available from Social Security Administration)[3]	$.................. x	.... =	....
4. Subtotal of projected pension and Social Security income (add lines 2 and 3)			....
5. Shortfall (if expenses are greater than income) that must be funded out of personal savings/investments (subtract line 4 from line 1)			....
6. Multiplied by 17[4]			x 17
7. Equals amount of savings/investments in future dollars that need to be accumulated by retirement age to fund retirement[5]			$..................

Explanations:

[1] Use inflation factor table for the appropriate calculation.

[2] Employers usually provide pension plan projections at retirement age, expressed in current dollars. If so, the amount should be multiplied by an inflation factor to approximate benefits in future dollars.

[3] Social Security estimates are expressed in current dollars, and therefore, they should be adjusted for inflation similar to footnote 2 above.

[4] As a general rule of thumb, for every $1,000 of annual income you will need to fund at retirement age, you will need to have at least $17,000 in savings/investments in order to keep up with inflation. If you plan to retire before age 62, use a factor of 20, rather than 17.

[5] You may be dismayed by the magnitude of the amount of personal resources that you will need to fund your retirement, which can easily exceed $1 million for younger persons and/or people with minimal pension benefits. Nevertheless, good savings habits combined with the power of compounding can usually close the gap between current resources and eventual needs.

Note: This is a *simplified* method. A professional planner can prepare a more detailed and individualized analysis.

(Continued on the next page)

Retirement Planning *Work Sheet Continued*

This section can be used to estimate the annual amount of savings that are required to accumulate the funds necessary to meet your retirement objectives. The amount computed on Line 7 equals the required *first year* savings. The annual savings should be increased by 5% in each succeeding year until you retire.

III. Retirement Savings Estimator

1. Amount of savings/investments in future dollars that need to be accumulated by retirement age to fund retirement (from Part II) $...................

2. Minus resources that are currently available for retirement purposes[1] $...................

3. Multiplied by appreciation factor (refer to annual appreciation factor table below)[2]   x ....

4. Equals estimated future value of retirement resources that are currently available (Multiply Line 2 by Line 3)   (...................)

5. Retirement funds needed by retirement age (Subtract Line 4 from Line 1)   ....

6. Multiplied by annual savings factor (Refer to annual savings factor table below)[3]   x ....

7. Equals savings needed over the next year (Multiply Line 5 by Line 6)[4] $...................

Appreciation Factor Table		Annual Savings Factor Table	
Number of Years Until Retirement	Factor	Number of Years Until Retirement	Factor
5	1.4	5	.1513
10	2.1	10	.0558
15	3.0	15	.0274
20	4.2	20	.0151
25	6.1	25	.0088
30	8.8	30	.0054
35	12.6	35	.0034
40	18.0	40	.0022

Explanations:

[1] Resources that are currently available typically include the current value of all of your investment-related assets that are not expected to be used before retirement. Don't include the value of your home unless you expect to sell it to raise money for retirement. Don't include any vested pension benefits if you have already factored them in on Line 2 of Part II of this work sheet.

[2] The appreciation factor is used to estimate what your currently available retirement resources will be worth when you retire. The appreciation factor assumes a 7.5% after-tax rate of appreciation.

[3] The annual savings factor computes the amount you will need to save during the next year in order to begin accumulating the retirement fund needed by retirement age as indicated on Line 5. The annual savings factor assumes a 7.5% after-tax rate of return.

[4] The annual savings needed to accumulate your retirement nest egg assumes that you will increase the amount of money you save by 5% each year until retirement.

Retirement Planning *Work Sheet: Sample*

Use this three-part work sheet to forecast the amount of retirement income you will require and to estimate the amount of savings you will have to accumulate to meet your retirement income needs.

I. Retirement Expense Forecaster

This section helps you approximate the amount of annual retirement income that will allow you to maintain your pre-retirement standard of living. First, the approximate income necessary to maintain your current living standard in current dollars is calculated. Then, by reference to future value tables and by using the assumed rate of inflation, you can project this amount to your estimated retirement date.

Current gross annual income[1]	$ 40,000
Minus amount of annual savings[2]	(4,000)
Subtotal (the amount you spend currently)	36,000
Multiplied by 75%[3]	x .75
Equals approximate annual cost (in current dollars) of maintaining your current standard of living if you were retiring this year	$ 27,000
Multiplied by inflation factor (Refer to inflation factor table below)[4]	x 2.2
Equals approximate annual cost (in future dollars) of maintaining your current standard of living when you retire	$ 59,400

Inflation Factor Table

Number of Years Until Retirement	Factor
5	1.2
10	1.6
15	1.9
20	2.4
25	3.0
30	3.7
35	4.7
40	5.8

Explanations:

[1] "Current gross annual income" includes all income from all sources.

[2] "Annual savings" includes, in addition to the usual sources of savings, reinvested dividends and capital gains, and any contributions to retirement plans that are taken from your annual income.

[3] The 75% multiplier is a general rule of thumb that says, in essence, that a retiree can maintain his/her pre-retirement standard of living by spending roughly 75% of his/her pre-retirement income. Of course, individual circumstances may dictate a higher or lower percentage. Ideally, you should prepare a retirement budget that details expected expenses. You may find a multiplier less than 75% in some circumstances (for example, low housing costs due to paid-off mortgage) or, in other circumstances, a higher multiplier (for example, extensive travel plans).

[4] In order to project retirement expenses to retirement age, current dollar living expenses must be multiplied by a factor to account for inflationary increases. The inflation factor table can be used for that purpose.

(Continued on the next page)

Retirement Planning *Work Sheet: Sample Continued*

This section can be used to forecast pension and Social Security benefits at retirement age and then to approximate the aggregate amount of savings/investments that will be needed by retirement age to cover any shortfall between Social Security/pension benefits and your total income needs.

II. Retirement Resources Forecaster

	Current Dollars	Times Inflation Factor[1]	Future (Retirement Age) Dollars
1. Estimated annual living expenses at retirement age (From Part I)			$ 59,400
2. Annual pension income (projection at retirement age available from employer)[2]	$ 10,000 x	2.2 =	22,000
3. Plus annual Social Security benefits (projection at retirement age available from Social Security Administration)[3]	$ 10,000 x	2.2 =	22,000
4. Subtotal of projected pension and Social Security income (add lines 2 and 3)			44,000
5. Shortfall (if expenses are greater than income) that must be funded out of personal savings/investments (subtract line 4 from line 1)			15,400
6. Multiplied by 17[4]			x 17
7. Equals amount of savings/investments in future dollars that need to be accumulated by retirement age to fund retirement[5]			$ 261,800

Explanations:

[1] Use inflation factor table for the appropriate calculation.

[2] Employers usually provide pension plan projections at retirement age, expressed in current dollars. If so, the amount should be multiplied by an inflation factor to approximate benefits in future dollars.

[3] Social Security estimates are expressed in current dollars, and therefore, they should be adjusted for inflation similar to footnote 2 above.

[4] As a general rule of thumb, for every $1,000 of annual income you will need to fund at retirement age, you will need to have at least $17,000 in savings/investments in order to keep up with inflation. If you plan to retire before age 62, use a factor of 20, rather than 17.

[5] You may be dismayed by the magnitude of the amount of personal resources that you will need to fund your retirement, which can easily exceed $1 million for younger persons and/or people with minimal pension benefits. Nevertheless, good savings habits combined with the power of compounding can usually close the gap between current resources and eventual needs.

Note: This is a *simplified* method. A professional planner can prepare a more detailed and individualized analysis.

(Continued on the next page)

Retirement Planning *Work Sheet: Sample Continued*

This section can be used to estimate the annual amount of savings that are required to accumulate the funds necessary to meet your retirement objectives. The amount computed on Line 7 equals the required *first year* savings. The annual savings should be increased by 5% in each succeeding year until you retire.

III. Retirement Savings Estimator

1. Amount of savings/investments in future dollars that need to be accumulated by retirement age to fund retirement (from Part II) $......261,800.

2. Minus resources that are currently available for retirement purposes[1] $........20,000.

3. Multiplied by appreciation factor (refer to annual appreciation factor table below)[2] x ....4.2.

4. Equals estimated future value of retirement resources that are currently available (Multiply Line 2 by Line 3) (.........84,000.)

5. Retirement funds needed by retirement age (Subtract Line 4 from Line 1) 177,800

6. Multiplied by annual savings factor (Refer to annual savings factor table below)[3] x 0151

7. Equals savings needed over the next year (Multiply Line 5 by Line 6)[4] $............2,684

Appreciation Factor Table		Annual Savings Factor Table	
Number of Years Until Retirement	Factor	Number of Years Until Retirement	Factor
5	1.4	5	.1513
10	2.1	10	.0558
15	3.0	15	.0274
20	4.2	20	.0151
25	6.1	25	.0088
30	8.8	30	.0054
35	12.6	35	.0034
40	18.0	40	.0022

Explanations:

[1] Resources that are currently available typically include the current value of all of your investment-related assets that are not expected to be used before retirement. Don't include the value of your home unless you expect to sell it to raise money for retirement. Don't include any vested pension benefits if you have already factored them in on Line 2 of Part II of this work sheet.

[2] The appreciation factor is used to estimate what your currently available retirement resources will be worth when you retire. The appreciation factor assumes a 7.5% after-tax rate of appreciation.

[3] The annual savings factor computes the amount you will need to save during the next year in order to begin accumulating the retirement fund needed by retirement age as indicated on Line 5. The annual savings factor assumes a 7.5% after-tax rate of return.

[4] The annual savings needed to accumulate your retirement nest egg assumes that you will increase the amount of money you save by 5% each year until retirement.

Retirement Action Plan *Work Sheet*

Retirement Action Plan

Current Status		
Needs Action	**OK or Not Applicable**	
		1. You must begin to plan for retirement now—it's never too early. Begin by preparing projections of your retirement income and expenses. If you are within 10 years of retirement, prepare these projections annually.
		2. You cannot rely on pension and Social Security benefits alone to provide for adequate retirement income. Therefore, get into the habit of setting aside some money each year that is earmarked for retirement. An IRA (whether or not it is deductible) is an inexpensive and effective means of getting into this habit.
		3. If you change jobs, roll over any vested pension benefits into an IRA immediately—no matter how small the amount may be and no matter how badly you want to use the money to buy something.
		4. If you are self-employed, set up a retirement plan that is appropriate to your circumstances and needs.
		5. If you have any net income from moonlighting (even if you are covered by a pension plan where you work), set up a simplified employee pension (SEP) plan or a Keogh plan to contribute tax-deductible money for retirement.
		6. One of the best things you can do during your working years to prepare for retirement is to be mortgage free by retirement age. If you are a renter or will still have a large mortgage when you retire, remember that you will need a considerably larger nest egg to cover your housing costs.
		7. Periodically review your retirement plan investments. Be sure to consider them in conjunction with your entire investment portfolio, personal investments, and retirement plan investments.

Comments:

CHAPTER 7

Basic Estate Planning Principles

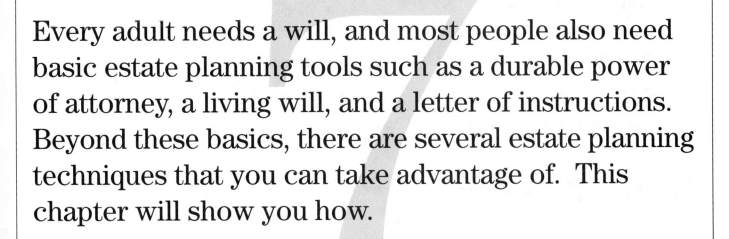

Every adult needs a will, and most people also need basic estate planning tools such as a durable power of attorney, a living will, and a letter of instructions. Beyond these basics, there are several estate planning techniques that you can take advantage of. This chapter will show you how.

Basic Estate Planning Principles

Questions

Isn't estate planning only for the very rich?
How should we get started in estate planning?
What are the basic components of an estate plan?
What important estate planning decisions do I need to make?
What objectives should we keep in mind when planning our estate?
If I become terminally ill, I don't want to be kept alive
by a machine. How can I ensure that my wishes are carried out?
Should we appoint a guardian for our children so that, should anything
happen to us, they will be taken care of?
What types of trusts are available to achieve my estate planning goals?

What Is Estate Planning?

Estate planning is the process of organizing your financial and personal interests, in accordance with prevailing laws, so that *your* wishes are met with a minimum of inconvenience and expense to your family. Estate planning also can assure that your estate incurs the minimum possible estate tax.

Effective estate planning need not be complicated. It has several straightforward objectives, including:

• Minimizing the problems and expenses of probate; to avoid potential family conflicts, where possible; and to pass on your estate in accordance with *your* wishes.

• Providing your spouse with as much responsibility and flexibility in estate management as desired, consistent with potential tax savings.

• Providing for the conservation of your estate and its effective management following the death of either or both spouses.

> "Estate planning also can assure that your estate incurs the minimum possible estate tax."

• Minimizing taxes at the time of death as well as estate taxes after death.

• Avoiding leaving the children too much too soon.

• Providing for adequate liquidity to cover taxes and other expenses at death without the necessity of a forced sale of assets.

• Providing for estate management in the event of the incapacity of either spouse.

• Organizing all important papers affecting your estate plan in a location known to all family members and to review them at least annually.

• Informing all family members about the overall estate plan.

(Continued on page 164)

Financial Snapshot | *Laurie and Peter Cooper*

Laurie and Peter Cooper are full of estate planning questions. "My husband and I are both 45 years old. Neither of us had given much thought to estate planning—it's hard to think of our house and the few investments that we do have as an 'estate.' My husband and I need to have a will. We're not sure if that's enough. A close friend of ours just died, and he didn't have a will. This is causing his wife and children some serious problems."

Beneficiary One who benefits or will benefit from a specified condition set forth in a trust or will. A beneficiary is a person designated to receive specific assets or income from the trust.

Bequest A broad term for a gift received through a will. A bequest can include real or personal property.

Charitable gift annuity An arrangement in which a donor transfers cash or other property to a qualified charitable organization in exchange for a commitment by the organization to pay the donor a specified amount each year during the remainder of the donor's life.

Charitable remainder trust A trust which provides for a specified distribution, at least annually, to one or more beneficiaries, at least one of which is not a charity, for life, or a term of years, with an irrevocable remainder interest to be held for the benefit of, or paid over to, charity. The two most common examples are the charitable remainder annuity trust and the charitable remainder unitrust.

Codicil A formal revision or addendum to a will.

Durable power of attorney A power of attorney is a written authority allowing one individual to act on behalf of another. A *durable* power of attorney ensures that if you ever become unable to manage your own financial and personal affairs, someone that you trust will continue to be able to act on your behalf.

Estate planning Determining your estate's value and how and to whom you want your assets distributed upon your demise.

Executor Person or persons designated to carry out the wishes in your will.

Legacy A gift by will of personal property.

Living trust Also known as an inter vivos trust, this is a trust created and executed during your life, as opposed to a testamentary trust, which takes effect upon your death and is created by your testament (will).

Living will A document that tells your health care provider that you do not want life-prolonging medical procedures when recovery from a condition is impossible and there is no chance of regaining a meaningful life.

Pooled income fund A trust created and maintained by a public charity rather than a private donor.

Probate The legal procedure of proving a will valid or invalid. The term probate also is used to encompass all matters concerning the administration of an estate or guardianship.

Trust A legal arrangement in which a person (i.e., settlor or grantor) transfers property to another person, persons, or organization which holds such property in a manner prescribed in a trust document for the benefit of the named person's beneficiaries.

Trustee A person or organization that holds control over the property in trust for the benefit of another in accordance with your trust's agreement.

Will A written declaration of how you would like the assets of your estate distributed. Your will directs the probate court as to how to divide your assets and to whom they should be distributed.

> "Chief among estate planning matters is a will, but other documents are also important."

This chapter concerns the establishment of a comprehensive estate plan—a key element in your financial planning that you shouldn't live and die without. Chief among estate planning matters is a will, but other documents are also important.

Many people don't complete even the most basic estate planning documents, nor do they revise their estate plan to reflect changes in personal circumstances or new laws and regulations. A reason for this may be a general reluctance to confront the fact that we are all mortal. While it's unpleasant to contemplate the possibility of our own demise, it is far more satisfying to know that our affairs have been put in order, and that our children have been taken care of. Beyond these basics, there are several more sophisticated estate planning techniques of which you should be aware, and you don't have to be wealthy to take advantage of them.

Even though you may have prepared an estate plan in the past, either your estate or your attitude toward it may have changed since you last reviewed matters. Some very important questions need answering. Have you had any children or grandchildren since you last revised your will? Have any of your intended heirs died, married, divorced, or become disabled since your last will was prepared? If so, these events may require a revision of your estate planning documents. It's certainly worth the time and expense to revise an out-of-date estate plan; you'll sleep more soundly, and your heirs will benefit from your foresight.

Minimum Estate Planning Needs

A simple estate plan can help save legal fees and unnecessary and costly probate delays and ensure that your estate is distributed in accordance with your wishes. It also may have some positive effects while you are still alive. Since it is unlikely that an estate will be distributed in accordance with individuals' wishes should they die before creating an estate plan, married and single people alike need to make adequate plans for the distributions of their estate. For example, you may want to leave at least a portion of your estate to a favorite charity or your alma mater. Yet, if you die without a will, this will never happen.

A minimum estate plan usually consists of the following four documents. Every adult is well advised to have these documents prepared.

Valid and Up-to-Date Will

Everyone knows that preparing and maintaining a will is important. But surprisingly, many adults do not have wills. A will specifies exactly how your estate is to be divided. It should be drawn up by an experienced attorney. Intestate estates (those of individuals who died without a will) may incur higher than necessary legal fees and unnecessary probate delays. Additionally, if you die intestate, state law, rather than you, will decide how your estate is to be distributed. Most importantly, you should periodically review and revise your will to reflect changes in your personal circumstances (including moving to another state) or changes in state and federal laws.

A lawyer can help you draw up a will to specify exactly how you want your estate divided. Your will does not prevent you from doing whatever you'd like with your property while you're still alive. If your circumstances change, you can always amend your will with a codicil or write a new one.

The following Will Planning/Review Checklist covers important considerations pertaining to the preparation or periodic review of a will, including the matter of guardianship for your children.

Will Planning/Review Checklist

Use this checklist either to plan a new will or to review an existing will.

Current Status

Yes	No	Unsure	N/A	
☐	☐	☐	☐	1. If there is an existing will, does it reflect the current situation, including birth of heirs and changes in the tax laws, and not contain obsolete sections, including state or residence and inappropriate selection?
☐	☐	☐	☐	2. Will any specific bequests or legacies be made?
☐	☐	☐	☐	3. Are there any bequests to charity, either outright or in trust?
☐	☐	☐	☐	4. Has the disposition of personal property—furniture, jewelry, and automobiles, for example—been planned?
☐	☐	☐	☐	5. Has provision been made for the disposition of real estate?
☐	☐	☐	☐	6. Does the will provide for the disposition of property if an heir predeceases you?
☐	☐	☐	☐	7. Will trusts be established for certain beneficiaries, or will they receive the assets outright?
☐	☐	☐	☐	8. Will certain beneficiaries be provided with periodic payments of income?
☐	☐	☐	☐	9. Does the will take advantage of the unlimited marital deduction to the most effective and practical extent allowed?
☐	☐	☐	☐	10. Has consideration been given to providing for marital and nonmarital trusts in the will?
☐	☐	☐	☐	11. Is the custody of minors satisfactorily addressed?
☐	☐	☐	☐	12. Has consideration been given to appointing a "financial" guardian for the children in addition to a personal guardian?
☐	☐	☐	☐	13. Does the will specify that any minor beneficiary's share of the estate will be held until he or she reaches maturity?
☐	☐	☐	☐	14. Does the will provide for a guardianship or trust to protect the inheritance of disabled or incompetent beneficiaries?
☐	☐	☐	☐	15. Have provisions been made to dispose of business interests?
☐	☐	☐	☐	16. Have appropriate and capable persons or institutions been appointed to serve as executor, trustee, and/or guardian?
☐	☐	☐	☐	17. Does the will name an alternate or successor executor, trustee, and/or guardian?
☐	☐	☐	☐	18. Should any special powers be given to or taken away from the executor?
☐	☐	☐	☐	19. Has the executor's bond requirement been waived?

(Continued on the next page)

Estate Planning

7

Current Status
Yes No Unsure N/A

☐ ☐ ☐ ☐ 20. Are specific powers granted to the executor, as necessary, such as to retain or sell property, to invest trust and estate assets, to allocate receipts and disbursements to income and principal, to make loans and borrow funds, or to settle claims?

☐ ☐ ☐ ☐ 21. Is the ownership of the assets complementary to the provisions of the will (i.e., some assets may pass outside of the will by contract or by type of ownership)?

☐ ☐ ☐ ☐ 22. Does the will state who will receive property if the beneficiary disclaims it? (Disclaimers can be an effective postmortem planning device.)

☐ ☐ ☐ ☐ 23. Have any special directions for the funeral or memorial been provided?

☐ ☐ ☐ ☐ 24. Have sources been identified from which debts, funeral expenses, and estate administrative costs will be paid?

☐ ☐ ☐ ☐ 25. Will the survivors have enough cash to pay ordinary family living expenses while the estate is in probate?

Durable Power of Attorney

There are basically two ways to protect personal assets and ensure that they will continue to be managed appropriately should you become incapacitated and unable to manage your financial affairs because of an accident, illness, or age. You can appoint a person to act for you by signing a durable power of attorney, or you can establish a living trust. Your right to manage your financial affairs may be revoked by a court order, and if you haven't provided for one in your durable power of attorney (or living trust), a court-appointed conservator (perhaps not the one you would have chosen) will oversee the management of *your* affairs.

"You can appoint a person to act for you by signing a durable power of attorney, or you can establish a living trust."

Signing a durable power of attorney ensures that if you ever become unable to manage your own financial and personal affairs, someone you trust will be able to act on your behalf. A power of attorney may be either special, applying to only certain situations, or general, giving the attorney-in-fact virtually limitless control over the financial affairs of the principal (the person who created the arrangement). General powers of attorney should be approached with caution as they can be subject to abuse; moreover, they're usually unnecessary.

A power of attorney may be either indefinite or for a specific length of time. No matter how the time is designated, it may be cancelled at any time as long as you're not incapacitated, and it terminates immediately upon the death of the principal.

If your state does not recognize durable powers of attorney, you can use a living trust to protect your rights in the event of incapacity. Since living trusts can accomplish more than a durable power of attorney, you may want to consider a living trust in lieu of a durable power. Living trusts are discussed later in this chapter.

Living Will

Medical dilemmas surrounding terminally ill patients abound and compound the difficulty of trying to accommodate the patient's wishes. Drafting a living will informs family members and physicians that under certain circumstances you do not wish to be kept alive by artificial means.

The fundamental shortcoming of living wills is that under most state statutes the circumstances are prescribed by law and you are *not* free to define the circumstances. Health care proxies and medical durable powers of attorney have appeared on the scene to provide this control. Living wills are legally recognized in most states. But even where they are not, experts suggest that preparing one anyway can be very helpful if, and when, the need to make these difficult decisions arises.

In conjunction with a living will, your attorney also may recommend (and many states require) a health care proxy (sometimes known as a durable power for health care). Generally, the health care proxy and living will each carry out a distinct function. The living will provides guidance to health care personnel and family members as to your wishes regarding life-sustaining treatment, and the health care proxy names the person who is responsible for making health care decisions on your behalf.

"The living will provides guidance to health care personnel and family members as to your wishes regarding life-sustaining treatment, and the health care proxy names the person who is responsible for making health care decisions on your behalf."

Letter of Instructions

A letter of instructions is not as crucial as other essential estate planning documents, but your heirs will be thankful you prepared one. A letter of instructions is an informal document (you don't need an attorney to prepare it) that gives your executor information concerning important financial and personal matters. Although it does not carry the legal weight of a will, the letter of instructions is very important because it clarifies any further requests to be carried out upon death and provides essential financial information, thus relieving the surviving family members of needless worry and speculation.

The Letter of Instructions Checklist, beginning on the next page, will help you decide what to include.

Letter of Instructions Checklist

A letter of instructions is not a legal document like a will. You have a lot more leeway in both the language and content. Your letter is a good place to put personal wishes and final comments, but your heirs will be very grateful if you include details about important financial matters.

☐ First Things to Do
- Acquaintances and organizations to be called, including Social Security, the bank, and your employer
- Arrangements to be made with funeral home
- Lawyer's name and telephone number
- Newspapers to receive obituary information
- Location of insurance policies

☐ Cemetery and Funeral
- Details of your wishes and any arrangements you have made

☐ Facts for Funeral Director
- Vital statistics, including your full name, residence, marital status, spouse's name, date of birth, birthplace, father's and mother's names and birthplaces, length of residence in state and in United States, military records/history, Social Security number, occupation, and life insurance information

☐ Information for Death Certificate and Filing for Benefits
- Citizen of, race, marital status, name of next of kin (other than spouse), relationship, address, and birthplace

☐ Expected Death Benefits
- Information about any potential death benefits from your employer (including life insurance, profit sharing, pension plan, or accident insurance), life insurance companies, Social Security, the Veterans Administration, or any other source

☐ Special Wishes
- Anything you want them to know

☐ Personal Effects
- A list of who is to receive certain personal effects, usually including details of who is to receive items such as golf clubs or some other special item and it could include autos, etc., in some states

☐ Personal Papers
- Locations of important personal documents, including your will, birth and baptismal certificates, communion and confirmation certificates, diplomas, marriage certificate, military records, naturalization papers, and any other documents (e.g., adoption, divorce)

☐ Safe-Deposit Box*
- Location and number of box and key and an inventory of contents

☐ Post Office Box
- Location and number of box and key (or combination)

☐ Income Tax Returns
- Location of all previous returns
- Location of your estimated tax file
- Tax preparer's name

☐ Loans Outstanding
- Information for loans other than mortgages, including bank name and address, name on loan, account number, monthly payment, location of papers and payment book, collateral, and information on any life insurance on the loan

☐ Debts Owed to the Estate
- Debtor, description, terms, balance, location of documents, and comments on loan status/discharge

* State law may require a bank to seal the deceased's safe-deposit box as soon as notified of his or her death, even if the box is jointly owned.

(Continued on the next page)

☐ Social Security
  • Full name, Social Security number, and the location of Social Security cards
☐ Life Insurance
  • Policy numbers and amounts, location of policy, whose life is insured, insurer's name and address, kind of policy, beneficiaries, issue and maturity date, payment options, and any special facts
☐ Veterans Administration
  • If you are a veteran, give information on collecting benefits from local Veterans Administration office
☐ Other Insurance
  • If any other insurance benefits or policies are in force, including accident, homeowners/renters, automobile, disability, medical, personal, or professional liability, give insurer's name and address, policy number, beneficiary, coverage, location of policy, term, how acquired (if through employer or other group), agent
☐ Investments
  • Stocks: Company, name on certificates, number of shares, certificate numbers, purchase price and date, and location of certificates
  • Bonds/notes/bills: Issuer, issued to, face amount, bond number, purchase price and date, maturity date, and location of certificates

  • Mutual funds: Company, name on account, number of shares or units, and location of statements and certificates
  • Other investments: For each investment, list amount invested, to whom issued, maturity date, issuer, and other applicable data, and location of certificates and other vital papers
☐ Household Contents
  • List of contents with name of owners, form of ownership, and location of documents, inventory, and appraisals
☐ Automobiles
  • For each car: Year, make, model, color, identification number, title in name(s) of, and location of title and registration
☐ Important Warranties and Receipts
  • Location and description
☐ Doctors' Names, Addresses, and Telephone Numbers
  • Including dentist, and children's pediatrician and dentist
☐ Checking Accounts
  • Name of bank, name on account, account number, and location of passbook (or receipt) for all accounts
☐ Credit Cards
  • For each card: company (including telephone and address), name on card, number, and location of card

(Continued on the next page)

Letter of Instructions Checklist *Continued*

☐ House, Condo, or Co-Op
- About the home: in whose name, address, legal description, other descriptions needed, lawyer at closing, and locations of statement of closing, policy of title insurance, deed, and land survey
- About the mortgage: held by, amount of original mortgage, date taken out, amount owed now, method of payment, and location of payment book, if any (or payment statements)
- About life insurance on mortgage: policy number, location of policy, and annual amount
- About property taxes: amount and location of receipts
- About the cost of house: initial buying price, purchase closing fee, other buying costs (real estate agent, legal, taxes), and home improvements
- About improvements: what each consisted of, cost, date, and location of bills

- For renters: lease location and expiration date

☐ Funeral Preferences
- Specify whether *or not* you would like to have any of the following done: Donate organs, autopsy if requested, simple arrangements, embalming, public viewing, least expensive burial or cremation container, or immediate disposition. Remains should be: donated (details of arrangements made), cremated (and the ashes: scattered, buried at), disposed of as follows (details), or buried (at)
- Specify which of the following services should be performed: memorial (after disposition), funeral (before disposition), or graveside to be held at: church, mortuary, or other
- Specify where memorial gifts should be given or whether to omit flowers
- If prearrangements have been made with a mortuary, give details

☐ Signature and date

The four basic estate planning documents described above—a will, durable power of attorney, a living will, and a letter of instructions—are the essential components of an estate plan. You may well be able to benefit from other estate planning techniques, including trusts, selecting the appropriate form of property ownership, and charitable giving.

Other Important Estate Planning Decisions

Property Ownership Designations

Joint ownership of property is common, particularly among married couples, and can be wise from an estate planning standpoint if the estate is fairly small. But jointly held property is not desirable in some instances. It is possible that the property may be subject to estate taxation twice in the case of property held jointly with someone other than a spouse. (See an attorney.)

Selection of an Executor

Close relatives are a natural choice for executor, and while that usually works out well, sometimes it does not. The reasons why relatives may not be appropriate executors include inexperience (particularly with complicated estates), lack of time to devote to any details of proper estate administration, or inability to get along with other relatives. (Once again, see an attorney.)

Guardianship for Children

One of the most important elements of a comprehensive will involves guardianship for your minor or incapacitated children. Guardianship generally refers to the responsibility of a minor child's or disabled adult's care and upbringing if the parents die early. Failure to make decisions in this area can lead to greater custodial and financial problems than families have encountered in the past. With the increasing number of nontraditional family situations, such as divorced parents and stepparents, possible complications may occur.

Your attorney may advise you to divide guardianship duties so that the responsibility for taking care of the child's health and well-being is given to one party, and the responsibility for taking care of the child's financial affairs is given to another. There are several reasons for separating responsibilities into those of the personal guardian (the former) and those of the property custodian, or conservator (the latter). The most important reason is that a particular relative or friend who you trust completely with the child's upbringing may not have the expertise to deal with money that will be left to the child.

Another important consideration is that if your potential estate is likely to be considerably greater than the resources of the guardian, you may want to consider empowering the property guardian to provide additional resources to the personal guardian's family to minimize the potential for resentment. For example, some parents have provided for the payment of college tuition out of their estate for the guardian's children as well as for their own.

Finally, regardless of how the guardianship arrangement is designed, it is vital that you discuss your wishes with the potential guardians prior to putting their names in the will or trust. If the children are old enough, they should be included in the discussion, too. Parents are too often embarrassed or afraid to start a fight within the family. Don't be. Realize that it is of the utmost importance to inform guardians. Otherwise, upon the event of your death, serious problems could arise when your designated guardians suddenly realize they have been selected to be responsible for the lives of your children. Also, if they have not agreed in advance, they may decline the responsibility, in which case you are back to not having solved the problem. You also should provide for successor guardians in case one of the guardians is unwilling or unable to serve.

"Guardianship generally refers to the responsibility of a minor child's or disabled adult's care and upbringing if the parents die early."

Spousal Transfers

The unlimited marital deduction allows one spouse to pass his or her entire estate to the other, completely free of federal estate taxes. State death tax regulations regarding marital transfers may differ. However, giving all of your estate to your spouse may not always be the best method of transferring property.

Lifetime Gifts

The annual gift tax exclusion allows you to give up to $10,000 per year to any number of people ($20,000 per year for married couples who file a split gift election), as well as direct payments of tuition to educational institutions and of medical expenses paid directly to a medical provider. While gifts to children and grandchildren are a convenient way for affluent families to reduce the size of their taxable estate during their lifetimes, you should be cautioned against being so generous that you end up jeopardizing your own financial well-being. Finally, the common practice of the elderly of giving money to relatives so that they can qualify for Medicaid in the event they have to go to a nursing home is full of pitfalls. The biggest problem is that they may not get the money back if and when they later need it.

Disposition of a Family Business

If you own a family business, you face particularly thorny estate planning problems. Careful planning is necessary to assure that your business can continue operating successfully should you die.

If and when you get ready to sell your business, whether to family members or outsiders, other complex estate planning matters may need to be considered, particularly if you intend to keep the business in the family. (See an attorney.)

Charitable Gifts

Charitable gifts made during your lifetime provide a dual tax advantage. First, you get a charitable deduction on your income taxes, and second, when such a gift is made, its value (plus any future appreciation) is removed from your estate. There are certain tax deduction limitations on charitable donations which you should become familiar with if you intend to make substantial charitable contributions. (See your tax advisor.)

A Matter of Trusts

Trusts can increase administrative convenience, protect you (or your loved ones) from lawsuits and creditors (if it is an irrevocable trust), allow for a speedier inheritance, and, in some cases, reduce your tax burden. Most importantly, a trust can be tailored to meet almost all of your estate planning desires. For example, a trust document can specify exact conditions about the distribution of assets (such as at what age a child will receive an inheritance), and can allow the trustee the discretion to withhold or distribute extra assets if prudent or necessary. In contrast, a simple will typically gives your assets to your heirs outright. A trust provides more assurance than a will that your wishes will be carried out.

Many people are uncomfortable with the prospect of their children or spouse receiving all of their assets at once—with no strings attached. A trust can be set up that will empower the trustee to distribute trust income to beneficiaries in accordance with their needs. This may be particularly useful if you have a disabled child or if you have children of widely differing economic circumstances.

You also can create a trust to shift the burden of management of your assets to a trusted third party, to transfer property to minors without the need to appoint a guardian, as a retirement tool to ensure that your assets will be well managed should you become incapable of managing them yourself, and even to safeguard your investments against unwise or extravagant spending during your lifetime, or after your death.

A Simple Will Can Be a $235,000 Mistake

The garden-variety will, which in essence says "all to my spouse," could end up costing your children or other heirs a lot of money if you have a reasonably sizable estate.

Assume that a husband has an estate of $1.2 million (which, by the way, is by no means an unusually large estate for older persons), and he dies leaving all of it to his wife. No federal estate taxes are owed because the transfer qualifies for the unlimited marital deduction. But what if the wife dies right after the husband? She has at least $1.2 million to bequeath but has only the $600,000 tax-free exemption available to reduce estate taxes. Her taxable estate, therefore, is $600,000 (the $1.2 million gross estate minus the $600,000 exemption). The federal estate tax on this $600,000 is a whopping $235,000, which could have been avoided altogether with some modest estate planning (no matter when the surviving spouse dies).

A better idea: the husband should limit the wife's taxable estate to the amount covered by her $600,000 exemption by not willing everything he owns to her. He can do this by allowing her the full use of all of the property to meet her needs but putting a part of his estate in a trust for her that will not be subject to estate tax at her death.

Of course, the wife might die first, but the estate can be structured to avoid some or all estate taxes, no matter who dies first. In the above example, the husband can, during his lifetime, give his wife $600,000 (there are no estate or gift taxes on transfers to a spouse), and she could leave that to him in her will to use if he survives her. These testamentary trust arrangements go under a variety of names, including marital trusts, unified credit trusts, credit shelter trusts, and qualified terminable interest property (QTIP) trusts.

Types of Trusts

Living Trust

A living, or inter vivos, trust is one created during your lifetime; a testamentary trust is one created by your will. A living trust's immediate advantage is that it can circumvent probate; if all your assets are held in the trust, there is nothing to transfer through the will. The trust is not obligated (in most states) to pay any remaining debts, and it ensures continuous management of the assets, uninterrupted by your death. If, at any point, you become disabled or otherwise unable to make an important decision concerning the assets, your cotrustee or successor trustee can take responsibility. (If you do not want to manage all your assets during the remainder of your life, you can appoint a cotrustee.)

A living trust, as compared with a simple will, provides more assurance that your wishes will be carried out; a trust document can specify exact conditions about the distribution of your assets (such as at what age a child will receive an inheritance), and can allow the trustee the discretion to withhold or distribute extra assets if prudent or necessary.

A living trust also can serve as a receptacle for estate assets and death benefits from your employee benefit plans and life insurance. Also, it can unify in one location all your assets and thus avoid administration of the estate in different places. When compared with a testamentary trust, this trust is protected from public inspection, and may be less vulnerable to attack on grounds of fraud, incapacity, or duress. Moreover, if your living trust is revocable, it permits you to alter it as is necessary or desired. However, while an irrevocable living trust in which you have no incidents of ownership or benefits is not included in your estate for estate-tax purposes, a revocable trust provides you with no tax savings (although if you die before revoking the trust, it automatically becomes irrevocable).

Revocable Living Trust

A living trust is usually set up to hold your property, naming yourself as the principal beneficiary. Regardless of your age or mental condition, the trustee is legally bound to act in the beneficiary's best interests according to the trust's instructions. A living trust's immediate advantage is that it can minimize or circumvent probate; if all the grantor's (the person who sets up the trust) assets are held in the trust, there is nothing to transfer through the will. The trust ensures continuous management of the assets, uninterrupted by death. If the grantor at any point is disabled or otherwise unable to make an important decision concerning the assets, a cotrustee can take responsibility. Typically, you will be the trustee, meaning that you control the assets of the trust. In this case, you also designate a successor trustee, who will take over upon your death or if you become incompetent or incapacitated. To appoint a successor trustee, you must state in the trust agreement that the successor is to take over if you are certified incompetent by a doctor. A living trust is particularly desirable in situations where your state probate laws are burdensome.

> "A living, or inter vivos, trust is one created during your lifetime; a testamentary trust is one created by your will."

Testamentary Trust

You may be unwilling to establish a living trust but you may still want to control the way in which your beneficiaries receive the estate after your death. This can be accomplished by creating a trust with instructions contained in your will, known as a testamentary trust. If you set up either a revocable living trust or a testamentary trust, you can either change or eliminate the trust during your lifetime.

Irrevocable Trust

Unlike the revocable trust, an irrevocable trust requires you to permanently give up any and all assets you transfer to it. Since the property in trust is no longer yours, it will be administered according to the terms of the trust both while you are alive and after your death. The best property to put into an irrevocable trust is that which has appreciation potential, like stocks and real estate, because if the property increases in value after you transfer it to the trust, the increase will not be subject to any estate tax. Irrevocable trusts incur legal and administrative fees, and most importantly, you lose control of the assets *forever*. Therefore, these trusts are suitable only if you can easily afford to part with the assets. Since this decision is a complex one, it's advisable to consult with an estate planning attorney.

> "Unlike the revocable trust, an irrevocable trust requires you to permanently give up any and all assets you transfer to it."

Charitable Trusts

There are a variety of ways to donate property to charity in exchange for a lifetime income and a partial income tax deduction. Some people have made good use of these arrangements to provide additional income during retirement, but they must be charitably inclined, because better investment returns can generally be garnered elsewhere. Those who can afford to donate a large amount of money to a charity during their lifetime can set up a charitable remainder trust. Those who are charitably inclined but want to donate lesser amounts ($5,000 to $10,000) should consider either a charitable gift annuity or a pooled income fund. If any of these arrangements interest you, check with your favorite charity. They will be happy to guide you through these rather complex arrangements.

Financial Snapshot *Continued* — *Laurie and Peter Cooper*

Laurie and Peter visited an estate planning attorney who helped them draw up a will, designate a durable power of attorney, and execute a living will (with a health care proxy). Their attorney pointed out that in a few years their estate will grow to the point where they may need to consider a trust.

"He also suggested that we draw up a letter of instructions and begin to think about guardianship for our children," states Peter. "Which we did the following weekend," chimes in Laurie. "We thought writing a will and getting started on our estate plan would be an anxiety-producing experience. Instead," says Peter, "we find that now that it's all done, it's one less thing to worry about."

Estate Planning Action Plan *Work Sheet*

The following action plan is designed to help you jump-start your estate planning.

Estate Planning Action Plan

Current Status		
Needs Action	**OK or Not Applicable**	
		1. Decide how you want your estate to be distributed.
		2. Have an attorney prepare a will that is consistent with your personal wishes and circumstances.
		3. Name an appropriate executor.
		4. Establish a durable power of attorney or living trust that protects you in the event of incapacity.
		5. Prepare and keep up-to-date a letter of instructions.
		6. Designate guardians for your children and, if applicable, disabled adults.
		7. Prepare a living will and a health care proxy.
		8. Prepare an estimate of your taxable estate so that you can determine the type of estate planning techniques that will be appropriate.
		9. Make sure sufficient cash will be able to be raised from your estate to meet the needs of your survivors; if not, take appropriate action to increase your estate liquidity.

(Continued on the next page)

Estate Planning Action Plan *Work Sheet Continued*

Estate Planning Action Plan

Current Status		
Needs Action	**OK or Not Applicable**	
		10. Make sure that the title in which you hold property (single name, jointly with your spouse, etc.) is appropriate for estate planning purposes.
		11. Any gifts to relatives and/or charitable contributions should take into consideration your financial condition and overall estate planning objectives.
		12. If you own property in more than one state, take appropriate action to minimize eventual probate problems.
		13. Consider the use of revocable and irrevocable trusts as part of your estate planning.
		14. If you own your own business, make provisions for its disposition in the event of your death.
		15. Inform your family and any other beneficiaries of your plans.

Comments:

Letter of Instructions *Work Sheet*

Letter of Instructions

A letter of instructions is an informal document that tells your survivors what to do upon your death. The work sheet that follows will help you figure out what to tell your survivors so that they can make your funeral arrangements and settle your other affairs as you wish. A letter of instructions is not a substitute for a will: you should treat it as a supplement to your will. Unlike your will, a letter of instructions—which is not legally binding—can be easily changed and updated.

Expected Death Benefits

1. From employer:

   • Person to contact: _____   Telephone: (   )

   • Life insurance: $

   • Profit sharing: $

   • Pension plan: $

   • Accident insurance: $

   • Other benefits:

2. From insurance companies—total amount: $

3. From Social Security—lump sum plus monthly benefits: $

4. From the Veterans Administration—amount: $
   (Note: The VA must be informed of the death for benefits to be disbursed.)

5. From other sources:

First Things to Do

1. Call:

2. Notify employer. Name and telephone:

3. Make arrangements with the funeral home. (See the "Cemetery and Funeral" section.)

4. Request at least 10 copies of the death certificate. (Usually, the funeral director will get them.)

5. Call lawyer. Name and telephone:

6. Provide the following newspapers with obituary information:

7. Contact the local Social Security office. (See the "Social Security" section.)

8. Retrieve and process insurance policies. (Policy locations are listed in the "Life Insurance" section.)

9. Notify the bank that holds the home mortgage.

10. Notify the following acquaintances and organizations:

(Continued on the next page)

Letter of Instructions

Cemetery and Funeral

Cemetery Plot

1. Location:

2. Date purchased: 19

3. Deed number:

4. Location of deed:

5. Other information (e.g., perpetual care):

Facts for the Funeral Director
  This list should be brought to the funeral home with the cemetery deed, if possible.

1. Full name:

2. Residence:

3. Marital status: Spouse's name:

4. Date of birth: 19   Birthplace:

5. Father's name and birthplace:

6. Mother's maiden name and birthplace:

7. Length of residence in state: In United States:

8. Military record:

   When:
   (Bring veterans discharge papers, if possible.)

9. Social Security number: Occupation:

10. Life insurance
    (Bring policy if proceeds will be used for funeral expenses.)

Insurer	Policy Number

Special Wishes

1.

2.

3.

(Continued on the next page)

Estate Planning **7** *Work Sheet*

Letter of Instructions *Work Sheet Continued*

Letter of Instructions

Personal Effects

The following personal effects should be given to the named person:

Item	Person

Funeral Preferences

1. Donate these organs:

2. Autopsy if doctor or family requests: ☐ Yes ☐ No

3. Simple arrangements:
   ☐ No embalming
   ☐ No public viewing
   ☐ The least expensive burial or cremation container
   ☐ Immediate disposition

4. Remains should be:
   ☐ Donated: Arrangements made on _____ , 19 ____ with _____
   ☐ Cremated and the ashes ☐ Scattered ☐ Buried at _____
   ☐ Disposed of as follows: _____
   ☐ Buried at _____

5. The following services:
   ☐ Memorial (after disposition)
   ☐ Funeral (before disposition)
   ☐ Graveside
   To be held at: ☐ Church ☐ Mortuary ☐ Other:

6. Memorial gift to: Omit flowers: ☐ Yes ☐ No

7. Prearrangements have been made with the following mortuary:

Location of Personal Papers

1. Last will and testament:

2. Birth and baptismal certificates:

3. Communion, confirmation certificates:

4. School diplomas:

5. Marriage certificate:

6. Military records:

7. Naturalization papers:

8. Other (e.g., adoption, divorce):

(Continued on the next page)

Letter of Instructions *Work Sheet Continued*

Letter of Instructions

Safe-Deposit Box

Note: In the event of the death of a safe-deposit box owner, state law may require the bank to seal the deceased's box as soon as notified of the death, even if the box is jointly owned.

1. Bank name and address:

2. In whose name: Number:

3. Location of key:

4. List of contents (if extensive, attach separate inventory):

Post Office Box

1. Address:

2. Owners:

3. Box number:

4. Location of key or combination:

Income Tax Returns

1. Location of all previous returns (federal, state, local):

2. Tax preparer's name: Telephone:

3. Location of estimated tax file:
   (Check to see if any estimated quarterly taxes are due.)

Doctors' Names and Addresses

1. Doctor's name: Telephone:

   Address:

2. Dentist's name: Telephone:

   Address:

3. Children's pediatrician's name: Telephone:

   Address:

4. Children's dentist's name: Telephone:

   Address:

(Continued on the next page)

Letter of Instructions *Work Sheet Continued*

Letter of Instructions

Checking Accounts
Attach a separate summary if there are multiple accounts.

1. Bank name and address:

2. Name(s) on account:

3. Account number: Type:

4. Location of passbook (or certificate receipt):

5. Special instructions:

Credit Cards
All credit cards in the deceased's name should be cancelled or converted to the survivor's name. Provide the following information for each card:

1. Company: Telephone:

   Address:

2. Name on card: Number:

3. Location of card:

Loans Outstanding
Provide the following information for each loan other than mortgages:

1. Bank name and address:

2. Name on loan:

3. Account number:

4. Monthly payment:

5. Location of papers and payment book (if any):

6. Collateral (if any):

7. Is there life insurance on the loan?   ☐ Yes   ☐ No

Debts Owed to the Estate

1. Debtor:

2. Description:

3. Terms:

4. Balance: $

5. Location of documents:

6. Comments on loan status/discharge:

(Continued on the next page)

Letter of Instructions *Work Sheet Continued*

Letter of Instructions

Social Security

1. Name: Number:

   Location of Social Security cards:

2. File a claim immediately to avoid possibility of losing any benefit checks. Call local Social Security Administration (SSA) office for appointment and follow SSA's instructions as to what to bring. SSA telephone:

3. Expect a lump sum of about $_____, plus continuing benefits for children under age 18, or for full-time students until age 22. A spouse may receive benefits until children reach age 18, between ages 50 and 60 if disabled, or if over age 60.

Life Insurance

To collect benefits, a copy of the death certificate must be sent to each insurance company. Provide the following information for each policy:

1. Policy number: Amount: $

2. Location of policy:

3. Whose life is insured:

4. Insurer's name and address:

5. Kind of policy:

6. Beneficiaries:

7. Issue date: , 19   Maturity date: , 19

8. How paid out:

9. Other options on payout:

10. Other special facts:

11. For $ _____ in veterans insurance, call the local Veterans Administration office. Telephone:

(Continued on the next page)

Letter of Instructions *Work Sheet Continued*

Letter of Instructions

Other Insurance

Accident

1. Insurer's name and address:

2. Policy number:

3. Beneficiary:

4. Coverage:

5. Location of policy:

6. Agent (if any):

Homeowners/Renters and Automobile

Provide the following information for each policy:

1. Coverage:

2. Insurer's name and address:

3. Policy number:

4. Location of policy:

5. Term (when to renew):

6. Agent (if any):

Medical

Provide the following information for each policy:

1. Coverage:

2. Insurer's name and address:

3. Policy number:

4. Location of policy:

5. Through employer or other group:

6. Agent (if any):

(Continued on the next page)

Letter of Instructions *Work Sheet Continued*

Letter of Instructions

House, Condo, or Co-Op

Contact the local tax assessor for documentation needed or for more information.

1. In whose name:

2. Address:

3. Lot: Block: On map called:

4. Other descriptions needed:

5. Lawyer at closing:

   Address:

6. Location of statement of closing, policy of title insurance, deed, land survey, and the like:

7. Mortgage:

   a. Held by:

   b. Amount of original mortgage: $

   c. Date taken out: , 19

   d. Amount owed now: $

   e. Method of payment:

   f. Location of payment book, if any (or payment statements):

   g. Is there life insurance on mortgage?   ☐ Yes   ☐ No

   • If so, policy number:

   • Location of policy:

   • Annual amount: $

8. House taxes

   a. Amount: $

   b. Location of receipts:

9. Cost of house

   a. Initial buying price: $

   b. Purchase closing fee: $

   c. Other costs to buy (e.g., real estate agent, legal, taxes):

   d. Improvements: Total: $

(Continued on the next page)

Letter of Instructions *Work Sheet Continued*

Letter of Instructions

House, Condo, or Co-Op Continued

10. House improvements
    Provide the following information for each improvement:

    a. Improvement:

    b. Cost: $ Date: , 19

    c. Location of bills:

11. If renting, is there a lease: ☐ Yes   ☐ No

    a. Lease location:

    b. Expiration date: , 19

Household Contents

1. Name of owners:

2. Form of ownership:

3. Location of documents:

4. Location of inventory:

5. Location of appraisals:

Automobiles

Provide the following information for each car:

1. Year, make, and model:

2. Body type:

3. Cylinders:

4. Color:

5. Identification number:

6. Title in name(s) of:
   Title to automobiles held in the deceased's name must be changed.

7. Location of papers (e.g., title, registration):

Important Warranties and Receipts

Item	Location

(Continued on the next page)

Letter of Instructions *Work Sheet Continued*

Letter of Instructions

Investments

Provide the following information (if necessary, attach a separate sheet):

Stocks

1. Company:

2. Name on certificate(s):

3. Number of shares: ' Certificate number(s):

4. Purchase price and date:

5. Location of certificate(s):

Bonds, Notes, and Bills

1. Issuer:

2. Issued to:

3. Face amount: $ Bond number:

4. Purchase price and date:

5. Maturity date:

6. Location of certificate:

Mutual Funds

1. Company:

2. Name on account:

3. Number of shares or units:

4. Location of statements, certificates:

Other Investments

For each investment, list the amount invested, to whom it is issued, the issuer, the maturity date, other applicable data, and the location of certificates and other vital papers.

Estate Planning *Questionnaire*

The following should make it easier for you to create an effective estate plan. Your goal is to make it as easy as possible for your loved ones to activate your estate plan. To ensure that your plan achieves this goal in fact as well as in spirit, review the following and revise your current plan accordingly.

Estate Planning

	Yes	No	NA
1. Have you clearly articulated your wishes regarding the ultimate disposition of your estate?			
2. Do you have an up-to-date will that is consistent with your personal wishes and individual circumstances?			
3. Have you named an appropriate executor?			
4. Have you designated an appropriate adult to be responsible for your financial affairs should you become incapacitated?			
5. Have you prepared a living will and health care proxy?			
6. Has an estimate been made of the size of your taxable estate?			
7. Have you calculated the impact of both federal estate taxes and state death taxes on your estate?			
8. Have provisions been made to provide adequate cash reserves upon your death to provide for your family?			
9. Have you made appropriate provisions in your overall estate planning for property owned in other states?			
10. Are trusts included in your current plan?			
11. Have the effects of current tax regulations on estate planning been evaluated and incorporated into your plan?			
12. Have you informed your family about your funeral plans?			

Comments:

Will Preparation *Checklist*

Will Preparation Checklist

The following items should be included in a will:

	Your full name and location of principal residence.
	Statement that the document is a will.
	Date.
	Statement revoking all previous wills.
	Instructions with respect to disposal of your body and funeral arrangements.
	Specific bequests with provisions for the death of the named beneficiaries. Specific bequests are for the transfer of a particular piece of property to a named beneficiary.
	General bequest, which does not specify from which part of the estate the property is to be taken, with provisions for the death of the named beneficiaries.
	Instructions for dividing the residuary, which is the amount of the estate remaining after these specific and general bequests have been made.
	Provisions for trusts, including the names of selected trustees and successor trustees.
	Statement of who should be presumed to have died first (either husband or wife) should both die in a common accident. This allows both wills to be processed without undue complications or tax effects.
	Names of guardians and alternate guardians for minor children, if necessary, or for a handicapped adult, child, or other relative under your care.
	Designation of what resources or assets are to be used to pay death taxes.
	Names of the executor and substitute executor.
	Signature. The will should be signed in the presence of all of the witnesses.
	Any major changes in the form of codicils. These, too, must be witnessed and signed, as was the original will.

Comments:

CHAPTER 8

Planning for the Times of Your Life

Life can be grand—as long as you keep your eyes on the prize of your financial well-being. This chapter will help you stay focused—in the best of times and in the worst of times—so that, no matter what, you will come out on top.

Planning for the Times of Your Life

This chapter explores several financially significant and personally challenging financial planning circumstances: from buying your first home to coping with a divorce, and aging parents. Many of the situations involve sophisticated technical issues, and you may find it necessary to hire professional advisors to help sort out everything.

Getting Started on the Right Financial Foot

You can do many things today to protect yourself from financial problems that will affect your future well-being. Of course, some problems are beyond your control, like a layoff. But you can avoid many potential financial problems by learning some sensible planning techniques right from the start.

The following strategies will help you take control of your financial future *now*, so that you can prepare for unavoidable problems that may pop up unexpectedly, and manage your money to avoid problems that might have developed otherwise.

> "One of the most important things you can do to protect against the unforeseen is to build a cushion of savings."

1. Build up your savings. One of the most important things you can do to protect against the unforeseen is to build a cushion of savings. In spite of what may look like limitless prospects for your future, it wasn't that long ago that many like-minded people had their hopes dashed. (In the early 1990s, the ranks of the unemployed were swelling by more than 15,000 *per week*.) Nothing can beat money in the bank (or in an investment account) to help you shoulder these burdens should they arise. Another benefit of setting aside emergency funds is that you'll worry a lot less about what's going to happen to you and your financial obligations. It is crucial that you begin to set aside some money: even a small amount like $5 or $10 per week is better than nothing. The easiest way to save is never to see the money. Most credit unions, banks, mutual fund companies, and stock brokerage firms will be more than happy to take your money out of your paycheck or checking account and put it into a savings or investment account through a systematic withdrawal program.

2. Get your debts under control. Many people take on too much consumer debt. How much is too much? One guideline is not to owe more than 15% to 20% of your yearly after-tax income (excluding your rent or mortgage payments). Another is not to owe more than one-third of your yearly discretionary income (income left over after the basics—food, clothing, and shelter—are paid for). Those who have too much debt are sitting on a house of cards: the slightest disruption in their personal financial situation, and they may be headed for big trouble. Whatever your debt situation, take the necessary steps to get your debts under control. First and foremost, don't add to your indebtedness. If necessary, take the scissors to your credit cards. Second, keep up-to-date on all of your obligations, and third, work to reduce your debts.

3. Maintain your good credit. Whether you have a lot of debt, a little debt, or no debt, you need to create a good credit history so that you can access credit when you need it (to buy your first car and your first home, or to cope with a financial emergency, for example). Another advantage to good credit that you may not yet have experienced is convenience. If you manage your credit properly, it allows you more flexibility to manage your day-to-day finances, and you won't have to waste time worrying about unpaid bills.

> "If there is one key to starting out on the right financial foot, it is learning to live *beneath* your means."

4. Prepare a budget, and review it regularly. This may sound like something only married people with children need to do. But it isn't. Ideally, you should be creating your first budget even before you get your first paycheck. You'll also need to review and revise it to reflect the many actual and/or expected changes in your income or expenses. If you think something particularly troublesome might happen, like a job loss, prepare a budget that reflects that condition, so you can figure out what you'll need to do to make ends meet.

5. Control your spending. If there is one key to starting out on the right financial foot, it is learning to live *beneath* your means. Until you get into the habit of spending less than you earn, you will never be able to save. If you can't save, you will never be able to acquire the very things that you should be working for: your first home or a financially secure retirement. Many people say that it's impossible for them to save: they claim that they spend their money only on absolute necessities and there is never anything left. These people simply haven't looked very hard at how and where they spend their money. There are always ways to cut spending, and most of them are painless.

6. Maintain your insurance coverage. Unfortunately, many people think little—if at all—about being insured. Insurance seems to be relatively unnecessary; after all, you're healthy now, and there hasn't been a burglary on your street for as long as anyone can remember. As a result, you may think a renters or health insurance policy is a waste of money. But don't be lulled into a false sense of security. Paying premiums for this type of protection represents money well spent.

The problem with leaving even a single gap in your insurance coverage—no matter how young you are—is that it exposes you to a possible uninsured loss, which could end up jeopardizing not only the few assets that you currently own, but also some of your *future* earnings.

7. Regularly invest some of your earnings. It's never too early or too late to start investing your money. Remember that while the opinions and advice of others may be helpful, you also can learn to make some of your own investment decisions. In this way, you'll understand what you're investing in and keep current on market conditions. A subscription to *Money* magazine, *Your Money*, or *Kiplinger's Personal Finance* can go a long way toward curing your lack of knowledge about investing. No matter what, avoid investing in extremes—liking stocks one week, loving bonds the next week, hating them both the next month. Instead, always take a long-term view and own both stocks and bonds in your portfolio.

8. Try to anticipate contingencies. You need to review your current financial situation periodically, so that you can anticipate any problems before they occur. The sooner you start, the more likely you'll be able to overcome whatever financial hurdles come your way, like the loss of your job, salary freezes or reductions, disability, or unexpected expenses.

* * *

Buying Your First Home

Questions

What is a buyer's broker?
What are points, and why do I have to pay them?
Is there an easy way to estimate how much house I can afford to buy?
What closing costs can I expect to pay?

Home ownership is the goal of most Americans. Yet, few of us take time to understand the ins and outs of home buying. This is an important oversight because, when it comes to buying a home, many people leave themselves at the mercy of the seller's broker. This is hardly the best way to start what, for many, proves to be the largest investment of their lives. This section will help you become a smarter home buyer.

> "Your total monthly debt obligations, including the mortgage, should not exceed 35% of your gross monthly income."

The decision to buy a particular home depends on several variables. The three most significant variables that must be factored into the purchase of a home are:

1. Location. Is the home convenient to work, shopping, school, and recreation? Is the general neighborhood declining or improving? How heavy are property taxes? Are there any crime or pollution problems? How good are the local school districts, community facilities, and services?

2. Type of home. The traditional single-family house is facing stiff competition from newer types of housing such as condominiums and multifamily units. Even traditional housing shows a tremendous amount of variety.

3. How much house can you afford? The amount of down payment and closing costs you will have to accumulate depends upon how much house you can afford. The following three rules of thumb should help you get an idea of how large a mortgage you can carry.

• Your monthly mortgage payment should not exceed more than one and a half week's worth of take-home pay.

• Your monthly mortgage payment should not exceed 28% of your gross monthly income.

• Your total monthly debt obligations, including the mortgage, should not exceed 35% of your gross monthly income.

Key Words

Buyer's broker A broker who negotiates the purchase price of a home on the buyer's behalf.

Points Fees paid by the buyer of a home at closing to the lender, usually 1% to 3% of the loan amount. (One "point" on a $150,000 mortgage would be $1,500.)

Purchase and sale agreement (P&S) A legal contract, specifying the terms and price of the sale between the buyer and seller of a home.

Real estate broker A broker who negotiates the sale of a home on the seller's behalf.

To determine how much house you can afford, you can also estimate what monthly mortgage payments might be. The following chart provides a way to estimate the amount of your monthly mortgage payment. For example, if you're thinking of qualifying for a $100,000 30-year mortgage at 8%, multiply 100 times the applicable amount—$7.34 per $1,000 borrowed—to determine that your monthly principal and interest payment will be approximately $734.

Payment Per $1,000 of Loan		
Interest Rate	15 Years	30 Years
7.00%	$8.99	$6.66
7.25	9.13	6.83
7.50	9.28	7.00
7.75	9.42	7.17
8.00	9.56	7.34
8.25	9.71	7.52
8.50	9.85	7.69
8.75	10.00	7.87
9.00	10.15	8.05
9.25	10.30	8.23

Also, don't forget about the down payment. Home buyers must save up a down payment which may be as low as 5% of the house value but more commonly is 10% to 20%. If the down payment is less than 20% of the market value of the home, most lenders will require the purchase of private mortgage insurance, which adds to the monthly payment. Thus, a $100,000 house may require an initial expenditure of as much as $20,000 plus closing costs.

Starting Your Home Search

To begin your search, read the real estate section of the Sunday newspaper. Chances are it will have an article or two about a particular neighborhood as well as extensive sale listings town by town. You can surmise, at a glance, the towns and areas you can afford.

While a property's location is important, affordability is just as important. Nevertheless, a location's advantages are tangible—in terms of conveniences, safety, public education, transportation, shopping areas, and cultural centers; all these factors need to be weighed against the costs of a home in a prime location. One strategy is to buy a less desirable home in the best possible location.

Finding a good Realtor is your next step. However, you need to remember that Realtors represent the seller, not you (the buyer). Nevertheless, a good Realtor knows the fair market prices for the homes he or she is selling.

Some real estate agents recently have switched camps and work exclusively for buyers. Known as buyer's brokers, these real estate professionals negotiate the purchase price on the buyer's behalf. A buyer's broker also may be able to help you locate areas where affordable housing exists. Buyer's brokers typically charge an hourly rate or a percentage of the selling price of the home that you purchase.

Once you've decided on the location, type of home, and Realtor, you'll need to begin to think about what type of mortgage to apply for.

Types of Mortgages

There are many types of mortgages to choose from. Familiarizing yourself with the most common types will help you select the most appropriate one for your needs. The two categories of mortgages are fixed-rate and adjustable-rate mortgages. A fixed-rate mortgage is a loan whose rate of interest does not change during the life of the mortgage. As a result, your loan payment will be a constant amount. By contrast, an adjustable-rate mortgage is a loan whose interest rate fluctuates throughout the life of the loan.

Within these categories, the most common types of mortgages are as follows.

30-Year Fixed Rate

The 30-year fixed-rate mortgage is still the standard. While an adjustable-rate mortgage may offer a lower interest rate at first, the security of knowing that the monthly payments will never change, and the lower monthly payments that a 30-year (as opposed to a 15-year) mortgage permits, seem to be the reasons why most home buyers opt for fixed-rate mortgages.

> "The two categories of mortgages are fixed-rate and adjustable-rate mortgages."

15-Year Fixed Rate

Your monthly payments will be higher than if you took out a 30-year fixed-rate mortgage, but the total interest you pay out over the life of the loan will be substantially lower. A 15-year fixed-rate mortgage is a good idea if you can afford the higher payments. Want to turn your 30-year mortgage into a 15-year mortgage at no cost? It's easy. Just make sufficient additional principal payments each month on your 30-year mortgage so that it will be paid off over the shorter period of time. You also can cut your mortgage repayment period down by taking out a biweekly mortgage, which means you make the equivalent of one extra monthly mortgage payment each year.

Two-Step Mortgage

This variation of the 30-year fixed-rate mortgage provides one fixed rate for the first phase of the loan—typically five to seven years—with a onetime adjustment for the remaining life of the loan. Two-steps are preferred by homeowners who are planning on moving before the first phase expires.

Adjustable-Rate Mortgage

Adjustable-rate mortgages offer extremely low rates that are subject to change. Many have a limit (ceiling) as to how high their interest rate can go—typically 18%, and a limit (floor) to how low they can go—typically 5.5%. The attraction of adjustable-rate mortgages is their low initial rate, but the danger is that the low rate will be left in the dust by rising interest rates. If you're contemplating staying in your new home for less than five years, then an adjustable-rate mortgage may be preferable.

Purchasing Your Home

A purchase and sale agreement (P&S) is the contract between buyer and seller that specifies the terms and price of the sale. Of course, the negotiation between buyer and seller occurs before the purchase and sale agreement is prepared. The P&S represents the legalization of the contract. That's why it's important for you to ask an attorney to review the P&S prior to signing it. You will want to include some contingencies in the agreement, regarding obtaining the financing (which will require the lender to appraise the property), a satisfactory home inspection, and a clear title.

The settlement is the legal sealing of the deal—where all legal documents (abstract of title and deed to property drawn up by the attorneys) are signed and all fees, including the broker's commission, are paid. Title insurance is another alternative worth considering. If a defect in the title is found after you purchase the home, the title insurance company is obligated to pay the damages—not you.

The buyer, seller, attorneys for both, real estate broker, and a representative of the lender usually attend settlement. The following is a list of typical fees, categorized according to who usually pays them (although most of them are negotiable):

Seller's Responsibility	Buyer's Responsibility
• Broker's commission	• Survey
• Seller's attorney fees	• Buyer's attorney fees
• Seller's percentage of property taxes, insurance policy insurance, and utilities	• Owner's title
	• Title examination fee
	• Financing fees
• Income tax from profit on sale	• Recording fees
• State transfer fees	

Closing Costs

Closing costs take many first-time home buyers by surprise. By now, you know that surprise is an element that works against successful financial planning. The following closing costs account for most of what you're likely to encounter when buying a home.

Mortgage Application Fee. Depending on the lender, this can run from nothing to several hundred dollars.

Origination Fee. This is the fee that a mortgage department or company charges to process your loan.

Private Mortgage Insurance Fee. If you don't have a 20% down payment but are still a candidate for a mortgage, you may be required to insure that the difference between your down payment and the 20% figure can be paid.

Appraisal Fee. You pay a professional to assess the market value of your desired home for the bank. Such fees start at $150, with no ceiling.

Home Inspection Fee. The fee—around $150—you pay a professional to inspect the house for defects. If you don't do this, you might end up with substantially less than you bargained for.

Credit Report Fee. The fee you pay the bank to run a credit check that tells them how creditworthy you are.

Check Your Credit Rating

Don't forget to check your credit rating. A clean credit record for at least two to three years is an important part of getting the mortgage you want.

Bank Attorney Fees. You pay the cost of the bank's legal work.

Points. Most lenders charge one or two points at closing: 1% to 3% of the loan amount. (Two points on a $125,000 mortgage would be $2,500.)

A problem with points is that they often pose a problem for home buyers trying to compare mortgage terms. The impact of points on total carrying costs compounds this confusion. Each point equals 1% of the loan amount. How much this affects the effective annual rate of the loan depends on how long you intend to own the house. One general rule of thumb if you plan to keep a house only a few years is to equate each point with about 0.25% on the interest rate. For example, a 9.5% loan with two points is roughly equivalent to a 9.75% loan with one point. The significance of points diminishes as the period of time you own the home increases.

* * *

How to Save and Invest for College Education Costs

Questions

How should I invest the money I set aside for my children's education? What kind of college financial aid does the federal government provide? How can I find out about sources of private financial aid?

Most experts, including the universities themselves, estimate that tuition costs will increase at an annual rate of 6% to 7%—well above the expected rate of inflation. But if inflation heats up again, college costs will escalate even more.

The following table projects current average four-year education expenses for tuition and room and board, assuming a 6% annual increase in costs. These figures do *not* include the students' out-of-pocket costs for such necessities as books and supplies, transportation, and entertainment. These extras could easily add many thousands of dollars to the four-year college tab.

AVERAGE FOUR-YEAR EDUCATION COSTS

Year Entering	Public School	Private School	Selective Private School
1993	$27,422	$69,780	$98,528
1994	29,067	73,967	104,440
1995	30,811	78,405	110,706
1996	32,660	83,110	117,348
1997	34,620	88,096	124,389
1998	36,697	93,382	131,853
1999	38,899	98,985	139,764
2000	41,232	104,923	148,150
2001	43,706	111,219	157,039
2002	46,329	117,893	166,461
2003	49,109	124,966	176,449
2004	52,055	132,464	187,036
2005	55,178	140,412	198,258
2006	58,489	148,837	210,153
2007	61,998	157,767	222,762
2008	65,718	167,233	236,127
2009	69,661	177,267	250,295
2010	73,841	187,903	265,313
2011	78,271	199,177	281,232
2012	82,967	211,127	298,106

How will you be able to afford to send your children to college? Part of the process of planning early to meet the high costs of higher education is to devise a realistic program that will help you meet the ever-rising costs of a college education.

Sources of Money for College

There are a variety of sources of funds for college including the following.

Parents' Income

While your child is in college, a portion of your income will more than likely go toward helping meet college expenses.

Key Words

Baccalaureate bond A specialized type of municipal bond sold as a college savings vehicle.

College work study A federally subsidized program designed to help provide part-time jobs to students on financial aid.

Federal Stafford Loan Popularly called guaranteed student loans, Federal Stafford Loans are made by the federal government directly to the student, rather than to his or her parents.

Student Jobs

There is no reason to expect your child not to work during the academic year and/or during vacations to help meet college expenses.

Gifts and Inheritances

Grandparents may be a source of help in meeting college expenses if they can comfortably afford it. Many seniors wish to know that money passed on after their death will be used to help educate the grandchildren or great-grandchildren.

Financial Aid

Financial aid is available only to the neediest families. Even with the relaxation of the rules in 1992, you will probably qualify for little or no financial aid. (To get an idea of what financial aid is available, see the section later in this chapter.)

Loans

Student and personal loans are a common way to bridge the gap between money needed for college and money available for college.

> "Savings need to be invested
> appropriately in order to
> keep up with the ever-rising
> costs of college."

Personal Investments

There are various investment alternatives for college-earmarked money which are described below.

College Investment Alternatives

Saving for your children's college tuition is critical. But, in most cases, saving goes only half way. Savings need to be invested appropriately in order to keep up with the ever-rising costs of college. The following is a summary of some smart places to invest college funds.

Investing for college, particularly when your child is young and you have a relatively long time to invest is like investing for any other worthwhile purpose. Three college-bound investment choices which make the grade are as follows.

Stock Mutual Funds

You may think that putting college funds in stocks is too risky, but if you're 10 years or more from writing out those tuition checks, stock mutual funds are an excellent place for a good portion of your college investments. (See Chapter 4 for details on mutual fund investing.)

Bonds

By timing the maturities to coincide with the years your child will be in college, you eliminate the potential loss of principal that can happen if you sell a bond before maturity after interest rates have risen.

What kinds of bonds should you buy? They run the gamut from ultra-safe U.S. Treasury bonds to municipal bonds to corporate bonds. Part of the decision will hinge upon your federal and state tax situation and whether the bonds are in your name or your child's name. An alternative to buying bonds directly is to invest in a bond mutual fund. (See Chapter 4 for more on bond investing.)

U.S. Savings Bonds

U.S. savings bonds' returns aren't spectacular, but the tax-deferred buildup feature and state tax exemption make Series EE bonds an excellent and safe place to put some of the money that's headed for college. An added benefit for savings bonds bought anytime after 1989 is that if you redeem them to cover college fees and tuition and you meet an income test (which rises each year with inflation), the interest on these bonds is tax free. But be careful, because the interest on these bonds when you cash them in is added to your income for purposes of determining whether your income level qualifies for tax exemption.

In general, it's hard to go wrong with a combination of stock mutual funds, U.S. savings bonds, and, when you have enough money to buy individual issues, bonds. There are also a few unique investments designed specifically for college savers that are described next.

Special College Savings Investment Plans

Prepaid Tuition Plans

A few states, colleges, groups of colleges, and banks offer prepaid tuition plans. Basically, you invest a certain amount of money which is guaranteed to meet the future tuition costs.

Baccalaureate, or College Saver, Bonds

These are municipal bonds that are sold by some states as a college savings vehicle. While the states may offer a variety of inducements to invest in them, the main advantage is tax-exempt interest. Before investing in a baccalaureate bond, compare it with other investment alternatives described here.

College Investment Strategies

Your college investment strategy will be influenced by the age of the college-bound child. The nearer your child is to entering college, the less risk you can afford to take with the money that will be needed to meet college costs. There aren't many times when we invest for the short term, but one of those times is when a child nears college age. Age and timing are important elements to any investment plan. The best time to invest for a child's future education is probably before he or she is born. But more realistically, the best time is as soon as you can do it.

Preteens

If your child is under age 13, you should be investing for the long term. Therefore, stock mutual funds and/or stocks should play an important role in your college savings plan. Why? Because over the long run, stocks have consistently provided better returns than bonds or short-term interest-earning investments like money market accounts. How much of a younger child's college fund should be in stocks? At least half, with the remainder in various kinds of bonds or bond mutual funds.

> "A few states, colleges, groups of colleges, and banks offer prepaid tuition plans."

Teenagers

If you have already set aside some money for college, when your child becomes a teenager you will need to gradually shift your money out of stocks into more conservative interest-earning securities. The reason is that you're becoming a short-term investor, since college is just a few years off. Therefore, you can't afford the risk of having too much money invested in stocks.

Be careful if you have been investing regularly in U.S. savings bonds—you have to hold them at least five years to benefit from the full interest rate. Also be careful not to invest too conservatively on behalf of your soon-to-be collegian. Rather than money market funds and savings accounts, consider short-term bonds or CDs to pick up a bit more yield.

> "If you have already set aside some money for college, when your child becomes a teenager you will need to gradually shift your money out of stocks into more conservative interest-earning securities."

A common college planning question is whether to keep the college savings fund in your name or your child's name. Many parents transfer a lot of money to their children. But this can backfire in more ways than one. For one thing, financial aid rules stipulate that most of the investments owned by the student will be used to meet college expenses, whereas, had the money been in the parents' name, a much lower percentage of these same investments would be required to go toward tuition.

Another way this can backfire is that once children reach the age of majority they can't legally be stopped from using the money any way they want.

Types of Financial Aid

As you can see from the college expense forecaster, meeting the cost of a college education is a struggle for all but the most affluent families—but it is not beyond your reach. As a result, most people need to learn as much as they can about the many ways to finance a college education. The following inventory of college funding sources will help you identify ways to help bridge the gap between college expenses and available resources.

Inventory of College Funding Sources

Grants and scholarships, and fellowships:
☐ Federal Pell Grant
☐ Federal Supplemental Education Opportunity Grant
☐ State financial assistance
☐ School financial assistance
☐ School scholarship or fellowship/ Private aid programs
☐ Military benefits or officer-training program
☐ Social Security benefits

Education loans:
☐ Federal Perkins Loan (formerly National Direct Student Loan)
☐ Federal Stafford Student Loan (formerly Guaranteed Student Loan)
☐ Federal Parent Loans for Undergraduate Students (PLUS loans)

☐ School loan programs
☐ State loan programs
☐ Private education loan programs

Personal loans:
☐ Home equity loan
☐ Other secured financing
☐ Unsecured loans

Personal resources allocable to funding education costs:
☐ Income of parents
☐ Income of student—school jobs
☐ Income of student—summer jobs
☐ Parents' savings/investments
☐ Student's savings/investments
☐ Gifts from relatives

Government Aid

The following types of government aid can help.

Federal Pell Grants. These are outright gifts from the federal government of up to $2,400. You apply simply by checking the appropriate box on the Family Financial Statement or the Financial Aid Form. Approximately four to six weeks after the information is sent in, your child receives a Student Aid Report assigning him or her an aid index that determines whether he or she is eligible. An index number lower than 1700 usually qualifies for a grant. The form comes in three parts and, whether or not your child is eligible, all three parts must be sent to the school that he or she will be attending.

Federal Stafford Loans (Guaranteed Student Loans). Commonly known as GSLs, but now officially known as Federal Stafford Loans, they're the most common and equitable way to help finance a college education today. Your child may take out a Federal Stafford Loan at an interest rate of 8%. The rate for the first loan taken out will remain the same for all subsequent loans. Your child may take out up to $2,625 in the first year, $3,500 for the second year, and up to $5,500 per year for the remaining two to three years that it takes to graduate. The total loan limit for an undergraduate is $23,000. Graduate students may borrow up to $8,500 per year of graduate study, amounting to not more than $65,500 including the undergraduate loans. Yearly loans cannot exceed tuition amounts.

The loan rate for subsidized Federal Stafford Loans, for loans received on or after July 1, 1993, is a variable rate based on the 91-day Treasury bill as of July 1 of each year, plus 3.1%. The rate is capped at 9%.

The government subsidizes the loan until six months after graduation. At this point, the student must start paying it back monthly and is allowed 10 years to repay. The school or the state loan guarantee agency can supply a list of lenders close by; you can also call the United Student Aid Fund agency's toll-free number, 1-800-428-9250.

Note: The check received will be somewhat less than the amount actually borrowed—there is a 5% origination fee. In addition, the guarantee agency in the state may charge an insurance premium.

Federal PLUS Loans. Federal Parent Loans for Undergraduate Students enable graduate students and the parents of undergraduates to borrow up to the annual cost of education minus any financial aid the student receives. The parents may receive this money in addition to the amount their child receives through the Federal Stafford program. Graduate students may borrow it in addition to their $65,500 maximum.

> **"Federal Stafford Loans.** Commonly known as GSLs, but now officially known as Federal Stafford Loans, they're the most common and equitable way to help finance a college education today."

All Federal PLUS loans carry an interest rate of 3.10% over the rate for one-year Treasury bills with a 10% cap. There's a catch: parents must start paying back the loan within 60 days. Graduate and independent undergraduate students can defer the principal until they leave school, but interest payments start within 60 days. Application is made in the same manner as for the Federal Stafford Loan, but *no* needs test is required, although parents may have to undergo a credit check.

Federal Supplemental Education Opportunity Grants (SEOG). These are for undergraduates only and range up to several thousand dollars. The difference between Federal Pell Grants and Federal SEOGs is that the government guarantees that the school will get enough money for all its Federal Pell Grant awards, whereas the school gets only a fixed amount for the Federal SEOG. Thus, Federal SEOGs are awarded on a first-come, first-served basis— another reason why it is important to send in application materials on time. The school will notify your child if he or she is going to receive a Federal SEOG and will either pay the student directly or credit his or her account.

Note: Part-time students also may be eligible for this grant and should check with the school.

Federal National Direct Student Loans (NDSL). These are special education assistance loans offered at below bank loan interest rates. An undergraduate may borrow a yearly sum with a cumulative maximum for the first four years. Graduate students can receive additional money on top of money borrowed as an undergraduate. Payments begin six months after graduation or after the student drops below half-time status, and loans must be paid back within 10 years. Students may defer payments by joining the Peace Corps, enlisting in the military, or teaching in an inner-city public school. The college's financial aid office is in charge of the program for that school.

Federal Subsidized Work Study. In Federal College Work Study (CWS) programs, your child finds a job with an approved employer, such as a nonprofit organization or a professor, either on or off campus. The government subsidizes a certain percentage of the payback, usually about two-thirds. By taking a CWS job, your son or daughter can become an attractive candidate for employment and thereby have an edge in getting a future job while, at the same time, helping share the cost of his or her current education. Wage rates vary but are at least the federal minimum, although the student is given a wage ceiling and may not earn more than that.

Campus-Based Federal Aid. Federal aid is available not only directly from the government, but also through the college of your son's or daughter's choice. The government gives the college a specific amount of money to distribute, to the college-designated recipients. This money is in the form of grants, loans, and subsidized jobs. A qualified student can participate in more than one program at a time for the purpose of meeting need that has not already been met.

Military Aid

The Army, Navy, Air Force, and Marine Reserve Officers Training Corps offer scholarships that pay all tuition, fees, books, and also provide a tax-free stipend per month to be used at the participating school. The student in turn incurs a long service obligation—six years, four of them on active duty. The school must have a base on campus to offer this scholarship, and the student must report to a Reserve Officers' Training Corps (ROTC) class weekly while enrolled in school. For more information write to:

Navy and Marines Recruiting Command
4015 Wilson Blvd.
Arlington, VA 22203-1991

Headquarters
U.S. Army ROTC Cadet Command
Fort Monroe, VA 23651-5000

Air Force ROTC
Public Affairs Division
Maxwell Air Force Base, AL 36112-6663

The National Guard also offers substantial tuition help after a two-year enlistment. Veterans benefits also may be applied toward a college education if the student is a veteran or is the spouse or child of a deceased or disabled veteran.

College Aid

Each school has its own way of packaging aid and will provide its students with information on available options. Installment plans, loans, merit scholarships, athletic scholarships, and discounts for more than one family member attending the university are all possible forms of aid. Many of the most competitive schools, including the Ivy League colleges, offer financial aid strictly on the basis of need. In fact, a group of these competitive schools meet every year to make sure that students applying to more than one of them get the same aid package from each school, so that qualified students will not have to forgo their first choice for financial reasons.

You may find that the more expensive colleges are a better source of financial aid. Many colleges offer scholarships on a non-need basis, such as for academic, athletic, or other talent. However, schools that give scholarships to attract better students may not continue the scholarships after freshman year. Always know the conditions and length of your award.

> "One option that is becoming available at more and more colleges is called the tuition prepayment option."

Tuition Payment Options. Many schools offer a variety of methods of payment to make the expense as painless as possible. Explore the available options. Many plans are unique to particular schools, and information is available for the asking.

One option that is becoming available at more and more colleges is called the tuition prepayment option. When the student enters, the entire four years are paid all at once at the price of the freshman year. The idea is to hedge against future increases in tuition, which has been increasing at a higher rate than inflation and is expected to continue to do so. The savings from such a plan can be in the thousands of dollars, but it is useful only to families who have sufficient capital to make the high prepayment. For parents who don't have a pile of cash, some schools have a loan plan to spread out the cost at a nominal interest rate.

Installment Plans. Another common type of payment option is the monthly payment plan, which allows the semester bill to be paid in monthly installments rather than all at once. This may be convenient for families who are paying a lot of the tuition bill out of their paychecks.

Private Aid

Scholarships that come from sources other than the school or the government are sometimes based on merit and are sometimes available through affiliation, such as via your employer, the Rotary Club or other community organization, or church. Finding out about such aid takes initiative, but the rewards can be very worthwhile. A good place to start looking is a school guidance counselor's office or your local library. Likewise, since this process may be overwhelming for all concerned, it is a good way to share with your child the hard work involved in making his or her dreams come true.

Organizing Your Approach to Financing College Costs

More often than not, parents delay planning for a child's education and are left with little time to organize financing. But even after maintaining a responsible savings program, parents may still find the cost of college far exceeds the amount saved. Both situations necessitate a methodical examination of financing alternatives, including the steps outlined below.

1. Assess all family resources available for funding college costs. Resources may include equity that has accumulated in the family home, gifts from grandparents, and inheritances.

2. Exhaustively review all sources of possible scholarships. A multitude of scholarship opportunities exist. Scholarships for academic, athletic, and leadership achievement are very common. Parents and students also should consider any military, company, union, trade, civic, religious, or ethnic affiliations they have that could lead to other sources of funds.

3. Investigate available loan and grant opportunities. Not all loans are created equal. Students displaying appropriate financial need may qualify for other federally sponsored low-interest loans aside from those discussed here. Also educational institutions themselves offer loans on favorable terms, although resources are usually limited. Candidates should apply for such loans as early as possible in order to be considered while funds last.

4. Pursue the aid package. Students should attempt to obtain packages that consist of few loans and many grants and work-study awards. Since much student aid is distributed on a first-come, first-served basis, students must be prompt in applying to college and financial aid programs. Don't be afraid to appeal the college's financial aid offer. They may up the ante. Obtaining outside sources of funding through scholarships is also an ideal way to reduce a student's loan obligation.

5. Try to minimize miscellaneous costs. Neither you nor your child should ever sacrifice quality of education for a few dollars' savings that can be repaid in the future when a fine education is finished. However, frugal living while in school is one way that a student may significantly reduce the amount of money, and therefore the amount of aid, needed. A few ways to minimize expenditures are:

• **Books.** Although it's easier to go to the campus bookstore and buy new supplies and textbooks, shopping for used books from fellow students, on-campus stores, or off-campus bookstores can result in substantial savings.

• **Room and board.** Many colleges provide a choice between on- or off-campus housing. Although it's often more convenient to live on-campus, a student may find room and board cheaper off-campus. Investigate the pros and cons of both possibilities.

• **Insurance.** Often, your medical insurance policies will cover your child through college until graduation. Therefore, don't pay for a college-sponsored program *if* your child is already insured under your plan.

Helpful Publications

There are several publications that give helpful information about dealing with college costs.
• *The Student Guide: Five Federal Financial Aid Programs* (Consumer Information Center, Dept. 522Y, Pueblo, CO 81009; (719) 948-3334). This guide describes all federal sources of financial aid in great detail and lists information sources for state aid for every state.
• *Applying for Financial Aid* (American College Testing Program, P.O. Box 168, Iowa City, Iowa 52243; (319) 337-1040).
• *The College Cost Book* (College Board Publications, Box 886, New York, NY 10101-0886; (800) 323-7155). This reference book is available in most libraries and high school guidance counselors' offices.
• *Don't Miss Out* (Octameron Associates, P.O. Box 2748, Alexandria, VA 22301; (703) 836-5480). This financial aid guide book contains need-analysis forms.
• *Paying Less for College* (Peterson's, Attention: Book Order Department, P.O. Box 2123, Princeton, NJ 08543; (800) 338-3282). This handbook gives financial information on 1,700 colleges in the nation, including the average percentage of need met at each school.

* * *

Special Financial Concerns of Retirees

Questions

Do people who have succeeded in achieving a secure retirement need to continue the financial planning process after they have retired? What sort of financial goals are appropriate for retired people?

Financial planning does not stop when you retire: even people who have successfully made the transition from the working world to retired life cannot rest on their laurels. As for the retiree who did not plan adequately, careful attention to financial planning is especially necessary if financial difficulties are to be avoided. The planning process continues as long as you live.

Continuing Financial Planning in Retirement

Retired people, like their working counterparts, need to manage their debts wisely, invest appropriately, and in many instances continue the savings programs they began in their working years. Keeping records in good order is especially important for retirees. Older people are more likely to become disabled or incapacitated, and the sudden onset of a disability could result in a child's or relative's having to assume responsibility for the disabled person's financial affairs. Should a disability occur, good, well-organized records will make matters a great deal simpler.

Retirees also need to maintain good insurance coverage, although in some instances life insurance can be scaled back. Finally, retired people have to pay special attention to their estate plans in order to see that they are appropriate and up-to-date.

Unfortunately, all too many older people assume that because they succeeded in meeting their retirement savings goals, short- and long-term goals are unnecessary. Yet people of all ages need to establish financial planning goals: they impose discipline and force you to consider where you want to be in the future. For retirees who have a comfortable amount of discretionary income, reasonable financial goals might include saving money for extensive travel, increased charitable giving, and transferring wealth to heirs before (and after) death.

The first thing a new retiree should do is reassess his or her current expenditure level. Now that the days of a weekly paycheck are over, a change in life-style may be necessary: the last thing the retiree wants is to run out of money. Like everyone else, the new retiree needs to establish a workable budget. Hopefully, the income derived from pensions, Social Security benefits, and personal investments will be sufficient to make a life-style change unnecessary.

> "The first thing a new retiree should do is reassess his or her current expenditure level."

Note: There are no new key words for this section. For key terms on retirement, please turn to Chapter 6.

Many older people think that retirement is a time to adopt a super-conservative approach to investing. However, playing it overly safe can be just as disastrous as being wild and reckless. The retiree is faced with a dual challenge: he or she must continue to grow an investment portfolio while ensuring that it provides a comfortable level of current income. Unlike younger investors, who generally rely on their salaries to meet living expenses, retirees often depend heavily on the performance of their investment portfolios. When the investment return on a retiree's portfolio sags, a decline in living standards is often the result. Because so many retirees are painfully aware of their dependence on current income, they tend to be excessively conservative in their investment habits.

Why is capital appreciation important to the retiree? The answers are longevity and inflation. Because of advancements in medical science, retirees today are living longer than ever. Many people who leave the work force at age 65 can look forward to another 30 years of life—and, unfortunately, another 30 years of inflation. Even at low inflation rates, living expenses could triple in 30 years. To avoid an erosion in living standards, the retiree's portfolio typically needs to contain enough stock and/or stock mutual funds to ensure that income will keep pace with inflation. Generally, at least a third of the retiree's portfolio should be invested in stocks.

Fortunately, retirees have one great advantage over everybody else—they have more time on their hands, which means that they have more time to manage their investments. Indeed, some newly retired people find that they can give their portfolio the attention it deserves for the first time in their lives, and do quite well closely managing their investments. Of course, very aged retirees may become incapable of managing their financial affairs due to ill health. For these people, the services of a good investment adviser may be crucial.

Selecting Your Investment Adviser

Finding the right advisors is well worth the effort. Word-of-mouth recommendation can be an important first step. It's also important to know that the person you are dealing with has your best interests at heart.

Investment Advisers

This umbrella term covers all those who provide investment advice for a fee—from mutual fund managers to publishers of investment newsletters, and the more familiar personal money advisors. Investment advisers must register with the Securities and Exchange Commission (SEC), although there's no specialized training or financial qualifications.

Some investment advisers operate individually, while others operate under the auspices of financial organizations such as insurance companies.

Charges for services rendered can be either fee-based or commission-based. Commission-based investment advisers charge you a commission on the investments you purchase. Fee-based investment advisers charge you either an hourly fee for the work they perform on your investment accounts or a fee based on a percentage of the total value of the investments they manage for you.

A good investment adviser can be an important part of your team of financial advisors. He or she can keep you current on economic trends that may affect the market, as well as keep a watchful eye over your investments' performance.

Stockbrokers

Many people think of stockbrokers as investment advisers. Stockbrokers may have a conflict of interest in advising you on your investments—their income is dependent upon the type of investments you buy and the frequency with which you buy and sell. Nevertheless, there are many excellent stockbrokers who can deal with these conflicts and still act in your best interest.

Estate Planning

Finally, every retiree needs a will, and most also need a durable power of attorney, living will, and letter of instructions. If you're a retiree and you don't have these basic documents, you will probably cause both yourself and your loved ones a lot of grief not only after your death, but also during your lifetime if you become incapacitated or terminally ill. Beyond these basics, there are several more sophisticated estate planning techniques that you should be aware of, and you don't have to be a millionaire to take advantage of them. How? Turn to Chapter 7, Basic Estate Planning Principles, to find out.

* * *

Death of a Family Member

Questions

What are the first steps to take when a family member dies? How do I meet financial needs and obligations until the deceased's estate is settled? How do I go about collecting proceeds from an insurance policy? What is the best way to cope with a sudden death?

> "The best thing to do is also the hardest thing to do—namely, to stay organized and focused on meeting your financial obligations under duress from the death of a family member."

The best thing to do is also the hardest thing to do—namely, to stay organized and focused on meeting your financial obligations under duress from the death of a family member. Staying in control of your emotions will be made easier if you can stay in control of your financial commitments. Your financial obligations fall into two categories: immediate and subsequent.

Key Words

Decedent A recently deceased person.

Estate The property belonging to the decedent—investments, real estate, and personal property—at the time of his or her death.

Executor or administrator The person appointed to oversee the disposition of the decedent's estate. Technically, an executor is appointed when a person dies with a will; an administrator when a person dies without a will.

Illiquid assets An investment or personal item that can't be easily or quickly sold for cash at a selling price near its fair market value. Examples include real estate and family businesses.

Liquid assets Cash and any other asset that can be quickly turned into cash, such as most stocks, bonds, money market accounts, savings accounts, and most mutual funds.

Meeting Financial Needs

To begin with, you must identify the resources available to meet your financial needs until the estate is settled. These expenses must account for everything from the $20 you still owe the milkman to the monthly mortgage, to insurance and taxes due on your property.

You will need cash on hand to meet these day-to-day expenses. You also will need readily accessible cash to pay funeral-related expenses, administration expenses, federal and state death taxes, and cash bequests (cash gifts to your designated beneficiaries). You or the executor of the estate (who may well be you) need to determine what liquid assets (in other words, readily accessible) are available, and what outside resources are available (your parents or children may be able to help you meet costs that you can't immediately cover yourself).

Even if your net worth is considerable, it may not be liquid (for example, it could be tied up in real estate holdings). This means that your assets may be inaccessible during the administration of the estate.

Fortunately, even if your (and the estate's) immediate cash needs have not been provided for by prudent advance estate planning, there are a number of ways that you or the executor may be able to obtain sufficient funds including the following.

- Joint checking or savings accounts and other assets that don't have to go through probate may help you cover immediate needs.

- If the executor—the person designated to settle the estate— receives the required authority to do so, he or she can distribute assets in lieu of cash bequests in some cases. Distribution of this kind will reduce the cash needs of the estate.

- If the decedent's will creates a trust, the executor may elect to place any illiquid assets in the trust and sell more marketable assets.

- The estate can raise cash by borrowing from a beneficiary of the estate, or from the beneficiary of a trust established by the estate.

- The estate tax on a family business interest (if meeting certain qualifying conditions) may be deferred for up to 14 years, with the estate making annual interest-only payments for the first four years and paying the balance in 10 annual installments of principal and interest. In order to qualify, the value of the business must exceed 35% of the value of the decedent's adjusted gross estate.

You will need to make some difficult money-related decisions. Make each one cautiously. Be extremely conservative. In fact, putting most or all death benefits or insurance proceeds in money market accounts, CDs, Treasury bills, or other short-term investments that are safe (federally insured) and accessible makes good sense over the first few months. You'll also be better able to allocate the resources later on.

The following checklist will help you determine what you need to do following the death of a family member.

Postdeath Checklist

Professional Help

☐ Contact the decedent's attorney. He or she should be helpful regarding the status and whereabouts of estate planning documents.

☐ Contact the decedent's financial advisors. There may be some financial details that you need to know about.

☐ If you are the executor of the estate, consider hiring an attorney to help you with the legal complexities of settling the estate.

☐ If you and yours are not familiar with financial, investment, and tax matters, then consider hiring an accountant, attorney, and/or financial planner to review all the ramifications of the deceased's estate.

Personal Affairs

☐ You will need at least 10 copies of the death certificate. Why? Because every time you make a claim for a benefit, you will be required to present a copy of the death certificate.

☐ Locate the *original* will and all life insurance policies. If they can't be found immediately, a good place to start is with a known safe-deposit box.

☐ The letter of instructions, if the deceased prepared one, should be read thoroughly so that the specific wishes of the deceased regarding his or her funeral are carried out. The letter of instructions will also provide useful information concerning the location of documents pertinent to the probate process and other matters of immediate concern to survivors.

> "You will need at least 10 copies of the death certificate."

☐ Obtain the deceased's Social Security number. You will need this more than once.

☐ If the deceased was married, obtain copies of the marriage certificate for purposes of making claims.

☐ If the deceased had children, then several copies of their birth certificates may need to be obtained. You won't be able to establish claims for certain Social Security benefits without them. Again, if you can't find the documents, contact the state and/or county where the children were born and request certified copies be sent to you immediately.

☐ You will need copies of the deceased's certificate of honorable discharge in order to claim any veterans benefits. If there isn't a readily available copy, write to the Department of Defense's National Personnel Record Center, 9700 Page Boulevard, St. Louis, MO 63132.

☐ Contact the deceased's employer for details about pension plans and other retirement plan (stock options, 401(k) plans) benefits. Request copies of pertinent documents.

☐ Determine titles/ownership of all personal property (for example, automobile, boat), real estate, and all stocks, bonds, and other investments.

☐ Ascertain the status of the deceased's credit accounts, mortgage, bank accounts, and utility bills to make sure they have been kept up-to-date.

☐ Notify the deceased's creditors.

Insurance

You'll need to determine the deceased's death benefits and advise the beneficiaries on the distribution of their proceeds. You also should review possible changes in your overall family insurance coverage. The following steps can help you through this process.

• You should notify the life insurance agent or company and file the necessary claims. Besides employee benefits and life insurance, you also may be eligible for Social Security or Veterans Administration benefits and should contact the appropriate offices.

• It's important to determine any death benefits that are due. If applicable, Social Security orphan's benefits also should be investigated. You also should notify the employee benefits office if the decedent was employed at the time of death. You may be eligible to receive a last paycheck, payment for accrued vacation and sick leave, company life insurance, a pension benefit, deferred compensation, profit sharing, and/or accident insurance.

• If you are the beneficiary of a life insurance policy, you may have several options of how to receive the money. These options should be very carefully evaluated. Don't rely solely on the insurance agent's recommendation. If necessary, pay for an independent opinion. You can always leave the insurance proceeds with the insurance company earning interest until a final decision is made.

Revise Your Coverage

Insurance coverage will need to be reviewed after the death of a spouse. If your spouse handled your insurance, you may be unfamiliar with the process. In this case, you will need to educate yourself on your insurance needs. Besides revising and changing the beneficiary designations on existing policies, you have to assess your own insurance needs as a result of the changed circumstances. If you were formerly covered as a spouse under a health insurance plan, continuing coverage will have to be acquired. Appropriate coverage in your name for auto, home-owners or renters, and umbrella liability insurance is also necessary. Depending on individual circumstances, you may need to acquire or increase the limits on disability and life insurance coverage.

Life Insurance Settlement Options

There are three main ways you can elect to receive the proceeds of a life insurance policy with lesser variations within each method.

Lump-Sum Settlements. Lump-sum payments—getting the whole amount at once—are usually appropriate for small policies and/or for those beneficiaries who are capable of investing wisely or who can rely on competent investment advisers. Lump-sum payouts occur automatically when insurance proceeds are payable into a trust.

> "Insurance coverage will need to be reviewed after the death of a spouse."

Fixed Payments. You can opt to have the insurance company distribute portions of the proceeds and interest thereon either over a fixed period of time or in installment payments of a fixed amount paid at stated intervals until the money is used up. Either way, make certain that you can change your mind and withdraw the entire sum at a later date. If you have not received the entire payment and have not exercised the power to withdraw a lump sum by the time of your own death, the unpaid balance will be payable at your election to your estate or to some other beneficiary.

Alternatively, the insurance company can pay you fixed payments of interest only, with the principal of the policy payable either to your estate or to a designated beneficiary. In any fixed-payment arrangement, the first payment must be made no later than 13 months after your loved one's death.

Annuities. With an annuity, the insurance company agrees to pay a certain monthly sum for life, the amount depending on the size of the insurance policy and your age. Annuities assure that you will never outlive the monthly payment.

Coping With a Sudden Death

A sudden death can wreak emotional havoc on surviving family members and friends. For the partner closest to the deceased, to whom most of the decisions regarding disposition and funeral services are left, the situation can be overwhelming.

For this reason it is imperative that, in the event that no preplanning was done, no one person be allowed to decide on the issues of disposition and interment—especially a spouse or child. If you or someone you know is in this situation, then consider this advice:

- **Do** call your closest and most trusted friend. You will need to rely on his or her help and judgment in the days to come.
- **Don't** go directly from the hospital to a funeral home. You will only risk agreeing on a too-elaborate funeral that will end up costing you time, emotion, and money.
- **Do** call up your immediate family members and ask them to convene as soon as possible and confer with you as a group.

- **Do** contact the deceased's attorney for legal guidance concerning the immediate matter of the will as it relates to funeral arrangements that you may not have been informed about.
- **Don't** commit to any funeral-related costs until you have discussed the items with your friend, family, and/or lawyer. It is an exhausting and unpleasant task but one that must be done. Never go it alone.
- **Don't** take any calls from strangers who claim to have known the deceased or want to help you with your future finances. Charlatans love to prey on grieving family members.

> "Don't commit to any funeral-related costs until you have discussed the items with your friend, family, and/or lawyer."

This option may be particularly useful where your resources and/or investment expertise is limited, where you have spend-thrift tendencies, or where there is danger of your exhausting all your savings through an uninsured nursing home stay.

If you want to purchase an annuity, the settlement option plan offered by the company that issues the life insurance policy may not be the best deal. Other insurance companies may offer you a higher monthly income. If you want to purchase an annuity from a company other than the one that paid the death claim, you should have the two companies transfer the funds directly to avoid adverse tax consequences.

* * *

Divorce

Questions

My husband and I recently divorced. What financial planning steps should I take?
If I get divorced, what happens to my pension?
What are the tax consequences of a legal separation?

The standard form of settlement for a divorce used to be alimony. Today, equitable distribution is increasingly more common. Knowing about both may help you on your way to a settlement you can live with.

> "Alimony is being replaced by distribution of marital assets."

The original reason for alimony was that it enforced the husband's obligation to continue to support his wife, for whom employment opportunities were very limited. (Authorities have differed as to whether alimony also was intended to compensate the wife for her contribution to the marriage.) The awarding of alimony is within the discretion of the court at a divorce trial, and it is generally only awarded in situations where the divorced spouse cannot support himself or herself or where sufficient marital assets currently do not exist to support both spouses.

Key Words

Alimony An allowance made to one spouse by the other for support pending or after legal separation or divorce.

Equitable distribution Not to be confused with meaning equal distribution, the determination of each party's claim to ownership is made by the court.

Mediation A less costly alternative to lawyer-based courtroom divorce settlement.

Premarital agreement Also known as antenuptial agreements, these contracts define each partner's separate property being brought into the marriage and describe your financial intentions after you're wed.

Separation agreement A document or court decree, often made up when a married couple separates, terminating the relationship and outlining the financial terms of the separation.

Alimony is being replaced by distribution of marital assets. The most common form is called equitable distribution, although a few states use community property to determine division. Equitable distribution does not mean equal distribution, and the determination of claim to ownership is made by a number of criteria. Basically, community property attempts to divide all marital property in which each spouse has a vested 50% interest between the divorcing spouses, whereas equitable distribution weighs each partner's contributions to the marriage, including nonfinancial considerations, to determine a fair claim. Many divorces negotiate some balance between maintenance and asset division. A spouse who receives a large property settlement, even when he or she is over age 50 and has never worked outside the house, can expect to have his or her alimony substantially decreased or eliminated from the settlement. In effect, property is traded for income.

Divorce Alternatives

If you are going to divorce, you need to consider the cost of the divorce process itself. Some people may not realize the range of legal fees and related expenses, including such costly minutiae as fees to property appraisers and accountants that may be incurred during divorce proceedings. Depending on the location and size of the firm, legal fees generally range from $75 to $350 an hour.

Although lawyers should be hired to review the final agreement, alternative professional help is available to mediate an agreeable settlement at a fraction of the legal eagles' cost.

Mediation

The most common alternative is a professional divorce mediator. While mediation is not recommended for hostile couples, it can help nonadversarial couples come to realistic and reasonable terms. Often, it helps both sides to understand and accept the finality of the divorce more easily than they might accept an extensively litigated decision imposed on them by the court. Mediation generally costs $70 to $100 an hour, and uncomplicated divorces can usually be resolved in less than 12 hours.

Do-It-Yourself Divorce

Another alternative to litigation is doing it yourselves. Amenable couples with no dependent children can, in many states, negotiate their own settlement and file for divorce themselves. Remember, if you choose this route, each party should consult with a lawyer before filing the final agreement so that nothing important will be overlooked.

Changes in Your Financial Planning

Divorce requires considerable financial planning. For one thing, you can expect your standards of living to decrease, at least temporarily, after your divorce. Why? The income and assets that once supported one household are now expected to support two. As a result, you will probably need to place increased importance on budgeting, planning, and revising your financial goals. The following are just some of the areas that you will need to address in light of your changed marital status.

Insurance

The status of your insurance policies and future coverage will need to be addressed in your final divorce settlement. It is very important that you notify your insurer of your change in marital status, because it affects the type and amount of coverage you will need. Premiums, for instance, may be affected by your revised insurance requirements.

Life Insurance. If you negotiate a lump-sum settlement without further spousal maintenance, you may wish to change the beneficiary designation on your existing life insurance policies. In cases where life insurance replaces alimony for the recipient spouse after the payor's death, the recipient spouse should insist on a clause in the agreement giving her or him authority to obtain information periodically from the insurance company.

There are several alternative ways to address the issue of insurance policies in a divorce settlement. The insured can give the ex-spouse the policy outright. However, the drawbacks for the insured are that he or she relinquishes all ownership rights, including the right to borrow against the cash value, even if the ex-spouse remarries and is no longer entitled to alimony.

The recipient can buy a policy on his or her ex-spouse's life. In this case, the divorce settlement should provide that the insured will comply with the requirements of the insurer (e.g., physical exam) if the ex-spouse ever wants to buy more insurance on his or her life.

The insured could retain ownership of the policies but name the ex-spouse as beneficiary as long as the ex-spouse remains unmarried. The advantage of this arrangement is that the policy reverts to the insured when the alimony obligation is terminated. The separation agreement should name the particular policy that will be kept in force for the ex-spouse and provide that he or she receive copies of all correspondence relating to it so that the ex-spouse will know it is being kept in force.

Health Insurance. Divorcing couples need to make sure that each spouse is adequately and continuously covered by health insurance. If one ex-spouse is fully insured under Social Security, the other is entitled to Medicare at age 65 as long as the ex-spouse is also age 65 or over (even if he or she is still working) or is deceased. An ex-spouse is entitled to the spouse's full disability benefits.

Pension Matters

A reasonable financial settlement takes projected income and assets into account. The division should provide for necessary and foreseeable expenditures, including the costs of medical or nursing home care. For older couples undergoing divorce, the allocation of pension and retirement plan benefits, which may be considered marital property, is obviously an extremely important issue. If the value of these retirement assets is not divided on an equal basis, you should make sure that you are otherwise compensated in your divorce settlement.

Borrowing and Credit

Credit may be a new and critical issue as the result of your changed marital status. Many newly single older adults have to establish credit on the basis of their changed financial position. However, in most instances, your credit rating cannot legally be affected by your marital status. If your credit was based in any way on your ex-spouse's income, you may have to reapply to the lender for credit. Your application will be accepted, rejected, or limited on the basis of several considerations, including current income. A divorcee applying for credit individually can cite as proof of creditworthiness the credit history of accounts carried in the name of the ex-spouse, if both spouses used them. A divorced person may also have to give reasons why a bad joint credit history does not reflect on personal ability or willingness to pay.

If you receive alimony, you need not reveal that fact to the creditor unless you wish to use it to demonstrate your creditworthiness. If you do include alimony as part of your income on your credit application, however, the lender is entitled to examine whether your ex-spouse can be depended upon to make regular payments. The creditor might conclude that your ex-spouse is a poor credit risk, in which case, alimony could be legally discounted as income, which could be detrimental to your application. Unless the lenders can prove that your ex-spouse is a poor risk, however, they cannot automatically discount alimony.

> "You should notify the credit bureau of both your and your ex-spouse's new addresses and specify that those accounts should henceforth be reported separately."

You should notify the credit bureau of both your and your ex-spouse's new addresses and specify that those accounts should henceforth be reported separately. Otherwise, transactions may be reported on the wrong spouse's account, and the records can get tangled, especially if one of the two remarries. Occasionally, one or both spouses will have credit problems during the separation period preceding the final divorce period, especially if the marital assets are frozen to negotiate the settlement. In this situation, the credit bureau and lenders should be informed of the circumstances. Lenders may be more lenient in restoring the credit ratings of the parties to a divorce once the situation stabilizes.

Tax Planning

While the emphasis in most contemporary divorces is on property division, income division (alimony) still exists, especially in cases where there are insufficient assets to support both households. For some couples, there are significant tax advantages to using ongoing support in structuring a settlement. For others, a lump-sum settlement is more advantageous. While the tax implications of your divorce may be the furthest thing from your mind as you undergo the stressful divorce experience, it is important that you understand the various alternatives available to you and your spouse.

Separation brings with it tax filing consequences. If you and your spouse are informally separated or have a signed separation agreement but no judicial decree of separate maintenance, each party may file tax returns in one of the following categories:

1. As long as you don't have a judicial decree of separate maintenance, you can still file jointly. This is an advantage for couples whose earnings are approximately the same, since joint returns are taxed at the lowest rate. (However, joint filers still incur the so-called marriage penalty, which results in a higher tax paid by joint filers than would be paid by two single people reporting the same total income.) The spouse whose income is lower, or who doesn't trust the other's accounting, may choose to file in one of the two remaining categories.

2. You may qualify to file as an unmarried head of household if you meet all the following conditions:
   a. You have lived apart from your spouse all year.
   b. You file a separate tax return.
   c. You pay more than half the cost of maintaining the household.

3. You can file as a single person if you meet the following conditions:
   a. You lived apart from your spouse all year.
   b. You file a separate tax return.
   c. You pay more than half the cost of maintaining the household.

Divorce can drain both your financial and psychological resources. There's no question that it sets you back financially. Nevertheless, if it's what you need to do for your well-being, the above information should help you make appropriate and cost-effective divorce decisions.

Premarital Agreements

One way to hold off the potential costs of a divorce is to consider premarital agreements, also known as prenuptial or antenuptial agreements. These agreements define each partner's separate property being brought into the marriage and describe your financial intentions after you're wed. It should be prepared with the advice and assistance of your lawyer—and your betrothed's lawyer—to avoid a potential conflict of interest.

> "One way to hold off the potential costs of a divorce is to consider premarital agreements, also known as prenuptial or antenuptial agreements."

Premarital agreements are advisable if one partner is much wealthier than the other and is concerned with the protection of assets should the marriage dissolve. In these situations, the agreement usually includes a transfer, or the promise of a transfer, of property from the wealthier spouse to the other. The transfer may either be outright or in a trust in exchange for a release of all claims the other may have for support or against the transferor's estate. Also, if you or your partner already has children from a previous marriage, a premarital agreement can protect each child's financial security.

In setting up a premarital agreement, it is often advisable for couples to use a trust instead of an outright transfer of property.

Legal precedent favors adherence to premarital agreements as long as both parties to the contract are open and honest about their assets and liabilities and both have access to legal advice. Most states permit a spouse to give up or limit his or her interest in a spouse's estate under certain conditions, but fewer allow contracts that limit or forbid alimony.

Another potential advantage of premarital agreements is that they may help you overcome some of the anxiety associated with remarriage. Then again, they could increase your partner's anxiety. So it's important to talk openly about this option with your partner in a way that considers both of your fears and anxieties, too.

* * *

Unemployment

Questions

If I am laid off, what severance benefits might I be able to receive?
What steps should I take once I am laid off?
What is a COBRA policy?

> "Be sure you understand your employer's severance benefits, such as salary continuation, payment for accrued vacation, and insurance benefits."

Unemployment can be psychologically traumatizing. However, if you take precautionary action, for example, having savings and investments totaling at least several months' salary, it won't be financially traumatizing. Even if you don't have much money safely tucked away for such a contingency, you can take corrective action so that your unemployment doesn't turn out to be financially devastating.

Key Words

COBRA A federal law that ensures continuing group health coverage for most former employees and their dependents. Passed in 1985, the Consolidated Omnibus Budget Reconciliation Act (COBRA) directs businesses with more than 19 employees to provide continuing group health coverage for at least 18 months after employee termination or resignation (36 months for the family of the employee, in the event of the employee's death).

Severance benefits Severance benefits from employers, such as salary continuation, payment for accrued vacation, and insurance benefits, may be available for laid-off workers.

Understanding Severance Benefits

Be sure you understand your employer's severance benefits, such as salary continuation, payment for accrued vacation, and insurance benefits. If you are about to be laid off or have just been laid off, it may be possible to negotiate additional severance benefits from your employer. Experts suggest that this be done within a day or two of the layoff when the employer is most apt to respond to your appeal.

Assessing Your Finances

If you have recently lost your job, you need to assess your financial situation so that you can cope with the loss of income. The following five steps will help you and your finances bounce back.

1. Assure continuation of health and life insurance coverage. It is advantageous to continue to carry your employer-provided health and life insurance coverage as well as all other insurance coverage. Most employers are required by the federal law COBRA to allow you to continue your company health insurance plan for up to 18 months without a medical checkup as long as you pay the premiums.

If your employer does not continue your life insurance coverage, you may be able to convert your employer's group policy to an individual policy. Otherwise, you may be able to purchase low-cost life insurance coverage to replace your company-provided policy by shopping around for the best rates. Unfortunately, you will not be able to continue or obtain disability insurance coverage while you are unemployed.

2. Apply for unemployment compensation benefits. If you've been let go, you are entitled to collect unemployment compensation benefits. Strange as it may seem, some people—perhaps out of pride or embarrassment—don't want to collect these benefits even though they are eligible.

3. Take stock of your ready resources. Your primary financial concern is how you're going to meet your financial obligations during your period of unemployment, so you should begin by taking stock of your available resources. Consider everything from your cash reserves as well as any investments that can be sold and converted into cash in a short period of time. The following work sheet will help you summarize your ready resources.

Summary of Ready Resources	
Cash in bank accounts	$
Savings, money market accounts	$
CDs and other interest-earning investments	$
Stock investments	$
Mutual funds	$
Other resources available	$
Total ready resources	$

Once you know how much (or how little) you have available, you can begin to prepare a budget that will sustain you during your period of unemployment.

4. Prepare your unemployment budget. Ideally, this budget should ensure that you will be able to meet important bills for the next six months. The budget work sheet provided in Chapter 2 may be used for this purpose.

First, determine what your income sources will be, including severance and unemployment benefits, income from your spouse's job, and investment income, unless you will have to liquidate those investments to meet living expenses. Next, summarize your expected expenses, starting with those that must be paid (rent/mortgage and groceries, for example) and ending with those expenses that can be forgone (restaurant dining and vacations, for example). After you have summarized your projected expenses, you can compare them with your expected income and decide how you are going to close the gap between income and expenses. The key to dealing with the financial strain of unemployment is to reduce expenses as much as possible. If your unemployment income is insufficient to meet your reduced expense level, you will have to use your ready resources to help meet expenses.

5. Curb spending. Chances are you will have to reduce your spending. Before you do this, summarize your past spending patterns so that you can identify realistic ways to curb them.

One of the best things to remind yourself about unemployment is that it provides the opportunity to start fresh. Take the time to reassess your career choice and path so that, when you reenter the work force—as you inevitably will—you will enter into the line of work that you most love to do.

* * *

Caring for Your Aging Parents

Questions

What should I look for when selecting a nursing home for my father or mother?
Are there other options besides a nursing home for a parent who needs care?
Is it important to talk with my elderly parents about their finances?

Key Words

Continuing care communities Communities that offer a variety of housing alternatives in one location: townhouses for independent, active older adults; apartment buildings with meals, homemaker, and laundry services; and, in many communities, a nursing home.

Homesharing An economical housing alternative in which an older person shares expenses and household tasks, typically with a younger person who needs affordable housing. This is also possible with another older person.

Medicaid State and federal government public assistance program that provides medical care for individuals whose incomes and total resources are below a certain level, without regard to their age.

Medicare A federal hospital insurance and supplementary medical insurance program for persons over age 65.

It's currently estimated that more than 8 million Americans provide personal care to their parents. Given the aging population, this number seems destined to increase. But few of us plan ahead effectively or prepare for the probability that our parents will, at least to some extent, rely on us during their old age. Besides, you can plan for your own senior years while you help your parents plan for theirs.

"It's currently estimated that more than 8 million Americans provide personal care to their parents."

Unpaid bills, unfilled prescriptions, an overdrawn bank account, or other indications of bouts of forgetfulness are all possible first signs that an elderly person's ability to take care of himself or herself may be waning.

While your parents are still healthy, it is important that you have a frank discussion with them about plans for and worries about the future. Housing, including the possibility of moving if the current location is inconvenient, is a critical topic. Many retirement homes and other elder care facilities have long waiting lists. To avoid having an elderly parent placed in an unsatisfactory home because of a sudden illness, you and your parents should discuss alternatives and possibly apply to a home before the need actually arises. Even if your parents are healthy, they should consider any housing decisions in anticipation of possible future health problems.

Meeting Major Medical Costs

One of the most important things to plan is how your parents expect to meet any major health care costs. Do they have sufficient health insurance? Remember that Medicare has many gaps in its coverage.

Whatever its deficiencies, the fact remains that Medicare is the core of most retired persons' medical coverage. The Medicare program provides health care benefits to every American over age 65 who is eligible for Social Security, plus certain disabled persons.

What Medicare Covers

Medicare consists of two parts: Part A pays for the costs of a hospital stay—it is provided at no cost for everyone who is automatically eligible for Social Security. Part B is an optional medical insurance plan designed to pay doctor bills. Medicare Part B participants pay a monthly premium, which is automatically deducted from their monthly Social Security checks.

Like any private insurance plan, Medicare does not cover all procedures, medicines, and doctor bills. It is important to know the ins and outs of the system to avoid unpleasant surprises.

Incapacity

It is difficult but prudent to raise the unpleasant issue of what will happen if your parents become incapable of managing their own affairs. They (as well as you) should have durable powers of attorney or similar documents prepared. Ask your parents how well they have been meeting expenses, keeping in mind that they may not wish to reveal any financial problems. Also, be sure your parents have a file, kept in a location known to you, containing copies of their wills, insurance policies, real estate papers, past tax returns, and other important documents.

Financial Concerns

Evaluate an elderly parent's future financial situation as well as current status. Even an elderly parent who is currently financially secure may eventually run into trouble. A retiree's typically fixed income is always in danger of having its purchasing power eroded by inflation. Of course, medical care and nursing care can reduce anyone's income and savings drastically. It is important to consider what measures you are willing or able to take to assist your parents financially. You should discuss with them how they are currently managing their own investments. Many elderly people either invest too conservatively or are susceptible to unscrupulous salespeople.

Where to Find Help

The National Association of Area Agencies on Aging, 1112 16th Street N.W., Washington, DC 20036, can help. You can write NAAAA to request information on agencies and elder-related services in your parents' locale. Services that can be arranged include:

- Emergency medical response system
- Daily visits by local residents
- Home care (e.g., laundry, housecleaning, cooking, small repairs, errands, and snow shoveling)
- Legal assistance
- Hot meals (at neighborhood centers or delivered to the home)
- Transportation services
- Day care centers

Seek further help through senior citizens centers, religious organizations, welfare services, nursing homes, local branches of the United Way, and major hospital social services departments or elderly outreach programs. If the elderly person requires substantial health-related assistance, a hospital-based social worker is often the best alternative. Of course, in choosing among these plans, parents should be included in all important discussions to the greatest extent possible.

> "Since every home you visit will present its best features, it's important to know what to look for and what to ask when you make your visits."

Guide to Selecting a Nursing Home

A variety of important considerations enter into selecting a nursing home, including location, recommendations, cost, and facilities. A final decision also rests on a thorough inspection and tour and your specific needs and preferences.

The decision to enter a nursing home—or to place a spouse or parent in one—is a difficult one, and can be very traumatic. However, once the decision is made, the trying task of selecting an appropriate nursing home begins. It's important to realize that few homes will offer everything you want. Since every home you visit will present its best features, it's important to know what to look for and what to ask when you make your visits. (Many of the following comments also apply to selecting a continuing care community or other senior housing facility.) Here are some tips on what to look for.

1. Nursing home licensing requirements. All nursing homes are required to have a current license from the state or a letter of approval from a licensing agency. You can ask for a copy of the nursing home's license, certification for participation in government programs, and reports of any recent violations.

2. Subjective opinions. The atmosphere of the home and the attitude of the staff and patients should be pleasant and cheerful. Most homes are trying to provide the best service they can within the limits of the income they receive, the staff they can afford to pay, and the cooperation they receive from the patients and their families. Pay attention to how patients, other visitors, and volunteers speak about the home and to whether the patients look well cared for and generally content. Most importantly, consider how the staff acts toward the patients; do they show them genuine interest and affection? Some nursing homes do not allow patients to wear their own clothes or decorate their rooms. Others enforce written statements of patients' rights.

3. Look for the obvious. Is the nursing home clean and orderly? Is it reasonably free of unpleasant odors? Is it well lighted? Are toilet and bathing facilities easy for handicapped patients to use? Are the rooms well ventilated and kept at a comfortable temperature? Are wheelchair ramps provided where necessary?

4. Safety is particularly important. Toilet and bathing facilities should have grab bars, and hallways should have handrails on both sides. Bathtubs and showers must have nonslip surfaces. One good indication of how seriously the home takes its patients' safety is how strictly it adheres to standard building safety ordinances. Exit signs should be clearly illuminated, and doors should be kept unobstructed and unlocked from the inside. Portable fire extinguishers should be evident and accessible. The sprinkler system and emergency lighting should be automatic. Emergency evacuation plans should be posted prominently.

5. How good is the quality of care? The best homes will have a physician available for medical emergencies at all times, either on staff or on call. At least one registered nurse per 20 patients—or a licensed practical nurse—should be on duty 24 hours a day. A registered nurse should serve as director of nursing services, and nurse call buttons should ideally be located at each patient's bed and in the bathrooms. Does the home have arrangements with nearby hospitals for quick transfer of patients? Nursing homes are required to give Medicaid recipients annual checkups. Are annual checkups given to patients paying privately?

6. Are there pharmaceutical services? Are the pharmaceuticals supervised by a qualified pharmacist in a room set aside for storage and preparation?

7. Is physical therapy available? Full-time physical, occupational, and speech therapy programs should be available to patients who need those services.

8. Don't simply take a guided tour. Try to check behind the scenes as much as possible. How clean is the kitchen? Is the food refrigerated properly? Is waste disposed of appropriately?

9. What about the menu? At least three meals should be served every day at normal hours (with no more than 14 hours allowed between the evening meal and breakfast the next morning). Time for leisurely eating and nutritious between-meal and bedtime snacks should be available. Sample a meal, and make sure it matches the one on the posted menu. It should look and taste appetizing and should be served at the proper temperature. The dining room should be attractive and comfortable. Are the patients given enough food? Are special meals prepared for patients on therapeutic diets? How are patients who need help eating assisted?

10. Insist on visiting patients' rooms. Make sure the rooms are shared according to the residents' preferences and compatibilities. Every room should open onto a hallway, and every room should have a window to the outside. Each patient should have a reading light, a comfortable chair, a closet, and a chest of drawers for personal belongings. Bathing and toilet facilities should have adequate privacy and be located conveniently, and each bed should have a curtain or screen to provide privacy. Does each patient have a locked drawer or safe box?

11. Check out provisions for exercise and relaxation. Is there an activities coordinator on staff who organizes a varied program of recreational, cultural, and intellectual activities? Suitable space, tools, and supplies should be provided for leisure activities, and activities also should be offered for patients who are relatively inactive or confined to their rooms. Activities should be scheduled each day and some evenings.

Besides the scheduled activities, is there a lounge where patients can chat, read, play games, watch television, or just relax away from their rooms? Is there an outdoor area where patients can get fresh air and sunshine? How easy is patient access to drinking water and telephones? Also find out what extra services are offered, how convenient they are, and how much they will cost. For example, will the resident have access to a barber or beautician, a manicurist, a masseur or masseuse, or a podiatrist? Are social services available to aid patients and their families? Do patients have an opportunity to attend religious services and talk with clergy both inside and outside the home?

Once you have established that the nursing home is clean, well kept, and treats its patients decently, compare the estimated monthly costs (including extra charges) with those of other homes. Make sure that the financial terms are clear and in writing and that the contract specifies that the home will provide a refund for unused days paid for in advance. The rate when you sign up should be guaranteed for a reasonable period of time. Is the home certified to participate in the Medicare and Medicaid programs? Will the patient be able to remain if he or she is forced to fall back on Medicaid?

Housing Options for People Who Need Extra Care

As many older Americans have discovered, healthy habits and good medical care have broken the link between advanced age and poor health. With the aging of the nation, more and more alternatives are being developed for the relatively healthy elderly—that increasingly large group who need a modest amount of help with the chores of daily living but can still manage pretty well by themselves. The following alternatives vary in the life-styles they promote and in the amount of medical and custodial care they offer.

Homesharing

Homesharing is a means for an older person to share expenses and household tasks with a younger person who needs affordable housing. A younger person might agree to do cleaning or yard work in exchange for inexpensive or free room and board. Local community groups or government agencies in most areas match homeowners with potential homesharers. Of course, you'll need to check the references of any potential homesharer thoroughly—from credit checks to personal references. You'll also need to prepare a written agreement spelling out the details of the arrangement. If you are considering the homesharing option for your parent or yourself, you should think carefully about the following:

• Are you—or is your parent—on a special diet that may differ from what the homesharer generally eats?
• Who will determine the menu?
• Who will shop and pay for food?
• How many meals a day will the homesharer be asked to provide?
• Do you expect the homesharer to eat meals with you—or your parent?

Home Care

Home care may be appropriate for people who wish to remain in their own homes but for whom the unskilled companionship and guardianship of a homesharer will not be adequate. Of course, when you remain in familiar surroundings, you usually feel more at ease, more in control, and more comfortable. Furthermore, it is much cheaper than moving into a nursing home or other institution. Home care is particularly appropriate for persons with Alzheimer's or other debilitating diseases and people who are recovering from recent hospitalization and still require nursing care or help with life's daily activities. Different levels of service are available, ranging from custodial care for people who need some assistance with daily tasks but don't need medical supervision to skilled nursing care. Many programs are also available for persons who need some help but don't require a live-in helper.

> "Homesharing is a means for an older person to share expenses and household tasks with a younger person who needs affordable housing."

Congregate Housing

This is a group living situation for older people who are basically in good health, but whose functional abilities are somewhat limited. Basic services include one to three meals per day in a central dining area, light housekeeping, laundry services, and organized recreational activities. Residents share common areas such as the living room, bathroom, kitchen, and dining room. The services of a social worker and/or homemaker, meal delivery, transportation, and recreational programs also may be available.

Congregate housing, which varies greatly in size and physical design, is sometimes sponsored by nonprofit organizations that offer the housing at a low rate. If you are considering the option of congregate housing, you should:

• Tour the facility, talk with residents, and, if possible, participate in a meal and some other activity.
• Examine the lease or contract carefully, checking to see if there is a penalty for terminating the lease. If you are hospitalized, is your room reserved for your return?
• Find out what the monthly fees are and what additional charges for extra services exist.
• Ask about regulations—for example, some facilities place restrictions on visitors or pets.

Many congregate housing facilities are being built in or near the urban areas of the North and Midwest. Residents who don't wish to relocate to the "retirement belt" of the Southeast and West can move in without losing touch with their families, friends, clergy, and community.

Continuing Care Communities

Designed to meet the changing needs of their residents, these communities offer a variety of housing alternatives in one location: townhouses for independent, active older adults; apartment buildings with meals, home-maker, and laundry services; and, in many communities, a nursing home. Continuing care communities usually require a sizable entry payment and a sizable monthly fee. Because this is a relatively new concept, you should check:

• The financial status of the owners and developers.
• The current level of occupancy.
• Whether the continuing care community has sufficient resources to keep it solvent.
• Whether the down payment is refundable if you move out.
• Whether any of the down payment is refundable to your estate upon your death.
• What services are included in the monthly fee.
• How much the monthly fee has increased over the community's history.
• Whether the facility is located near public transportation and is accessible to family, friends, and shopping.

As with any housing option, you always should visit the community and talk with residents, and have a lawyer review any contract documents. Unfortunately, several such communities have failed, leaving their residents in the lurch.

"Continuing care communities usually require a sizable entry payment and a sizable monthly fee."

> ## "When choosing an adult day care center, ask what is included in the daily rate."

Many seniors faced with or concerned about declining health and increasing medical costs enter continuing care communities to protect themselves against these risks, because no additional costs will be incurred even if their health care expenses increase. Continuing care contracts offer the elderly person the advantages of independent living, long-term security, and more affordable nursing home care.

Adult Day Care

Adult day care is often appropriate for elderly persons who are still mobile and have their faculties but who may not be entirely self-sufficient. Adult day care is available at a lower cost than residential care, and retirement communities often offer this care daily or several times a week at a much lower cost than nursing home or home nursing care.

Transportation, games and puzzles, exercises, physical therapy, field trips, performances, classes, snacks, and hot midday meals are the staples offered by adult day care centers, in addition to having registered and licensed practical nurses on hand to monitor the participants' health.

When choosing an adult day care center, ask what is included in the daily rate. Program supplies, transportation, and excursions may cost extra, and individualized services for the severely handicapped, physical therapy, and psychiatric care will add substantially to the total cost that is not covered by Medicare or most private medical insurance. Some insurers are beginning to offer policies that cover adult day care.

Points to consider in choosing a center include the center's conformity to state regulations, the sufficiency of available medical staff and services, quality of the meals and the center's capacity to accommodate special dietary regimens, client-to-staff ratio, and safety and cleanliness of the facilities. Social workers and consultants can assist you in evaluating the suitability for this level of care and in identifying an appropriate center.

Resources

American Association of Homes for the Aging

901 E Street N.W., Suite 500
Washington, DC 20004
(202) 783-2242

"Consumer Information on Continuing Care"

American Association of Retired Persons Research Information Center
601 E Street N.W.
Washington, DC 20049
(202) 434-6240

National Council of Senior Citizens
1331 F Street N.W., Fifth Floor
Washington, DC 20004
(202) 347-8800

National Association for Home Care
519 C Street N.E.
Washington, DC 20002
(202) 547-7424

"Directory of Accredited Approved Homemaker-Home Health Aide Services" and **"All About Homecare"**

Foundation for Hospice and Home Care
513 C Street N.E.
Washington, DC 20002
(202) 547-4273

* * *

Funeral Planning

Questions

How can I go about selecting an appropriate funeral home before I die?
What are some less expensive funeral alternatives?
Do veterans receive any funeral benefits?

It's a grim topic, but don't let that fact keep you from discussing it. In fact, you can ease a good deal of the emotional trauma and confusion—and the associated cost—by planning your funeral in advance. This final section of this chapter focuses on planning a cost-effective funeral. Planning one's own funeral is certainly the most emotionally difficult aspect of financial planning, but your heirs will be better off if you make the hard decisions yourself.

The Importance of Making Your Wishes Known

If you haven't already done so, talk with your parents about their funeral plans (or talk to your adult children about your own plans.) It's not an easy subject to discuss, but it is a matter of great importance. The reason: funerals have become increasingly and needlessly expensive.

> "You are probably better off using a home that charges separately for each item, and avoiding funeral homes that tout package deals."

Key Words

Memorial service A cost-effective alternative to a funeral service, typically taking place after the body has been cremated or interred.

Organ donation The process of authorizing the use of your healthy organs for transplant purposes.

Choosing a Funeral Home

Most people decide to have a funeral home handle the final arrangements. This entails finding an appropriate funeral home—the most important step in your funeral preplanning if this is the route you're going to take.

A funeral home takes care of all the details concerning disposal of the deceased's body, especially in the case of an earth burial. But be sure it will do so in accordance with your personal approval and financial means. One tip: you are probably better off using a home that charges separately for each item, and avoiding funeral homes that tout package deals. The prices of these deals may well include a good deal of padding—just like the option-loaded packages car dealers try to sell you. At the very least, you could end up paying for frills you don't need and don't want.

When paying for a funeral in advance, make sure that the funds can be refunded if you change your mind about what sort of arrangements you want.

Funeral Planning and the Letter of Instructions

A letter of instructions, as discussed in Chapter 7, helps ensure that survivors know exactly how to proceed at the time of your death. A letter of instructions should include the following information pertaining to your funeral:

• Previously arranged or preferred funeral arrangements.

• Notification and pertinent information if you are an organ or body donor. (Include the location of your uniform donor card.)

• Names and addresses of the memorial society, funeral home, and/or crematory with which you contracted.

• Type of ceremony and details of service.

• Casket and grave-marker preferences.

• Preferred death notice.

Disposing of the Remains

Mankind has devised countless ways to dispose of the dead; the methods common to late 20th-century America are discussed below. Naturally your religious beliefs and/or secular attitudes about death will influence the route you decide to take. At the very least, however, the following information will allow you to compare the available alternatives on a practical level.

> "If you are interested in donating organs, ask your doctor for information on making the appropriate arrangements."

Donation to Medical Schools

If you are of a practical and unsentimental turn of mind, donating your body to a medical institution is the most cost-effective way to dispose of your body. Many people who choose to donate their bodies to science also have humanitarian motives—they know that their actions will support medical research while saving their heirs money.

Check with the medical school or institution of your choice about its detailed requirements for accepting the remains. Some bodies may be unsuitable. Make sure that the institution will accept your body, and pay for its transportation. Also, be sure to have a backup plan for unexpected events, such as death occurring at a place too far away to transport your body to the medical school.

Organ Donations

An alternative to donating the entire body is to donate only specific organs for transplant. The designated organs must be removed immediately after death in order for them to have any value. The rest of your body will be released in time for the funeral. If you are interested in donating organs, ask your doctor for information on making the appropriate arrangements.

Cremation

Next to donating your body to a medical school, cremation is the best choice from a purely financial standpoint: it is cheap and straightforward. No casket is required for cremation: a simple, low-cost fiberboard container is all you need. If the body is delivered directly to the crematorium, even the presence of a funeral director is unnecessary, further reducing the cost.

After cremation, there are a number of economical ways to handle your remains. Most families scatter or bury the ashes in a place familiar to the deceased, although local laws may prohibit or restrict this. As an alternative, the urn can be placed in a niche at a special mausoleum called a columbarium, or in a cemetery's mortuary chapel.

Earth Burial

Earth burial is the most expensive and complicated way to dispose of your body. If you want to have an earth burial, it can take place either immediately after death or after a funeral-home viewing and/or church (or graveside) service have taken place. In any case, the largest expense involved in an earth burial is the cost of the coffin. Because so many expensive coffins are on the market, you should choose one yourself in advance and make sure that your letter of instructions makes your choice clear. That way, if you want a simple coffin, your heirs won't be overcharged by an overzealous funeral director. If you're not prepared to select your own coffin now, at least inform family members about your wishes to be buried in a simple coffin.

A funeral home also might try to sell burial vaults to enclose the casket, asserting that the cemetery requires it. Even if the cemetery does require a grave lining (to prevent cave-ins) a simple metal or concrete liner is more than sufficient and is far less costly than a vault.

As far as embalming is concerned, it is unnecessary if burial occurs soon after death. Embalming is only required when there will be a delay in burial or when the body is to be shipped a great distance.

Choosing a Cemetery

If you've made up your mind to be interred, you have to think about where you want to be buried. Consider a place where family and friends won't be too inconvenienced. Then, consider the costs—they vary widely. Municipal cemeteries are usually less expensive than private ones. Urban areas are generally more expensive than rural locations. Above-ground mausoleums tend to be more costly than earth burial. Different areas within the same cemetery may cost more or less depending on the specific location.

Buying a Cemetery Plot

Consider buying the plot in advance. You may save some money by locking into today's price for tomorrow's plot. It's also a good anti-inflation investment—plot prices have risen dramatically in the past, far outstripping inflation rates. But keep in mind that if you end up moving to a new place far away from the purchased plot, prepurchasing a lot may complicate rather than simplify your plans. Exchange plans are available but often have many restrictions. If you don't have an exchange plan, you have to arrange for a private sale.

Final Rites

After deciding on the disposition of the body, the second most important consideration is the funeral service. A great deal of money can be either spent or saved depending on how well you plan. Remember that the purpose of the service is to assuage the survivors' emotional needs. For example, a family may feel that the deceased deserves a big send-off. But they're the ones who may live to regret the expense.

Funeral Service

The most expensive type of ceremony is the funeral service. By definition, a funeral service is one held in presence of the body. If there is a time lapse before the burial, the body will have to be embalmed, and for an open coffin ceremony, cosmetic work is required. Also, if there is a viewing, rental charges may be imposed. A funeral parlor is usually rented for the ceremony, but the funeral director may transport the body to another meeting place, or church. These details add up. Remember, a memorial society can be of great help. If you're not getting assistance from a memorial society, choose a trusted friend or relative to help you make your preferred arrangements.

Memorial Service

The second type of ceremony is a memorial service. It differs from a funeral service in that it typically takes place after the body has been cremated or interred. The focus of a memorial service therefore tends to be on the life of the deceased. Also, because there are no calendar constraints on the disposal of the body, a memorial service offers greater flexibility in location and time. It can be performed at virtually any place and does not require the assistance of a funeral home. A memorial service can be far less expensive than a funeral service, as cosmetic work, elaborate coffin, and funeral parlor are unnecessary. In general, memorial services tend to be less elaborate and more thoughtful than funeral services. A common feature is to suggest that friends make a donation to some specified charitable organization. They will be thankful because such donations are thoughtful—and tax deductible.

> "A memorial service can be far less expensive than a funeral service."

Financing the Funeral

Making your family aware of all the anticipated and contracted funeral expenses, including any possible special sources of funds you've set aside to cover them, can make the whole funeral ordeal less stressful.

A regularly renewed certificate of deposit (CD) is a good vehicle for this purpose, especially since the penalty for early withdrawal does not apply if the owner dies.

Along with your own funeral savings, you also may be able to find some outside sources that can help reduce the burden. Double-check the following sources:

• Check your life insurance policy to see if it provides for burial and cremation costs. If you have burial insurance, be sure your family knows about it.

• Notify your family in advance about any job-related death benefits. For example, they may be eligible for assistance through your worker's compensation plan. In any event, ask them to notify the employee benefits office at your work place, as there may be some benefit connected with the pension or the company's life insurance program.

Sources of Death Benefits

If you're a fully insured worker under Social Security or have credit for a year and a half out of the three years before death, there is a $255 lump-sum death benefit. However, as with other Social Security benefits, a survivor has to apply to the Social Security Administration to receive the benefit.

Who can be considered a survivor? Your spouse, and if your spouse is left to care for children who are under age 16 or disabled, he or she is eligible for benefits regardless of age. Furthermore, your unmarried children under age 18 (or 19 if they are full-time students) would be eligible for benefits. Finally, grandchildren (under limited circumstances) and dependent parents age 62 or older are also eligible for survivor's benefits.

If you're an honorably discharged wartime or peacetime veteran, you may qualify for funeral-expense-related benefits.

Despite the difficulties associated with this area of personal financial planning, the fact remains that it is one of the most thoughtful things you can do for those who will survive you.

CHAPTER 9

Common Mistakes to Avoid

This chapter will show you some of the most common financial planning mistakes so that you can steer clear of them. Knowing how to avoid common pitfalls is one great way to keep your finances up and running toward your goals.

Common Mistakes to Avoid

The following are common mistakes to avoid as you proceed along the road of personal financial planning. Mistakes are grouped according to their corresponding chapter in this book.

Chapter 2

Common Personal Financial Planning Mistakes*

*Please refer back to Chapter 2, where common mistakes are already included in the text.

Chapter 3

Common Insurance Planning Mistakes

- Leaving gaps in insurance coverage.
- Maintaining low deductibles.
- Renewing a policy without examining whether policy changes need to be made.
- Failing to insure valuables.
- Having insufficient disability insurance.
- Taking too little—or too much— life insurance.

Chapter 4

Common Investment Mistakes

- Taking too much or too little risk.
- Chasing after high-yield investments.
- Holding on to investments for sentimental reasons.
- Maintaining too many investment accounts.
- Failing to take advantage of mutual funds.
- Neglecting to learn about investing.

Chapter 5

Common Tax Planning Mistakes

- Overlooking common deductions.
- Overemphasizing taxes in making investment decisions.
- Neglecting to learn about tax-saving techniques.
- Waiting too long to undertake tax-saving techniques.
- Failing to maintain good tax records.

Chapter 6

Common Retirement Planning Mistakes

- Failing to consider the toll inflation takes on retirement savings.
- Failing to participate in retirement savings plans.
- Neglecting to prepare retirement income and expense projections during all working years.
- Failing to take out required IRA minimum withdrawals after age 70-1/2.
- Taking early retirement incentive plans without a thorough analysis of their financial consequences.
- Failing to take advantage of tax-exempt and tax-advantaged retirement investment plans.
- Relying on Social Security for more than one-fourth of retirement income needs.

Chapter 7

Common Estate Planning Mistakes

- Neglecting to prepare a will and other important estate planning documents.
- Failing to prepare a letter of instructions.
- Assuming that trusts are only for the very rich.
- Giving away too much too soon.
- Selecting an inappropriate executor.
- Failing to inform family members about your estate plan.

Index

Index

E

F

G

H

Index

I

Index

Index

U

V

W

Y

Z

Work Sheets

Index

Checklists

Appendix A

Financial Planning Resources

For more information on financial planning, contact the organizations on the following page.

Financial Planning Resources

National Endowment for Financial Education (NEFE), 4695 South Monaco Street, Denver, Colorado 80237, (303) 220-1200. The National Endowment for Financial Education (NEFE) is a nontraditional provider of education and testing services for the financial services industry. The College for Financial Planning, perhaps the best-known division of NEFE, as well as the creator of the Certified Financial Planner® designation, offers self-study adult education for financial services professionals. Curricula include the Certified Financial Planner Professional Education Program, which leads to the CFP® designation; Advanced Studies courses; a master's degree program with emphasis in financial planning; the High School Financial Planning Program for youths; Foundations in Financial Planning for financial services employees; and continuing education for financial planning professionals. NEFE's other divisions include the Institute for Tax Studies, the Institute for Retirement Planning, the new Institute for Wealth Management, a Public Education Center, and the NEFE Press, a publishing arm.

International Board of Standards and Practices for Certified Financial Planners, Inc. (IBCFP), 1660 Lincoln Street, #3050, Denver, Colorado 80264, (303) 830-7543. The IBCFP is the independent, nonprofit organization that administers the IBCFP comprehensive exam and licenses individuals to use the CFP and Certified Financial Planner marks. One of its functions is to act in the public's interest to ensure that CFP licensees practice in accordance with recognized standards of conduct, and to further ensure that they perform their work effectively, ethically, and in the best interests of their clients.

Institute of Certified Financial Planners (ICFP), 7600 East Eastman Avenue, Suite 301, Denver, Colorado 80231, 1-800-282-PLAN. This professional organization of Certified Financial Planner licensees offers brochures on such matters as selecting qualified financial planning professionals, identifying fraudulent investments, funding college expenses, planning for retirement, and analyzing issues regarding personal economics in society. The ICFP also can provide names of Certified Financial Planner professionals in your area.

International Association for Financial Planning (IAFP), Two Concourse Parkway, Suite 800, Atlanta, Georgia 30328, 1-800-945-IAFP. The IAFP represents financial professionals who help people manage and invest their money to meet specific financial needs and goals. The IAFP also offers a referral service to locate qualified financial planners in your area.

National Association of Personal Financial Advisors (NAPFA), 1130 Lake Cook Road, Suite 150, Buffalo Grove, Illinois 60089, 1-800-366-2732. This is a professional membership organization for financial advisors who work on a fee-only (no-commission) basis. NAPFA provides a toll-free number consumers can call for information on fee-only financial planning, financial planner interview forms, and the names of local NAPFA members.

Appendix B

Work Sheets and Checklists

The following are duplicates of the work sheets and checklists that appear in Chapters 1 through 7. These forms are perforated so that you can remove them for easy use in your personal financial planning.

Appendix B

Work Sheets and Checklists

The following are duplicates of the work sheets and checklists that appear in Chapters 1 through 7. These forms are perforated so that you can remove them for easy use in your personal financial planning.

Establishing Objectives *Checklist*

Establishing Objectives

Objectives	Very Important	Somewhat Important	Not Important
• Improving personal record keeping (Chapter 2)			
• Reducing debt (Chapter 2)			
• Ensuring complete insurance coverage (Chapter 3)			
• Investing more regularly (Chapter 4)			
• Reducing income taxes (Chapter 5)			
• Assuring a comfortable retirement (Chapter 6)			
• Making sure the estate is properly planned (Chapter 7)			
• Buying a home (Chapter 8)			
• Meeting college education costs (Chapter 8)			

Comments:

Statement of Personal Assets and Liabilities *Work Sheet*

Use this work sheet to summarize your assets and liabilities. Three columns are included so that you can periodically monitor your progress. Prepare this statement at least once per year. Many people prepare it more frequently.

Assets and Liabilities

	19	19	19
Assets			
1. Cash in Checking and Brokerage Accounts	$	$	$
2. Money Market Funds and Accounts			
3. Fixed-Income Investments			
• Savings account			
• CDs			
• Government securities and funds			
• Mortgage-backed securities and funds			
• Corporate bonds and bond funds			
• Municipal bonds and bond funds			
• Other fixed-income investments			
4. Stock Investments			
• Common stock in publicly traded companies			
• Stock mutual funds			
• Other stock investments			
5. Real Estate Investments			
• Undeveloped land			
• Directly owned, income-producing real estate			
• Real estate limited partnerships			
6. Ownership Interest in Private Business			
7. Cash Value of Life Insurance Policies			
8. Retirement-Oriented Assets			
• Individual retirement accounts			
• Salary reduction 401(k) plans			
• Keogh or simplified employee pension plans			
• Employee thrift and stock purchase plans			
• Vested interest in corporate pension and profit sharing plans			
• Tax-deferred annuities			
• Other retirement-oriented assets			

(Continued on the next page)

Statement of Personal Assets and Liabilities *Continued*

Assets and Liabilities

	19	19	19
9. Personal Assets			
• Personal residence(s)	$	$	$
• Automobile(s)			
• Jewelry			
• Personal property			
10. Other Assets			
•			
•			
•			
11. Total Assets	$	$	$
Liabilities			
1. Credit Cards and Charge Accounts	$	$	$
2. Income Taxes Payable			
3. Miscellaneous Accounts Payable			
4. Bank Loans			
5. Policy Loans on Life Insurance Policies			
6. Automobile Loans			
7. Student Loans			
8. Mortgages on Personal Residence(s)			
9. Mortgages on Investment Real Estate			
10. Broker's Margin Loans			
11. Limited Partnership Debt			
12. Other Liabilities			
•			
•			
•			
13. Total Liabilities	$	$	$
14. Net Worth (total assets less total liabilities)	$	$	$

Note: Assets should be listed at their current market value. Be realistic in valuing those assets that require an estimate of market value, such as your home and personal property.

Personal Record-Keeping Organizer *Work Sheet*

The following Personal Record-Keeping Organizer serves two purposes. First, you can indicate next to each item where that particular item is now located. Second, you can organize your personal records by consolidating your documents into the three files noted below.

I. Items for Storage in a Safe-Deposit Box

Personal

1. Family birth certificates	
2. Family death certificates	
3. Marriage certificate	
4. Citizenship papers	
5. Adoption papers	
6. Veterans papers	
7. Social Security verification	

Ownership

1. Bonds and certificates	
2. Deeds	
3. Automobile titles	
4. Household inventories	
5. Home ownership records (e.g., blueprints, deeds, surveys, capital addition records, yearly records)	
6. Copies of trust documents	

Obligations/Contracts

1. Contracts	
2. Copies of insurance policies	
3. IOUs	
4. Retirement and pension plan documents	

Copies of Estate Planning Documents

1. Wills	
2. Living wills	
3. Trusts	
4. Letters of instruction	
5. Guardianship arrangements	

(Continued on the next page)

Personal Record-Keeping Organizer *Continued*

II. Items for Storage in Home Active File

Current Income/Expense Documents

1. Unpaid bills	
2. Current bank statements	
3. Current broker's statements	
4. Current cancelled checks and money order receipts	
5. Credit card information	

Contractual Documents

1. Loan statements and payment books	
2. Appliance manuals and warranties (including date and place of purchase)	
3. Insurance policies • Home • Life • Automobile • Personal liability • Health and medical • Other:	
4. Receipts for expensive items not yet paid for	

Personal

1. Employment records	
2. Health and benefits information	
3. Family health records	
4. Copies of wills	
5. Copies of letters of instruction	
6. Education information	
7. Cemetery records	
8. Important telephone numbers	
9. Inventory and spare key to safe-deposit box	
10. Receipts for items under warranty	
11. Receipts for expensive items	

Tax

1. Tax receipts	
2. Paid bill receipts (with deductible receipts filed separately to facilitate tax preparation and possibly reduce taxes)	
3. Brokerage transaction advices	
4. Income tax working papers	
5. Credit statements	
6. Income and expense records for rental properties	
7. Medical, dental, and drug expenses	
8. Records of business expenses	

(Continued on the next page)

Personal Record-Keeping Organizer *Continued*

III. Items for Storage in Home Inactive File

1. Prior years' tax returns	
2. Home improvement records	
3. Brokerage advices (prior to three most recent years)	
4. Family health records (prior to three most recent years)	
5. Proof that major debts or other major contracts have been met	
6. Cancelled checks (prior to three most recent years)	

Personal Budget Planner *Work Sheet*

Individuals and families should prepare budgets just as businesses do. Use this Personal Budget Planner either to record your past cash income and cash expenses and/or to budget future income and expenses. You may want to use the first column to record your past income and expenses, the second column to list your budget over the next month, quarter, or year, and the third column to compare your actual future income and expenses against your budget in the second column. If you budget over a period of less than one year, be sure to consider those expenses that you pay less frequently than monthly, such as insurance, vacations, and tuition. You should be setting aside an amount each month that will eventually cover those large bills.

Indicate at the top of each column whether the amounts in that column are actual or estimated past figures or budgeted future figures. Also indicate the time period in each column, e.g., "March 1995" or "Year 1994."

Budget Planner

Indicate if actual or budgeted			
Indicate the time period			
Cash Income			
1. Gross salary	$	$	$
2. Interest			
3. Dividends			
4. Bonuses/profit sharing			
5. Alimony/child support received			
6. Distributions from partnerships			
7. Income from outside businesses			
8. Trust distributions			
9. Pension			
10. Social Security			
11. Gifts			
12. Proceeds from sale of investments			
13. Other • • •			
14. Total cash income	$	$	$

(Continued on the next page)

Personal Budget Planner *Continued*

Budget Planner

Cash Expenses			
1. Housing (rent/mortgage)	$	$	$
2. Food			
3. Household maintenance			
4. Utilities and telephone			
5. Clothing			
6. Personal care			
7. Medical and dental care			
8. Automobile/transportation			
9. Child-care expenses			
10. Entertainment			
11. Vacation(s)			
12. Gifts			
13. Contributions			
14. Insurance			
15. Miscellaneous out-of-pocket expenses			
16. Furniture			
17. Home improvements			
18. Real estate taxes			
19. Loan payments			
20. Credit card payments			
21. Alimony/child support payments			
22. Tuition/educational expenses			
23. Business and professional expenses			
24. Saving/investments			
25. Income and Social Security taxes			
26. Other • • •			
27. Total cash expenses	$	$	$
Excess (Shortfall) of Cash Income Over Cash Expenses	$	$	$

Establishing Goals and Objectives

Checklist

Current Status		
Needs Action	**OK or Not Applicable**	
		1. Set some realistic financial planning goals, and plan how you are going to achieve them.
		2. If you experience any major changes in your personal or financial status (major life events), review how your new circumstances will affect your overall financial planning.
		3. Discuss money matters openly and regularly with your spouse.
		4. Create a personal record-keeping system that is comprehensive enough to be useful yet simple enough that you will use it.
		5. Prepare a statement of personal assets and liabilities periodically to measure your financial planning progress.
		6. Select your financial advisors with care, and be aware of potential conflicts of interest they may have.
		7. If you are not satisfied with any of your financial advisors, don't hesitate to make a change.
		8. Be particularly careful in selecting a financial planner. Be sure he or she has the qualifications that are necessary to meet your needs.

Comments:

Insurance Evaluation *Checklist*

The following insurance checklist corresponds to the subsections in Chapter 3. Using checklists is a good way to ensure that you have attended to important insurance matters.

Insurance Evaluation

General Guidelines

- Look for comprehensive policies and avoid narrowly defined coverage (e.g., cancer policies).
- To reduce premiums, take the largest deductible you can afford.
- Ask your agent to shop around for the best policy at the best price.

Life Insurance

- Determine how much life insurance you need. One rule of thumb is that a worker with a spouse and two children should carry at least enough insurance to cover five to seven times his or her net annual income. (Add another year of income for each additional dependent.)
- Determine whether term or cash value life insurance (or a combination) will best meet your needs. Term insurance buys the most protection per premium dollar over the short run, but cash value insurance can provide more flexibility and tax advantages. Often a combination of term and cash value is the best way to acquire life insurance protection.

Health Insurance

- Review your health insurance policy to make sure you fully understand the extent of its coverage and its limitations.
- Make sure *all* family members have adequate major medical insurance, including children away at school, parents, and adult children.
- If you become unemployed, disabled, or divorced, take advantage of the provisions under COBRA to continue health care coverage.
- If your employer does not offer health insurance coverage, or if you are self-employed, investigate the purchase of insurance on your own, preferably through an association, but, if necessary, on an individual basis.

Disability Insurance

- Obtain and maintain sufficient disability insurance coverage to replace 60% to 70% of your work income. (Keep in mind that employer-provided disability benefits are taxable.)
- Make sure you understand your disability insurance policy's features and limits, particularly your company's disability policy.
- If you need to purchase a disability policy individually, compare several policies and evaluate carefully the various features they offer.

Automobile Insurance

- Buy sufficient automobile insurance coverage in essential areas, but reduce or eliminate unnecessary coverage.
- Look for ways to reduce your automobile insurance premiums.

(Continued on the next page)

Insurance Evaluation *Continued*

Insurance Evaluation

Homeowners and Renters Insurance

	Always maintain adequate homeowners or renters insurance coverage.
	Review your coverage at least every two years, and change it when necessary.
	Maintain replacement cost coverage on your home.
	Maintain replacement cost coverage on your personal possessions.
	If you have valuables, insure them separately with a floater or with an endorsement on your policy.
	Take a personal inventory of your household possessions, and keep that inventory up-to-date.

Umbrella Liability Insurance

	Protect yourself and your family from financially devastating lawsuits with umbrella liability insurance.
	Examine your umbrella policy to make sure that you understand its limits and that all family members are covered.
	If you are a self-employed professional or small-business owner, you probably need professional or business liability insurance.

Comments:

Insurance Coverage *Work Sheet*

Evaluate your insurance coverage status with the following work sheet. This will help you pinpoint weaker areas of coverage so that you can insure accordingly.

Insurance Coverage

Date:_____

Type of Insurance	Source of Coverage	Coverage Adequate	Coverage Not Necessary	Improved Coverage Needed	Coverage Needed but Not Yet Obtained
Life					
Health					
Disability					
Homeowners/Renters					
Automobile					
Umbrella liability					
Professional liability					

Comments:

Life Insurance Needs *Work Sheet*

Use the following work sheet to estimate your life insurance needs. If you enter amounts for each category of need, the resulting estimate should be viewed as a *maximum* amount of insurance that will meet all foreseeable needs of your survivors. **Note:** All amounts should be expressed in terms of current dollars.

Life Insurance Needs

Expenses

1. Final expenses (onetime expenses incurred by your death)

   a. Final illness (medical costs will probably exceed health insurance deductibles and coinsurance, so assume that you will have to fund at least those amounts) $....................

   b. Burial/funeral costs   ....

   c. Probate costs (if unsure, assume 4% of assets passing through probate process)   ....

   d. Federal estate taxes (for most estates over $600,000 willed to someone other than spouse)   ....

   e. State inheritance taxes (varies by state)   ....

   f. Legal fees, estate administration   ....

   g. Other   ....

   h. Total final expenses $....................

2. Outstanding debt (to be paid off at your death)

   a. Credit card/consumer debt   ....

   b. Car   ....

   c. Mortgage (if it's to be paid off at your death; otherwise, include payments in life income)   ....

   d. Other   ....

   e. Total outstanding debt $....................

(Continued on the next page)

Life Insurance Needs *Continued*

Life Insurance Needs

3. Readjustment expenses (to cover the transition period of immediate crisis)

   a. Child care ....

   b. Additional homemaking help ....

   c. Vocational counseling/educational training (for a nonworking
      or underemployed spouse who expects to seek paid employment) ....

   d. Other ....

   e. Total readjustment expenses $............................

4. Dependency expenses (until all children are self-supporting)

   a. Estimate your household's current annual expenditures ....

   b. To remove the deceased person's expenses, multiply this figure by:
      .70 for a surviving family of one
      .74 for a surviving family of two
      .78 for a surviving family of three
      .80 for a surviving family of four
      .82 for a surviving family of five

      $.................... (Line 4a) x .... (factor) = ...

   c. Deduct spouse's estimated annual income
      from employment (....................)

   d. Equals current annual expenses to be covered by currently
      owned assets and insurance ....

   e. To determine approximate total dependency expenses
      required, multiply by number of years until youngest child
      becomes self-supporting:

      .... (Line 4d) x .... (years) = ...

   f. If support for dependent parent(s) is to be provided,
      multiply annual support by the number of years such
      support is expected to continue:

      $.................... x .... (years) = ...

   g. Total dependency expenses (add Lines 4e and 4f) $....................

(Continued on the next page)

Life Insurance Needs *Continued*

Life Insurance Needs

5. Education expenses

    a. Annual private school tuition in current dollars
       (if desired) ....

    b. Multiply by number of years and children left to attend:

       $.................... (Line 5a) x .... (years) = ...

    c. Annual college costs in current dollars   ....

    d. Multiply by number of years and children left to attend:

       $.................... (Line 5c) x .... (years) = ...

    e. Total education expenses (add Lines 5b + 5d) $....................

6. Life income (for the surviving spouse after the children
   are all self-supporting)

    a. Annual amount desired (in current dollars)   ....

    b. Deduct spouse's estimated annual income
       from employment   (....................)

    c. Equals annual expenses to be covered by currently
       owned assets and insurance   ....

    d. Multiply by number of years between when the youngest
       child becomes self-supporting and the surviving spouse
       begins receiving Social Security benefits and other
       retirement income, if any:

       $.................... (Line 6c) x .... (years) = $....................

7. Retirement income for surviving spouse

    a. Annual amount desired in current dollars
       (less Social Security and any pension income)   ....

    b. Multiply by number of years of life expectancy after
       retirement begins:

       $.................... (Line 7a) x .... (years) = ...

8. Total funds needed to cover expenses:
   (add lines 1h, 2e, 3e, 4g, 5e, 6d, 7b)   ....

(Continued on the next page)

Life Insurance Needs *Continued*

Life Insurance Needs

Assets currently available to support family

Proceeds from life insurance already owned	$....................
Cash and savings	....
Equity in real estate (if survivors will sell)	....
Securities	....
IRA and Keogh plans	....
Employer savings plans	....
Lump-sum employer pension benefits	....
Other sources	....

9. Total assets   ....

Additional life insurance required

10. Subtract available assets (Line 9) from total funds needed to cover expenses (Line 8). This shortfall represents the estimated amount that must be covered through life insurance. $....................

Disability Income Needs *Work Sheet*

The following work sheet will help you determine how much disability insurance you need.

Disability Income Needs

Resources needed

1. Total annual family living expenses $...................

2. Subtract annual expenses which go away if you become disabled, such as taxes (disability benefits may be partly or fully tax free)*, work-related expenses, entertainment, and travel   (...................)

3. Adjusted annual family living expenses (subtract Line 2 from Line 1)   ....

Resources available

4. Annual income from savings and investments (dividends and interest)   ....

5. Annual income from spouse's job   ....

6. Disability benefits provided by employer's policy   ....

7. Disability benefits provided by other disability policies currently owned   ....

8. Total available resources (add lines 4, 5, 6, and 7)   ....

9. Additional resources needed either from liquidating assets or additional disability insurance (subtract Line 8 from Line 3) $...................

*If you become disabled, very few expenses go away, but only benefits for which the insured paid the premium are tax free.

Automobile Insurance Rate Comparison *Work Sheet*

Use this work sheet to compare automobile insurance premium quotations.

Auto Rate Comparison

	Amount of Coverage	Annual Premium Quotations	
Minimum coverage state requires for:		Name of Insurer:	
Bodily injury liability	$..................	$..................	$..................
Property damage liability	....	....	....
Personal damage protection (no-fault states)	....	....	....
Uninsured motorist	....	....	....
		Subtotal: $..................	$..................

	Amount of Coverage	Annual Premium Quotations	
Level of coverage desired for:			
Bodily injury liability	....	....	....
Property damage liability	....	....	....
Medical payments	....	....	....
Personal-injury protection (no-fault states)	....	....	....
Collision with:			
a. $100 deductible	....		
b. $250 deductible	....		
c. $500 deductible	....	....	....
d. $1,000 deductible	....		
Comprehensive with:			
a. No deductible	....		
b. $100 deductible	....		
c. $250 deductible	....	....	....
d. $500 deductible	....		
e. $1,000 deductible	....		
Uninsured motorist	....	....	....
		Subtotal: $..................	$..................

(Continued on the next page)

Automobile Insurance Rate Comparison *Continued*

Auto Rate Comparison

	Amount of Coverage	**Annual Premium Quotations**	
Other coverage:			
Towing and labor	$..................	$..................	$..................
Rental car reimbursement	....	....	....
Subtotal:		$..................	$..................
Other applicable charges:			
Membership fee	....	....	....
Surcharges	....	....	....
Subtotal:		$..................	$..................
Total annual premium:		$..................	$..................
Less estimated dividends, if any:		(..................)	(..................)
Net annual premium:		$..................	$..................

Comments/recommendations:

Investment Management Action Plan *Work Sheet*

Investment Management Action Plan

Current Status		
Needs Action	**OK or Not Applicable**	
		1. Summarize all of your investments, including any retirement plan investments that you manage.
		2. Determine how your investments are allocated, in total, among the three investment categories: stock, interest-earning, and real estate.
		3. Plan how you are going to re-deploy your investments to achieve a more appropriate allocation.
		4. Begin, if you haven't already, to save at regular intervals to build up your investment portfolio.
		5. If your income is likely to fluctuate, adjust your saving and investing to assure that sufficient resources will be available to meet living expenses.
		6. Spend some time learning about investments and the current investment climate.
		7. Periodically review the status of your portfolio.
		8. Coordinate your investing with other areas of financial planning, particularly taxes and estate planning, but don't let the desire to save on taxes dominate your investing.
		9. Recognize that a buy-and-hold strategy is almost always the most beneficial way to manage a personal portfolio.
		10. Keep in mind that mutual funds, preferably no-load funds, should play a role in every portfolio.
		11. While real estate is often a sound long-term investment, never invest in a property that violates general guidelines outlined in this chapter.
		12. Select and control your investment advisers carefully.
		13. Above all, be consistent in carrying out your investment objectives.

Comments:

Investment Summary *Work Sheet*

Use this work sheet to facilitate the often-laborious process of summarizing your investment portfolio.

Date at which market values are indicated:_____

Investment Summary

Description	Number of Shares or Face Value	Date Acquired	Original Cost	Current Market Value	Estimated Annual Interest or Dividend
1. Cash-equivalent investments: Money market funds and accounts			$	$	$
Savings accounts					
CDs					
Other cash-equivalent investments					
Total cash-equivalent investments			$	$	$

(Continued on the next page)

Investment Summary *Work Sheet Continued*

Investment Summary

Description	Number of Shares or Face Value	Date Acquired	Original Cost	Current Market Value	Estimated Annual Interest or Dividend
2. Fixed-income investments: U.S. government securities			$	$	$
U.S. government securities funds					
Mortgage-backed securities					
Mortgage-backed securities funds					
Corporate bonds					
Corporate bond funds					
Municipal bonds					
Municipal bond funds					
Other fixed-income investments					
Total fixed-income investments			$	$	$

(Continued on the next page)

Investment Summary *Work Sheet Continued*

Investment Summary

Description	Number of Shares or Face Value	Date Acquired	Original Cost	Current Market Value	Estimated Annual Interest or Dividend
3. Equity investments: Common stock in publicly traded companies			$	$	$
Stock mutual funds					
Precious metals and precious metal funds					
Other equity investments					
Total equity investments			$	$	$

(Continued on the next page)

Investment Summary *Work Sheet Continued*

Investment Summary

Description	Description	Date Acquired	Original Cost	Current Market Value	Estimated Annual Interest or Dividend
4. Real estate investments: Undeveloped land			$	$	$
Directly owned, income-producing real estate					
Real estate limited partnerships					
Total real estate investments			$	$	$
5. Interests in privately held businesses:			$	$	$
Total interests in privately held businesses			$	$	$
Grand total investments			$	$	$

Asset Allocation *Work Sheet*

This work sheet allows you to view the percentage allocation of your total portfolio versus your desired, or target, allocation. Transfer the current market value totals for each investment category from the Investment Summary into the first column below. Then calculate the percent of your total investment portfolio in each category. Compare these percentages with your desired portfolio allocation, which can be entered in the right column. This analysis should be prepared at least annually.

Date at which market values are indicated:_____

Asset Allocation

| Investment Category | Current Market Value | | | | |
	Personal Investments	Retirement Plan Investments*	Total	Percent of Portfolio	Target Percent of Portfolio
Stock	$	$	$	%	%
Interest-earning investments					
Real estate					
Grand total	$	$	$	%	%

Comments:

*List all retirement plan investments in which you control the investment allocations, including IRA and 401(k) plans.

Investment Allocation Planner *Work Sheet*

It's now time for you to plan how you should allocate your investments just as has been done in the chapter. If you don't yet have any investments, you can still plan for the day when you will, because that day (hopefully) won't be far off.

Allocation Planner

Method of ownership	Investment Category		
	Stock	Interest-Earning	Real Estate
Direct ownership			
Indirect Ownership (Mutual Fund/Partnership)			

Comments:

Investment "To Do" List:

Tax Planning Action *Checklist*

Tax Planning

Current Status		
Needs Action	**OK or Not Applicable**	
		1. Familiarize yourself with the many available ways to reduce taxes.
		2. Coordinate your income tax planning with other important personal financial planning areas, including investments and retirement planning.
		3. Don't lose sight of the role of old-fashioned tax-advantaged investments like tax-exempt bonds and buying and holding stock and real estate.
		4. Maintain complete and well-organized income tax records throughout the year. Your tax record keeping should be coordinated with your personal record-keeping system.
		5. Effective income tax planning is both a year-round process and a multiyear process. Spend some time after tax season—with your advisor, if applicable—planning your income tax strategies over the next five years.

Comments:

Tax-Free Investing Yield Calculation *Work Sheet*

Tax-Free Investing Yield Calculation

To determine the **after-tax yield** on each interest-earning investment you're considering:

Interest rate on the investment		%
Times (1 – tax rate paid on the investment*)	x	
Equals **after-tax yield**	=	%

* The tax rate paid on the investment depends on the type of security:

Type of Investment	Tax Rate Paid on Investment
Corporate and mortgage-backed securities:	Combine both your federal and state tax rates
Treasury securities:	Federal income tax rate
Out-of-state municipal securities:	State income tax rate
In-state municipal securities:	Exempt from both federal and state income taxes

Example: Say you're in the 31% federal and 6% state income tax brackets. You're considering investing in one of four securities: a corporate bond yielding 8%, a Treasury bond yielding 7%, an out-of-state municipal bond yielding 6%, and an in-state municipal bond yielding 5%. Which pays the most **after-tax** interest income?

	Corporate bond	Treasury bond	Out-of-state municipal bond	In-state municipal bond
Interest Rate on the Investments	8%	7%	6%	5%
x (1 – Tax rate paid on the investment)	x .63	x .69	x .94	x 1.0
= **After-tax yield**	5.0%	4.8%	5.6%	5.0%

Conclusion: In this example, the out-of-state municipal bond has the highest after-tax yield. Therefore, it pays the most after-tax interest income.

Year-End Tax Planning *Checklist*

Tax Planning

1. Consider making year-end charitable contributions of personal property such as clothing and furniture.

2. Consider making a contribution of appreciated securities to avoid paying capital gains tax (but be wary of possible adverse alternative minimum tax (AMT) consequences).

3. Consider bunching miscellaneous expenses, including professional dues, tax preparation fees, and unreimbursed employee business expenses, into the current year so that the total exceeds 2% of adjusted gross income (AGI).

4. If the 2% threshold will not be exceeded even through bunching, consider postponing as many of these expenses as possible until next year.

5. If enough money has not been withheld to meet the current year's tax liability, consider increasing the amount withheld from pay late in the year.

6. Make the maximum possible deductible individual retirement account contribution.

7. Increase participation in employer's 401(k) plan.

8. If there is any income from self-employment, consider opening a Keogh account on or before December 31 to shelter up to 20% of net earnings from self-employment.

9. If taxable income is nearing the 33% bracket, consider deferring income, to the extent permissible, until the succeeding year.

10. Consider paying the last installment of estimated state income tax payments in December rather than in January.

11. Determine AMT liability and shift itemized deductions that are treated as exclusion items for AMT purposes into years in which no AMT liability will be incurred. These include personal interest, state and local taxes, and most miscellaneous itemized deductions.

12. Determine whether medical expenses are likely to exceed the 7.5% of AGI hurdle. If so, bunch them in current year. If not, defer them.

13. Consider realizing capital losses to offset capital gains and investment interest or vice versa if you currently have net capital losses in excess of $3,000.

(Continued on the next page)

Year-End Tax Planning *Checklist Continued*

Tax Planning

14. Use installment sales method to defer capital gain recognition, particularly if it is likely that you will be in a lower tax bracket in later years.

15. If a change in filing status is expected in the succeeding year, defer current income and accelerate deductions if the change in status will lower tax rates. If higher rates are expected, reverse the strategy.

Comments/recommendations:

Retirement Planning *Work Sheet*

Use this three-part work sheet to forecast the amount of retirement income you will require and to estimate the amount of savings you will have to accumulate to meet your retirement income needs.

I. Retirement Expense Forecaster

This section helps you approximate the amount of annual retirement income that will allow you to maintain your pre-retirement standard of living. First, the approximate income necessary to maintain your current living standard in current dollars is calculated. Then, by reference to future value tables and by using the assumed rate of inflation, you can project this amount to your estimated retirement date.

Current gross annual income[1] $..................

Minus amount of annual savings[2]   (..................)

  Subtotal (the amount you spend currently)   ....

Multiplied by 75%[3]   x .75

Equals approximate annual cost (in current dollars) of maintaining
  your current standard of living if you were retiring this year $..................

Multiplied by inflation factor
  (Refer to inflation factor table below)[4]   x..................

Equals approximate annual cost (in future dollars) of maintaining
  your current standard of living when you retire $..................

Inflation Factor Table

Number of Years Until Retirement	Factor
5	1.2
10	1.6
15	1.9
20	2.4
25	3.0
30	3.7
35	4.7
40	5.8

Explanations:

[1] "Current gross annual income" includes all income from all sources.

[2] "Annual savings" includes, in addition to the usual sources of savings, reinvested dividends and capital gains, and any contributions to retirement plans that are taken from your annual income.

[3] The 75% multiplier is a general rule of thumb that says, in essence, that a retiree can maintain his/her pre-retirement standard of living by spending roughly 75% of his/her pre-retirement income. Of course, individual circumstances may dictate a higher or lower percentage. Ideally, you should prepare a retirement budget that details expected expenses. You may find a multiplier less than 75% in some circumstances (for example, low housing costs due to paid-off mortgage) or, in other circumstances, a higher multiplier (for example, extensive travel plans).

[4] In order to project retirement expenses to retirement age, current dollar living expenses must be multiplied by a factor to account for inflationary increases. The inflation factor table can be used for that purpose.

(Continued on the next page)

Retirement Planning *Work Sheet Continued*

This section can be used to forecast pension and Social Security benefits at retirement age and then to approximate the aggregate amount of savings/investments that will be needed by retirement age to cover any shortfall between Social Security/pension benefits and your total income needs.

II. Retirement Resources Forecaster

	Current Dollars	Times Inflation Factor[1]	Future (Retirement Age) Dollars
1. Estimated annual living expenses at retirement age (From Part I)			$...................
2. Annual pension income (projection at retirement age available from employer)[2]	$................... x	.... =	....
3. Plus annual Social Security benefits (projection at retirement age available from Social Security Administration)[3]	$................... x	.... =	....
4. Subtotal of projected pension and Social Security income (add lines 2 and 3)			....
5. Shortfall (if expenses are greater than income) that must be funded out of personal savings/investments (subtract line 4 from line 1)			....
6. Multiplied by 17[4]			x 17
7. Equals amount of savings/investments in future dollars that need to be accumulated by retirement age to fund retirement[5]			$...................

Explanations:

[1] Use inflation factor table for the appropriate calculation.

[2] Employers usually provide pension plan projections at retirement age, expressed in current dollars. If so, the amount should be multiplied by an inflation factor to approximate benefits in future dollars.

[3] Social Security estimates are expressed in current dollars, and therefore, they should be adjusted for inflation similar to footnote 2 above.

[4] As a general rule of thumb, for every $1,000 of annual income you will need to fund at retirement age, you will need to have at least $17,000 in savings/investments in order to keep up with inflation. If you plan to retire before age 62, use a factor of 20, rather than 17.

[5] You may be dismayed by the magnitude of the amount of personal resources that you will need to fund your retirement, which can easily exceed $1 million for younger persons and/or people with minimal pension benefits. Nevertheless, good savings habits combined with the power of compounding can usually close the gap between current resources and eventual needs.

Note: This is a *simplified* method. A professional planner can prepare a more detailed and individualized analysis.

(Continued on the next page)

Retirement Planning *Work Sheet Continued*

This section can be used to estimate the annual amount of savings that are required to accumulate the funds necessary to meet your retirement objectives. The amount computed on Line 7 equals the required *first year* savings. The annual savings should be increased by 5% in each succeeding year until you retire.

III. Retirement Savings Estimator

1. Amount of savings/investments in future dollars that need to be accumulated by retirement age to fund retirement (from Part II) $....................

2. Minus resources that are currently available for retirement purposes[1] $....................

3. Multiplied by appreciation factor (refer to annual appreciation factor table below)[2]   x ....

4. Equals estimated future value of retirement resources that are currently available (Multiply Line 2 by Line 3)   (....................)

5. Retirement funds needed by retirement age (Subtract Line 4 from Line 1)   ....

6. Multiplied by annual savings factor (Refer to annual savings factor table below)[3]   x ....

7. Equals savings needed over the next year (Multiply Line 5 by Line 6)[4] $....................

Appreciation Factor Table		*Annual Savings Factor Table*	
Number of Years Until Retirement	Factor	Number of Years Until Retirement	Factor
5	1.4	5	.1513
10	2.1	10	.0558
15	3.0	15	.0274
20	4.2	20	.0151
25	6.1	25	.0088
30	8.8	30	.0054
35	12.6	35	.0034
40	18.0	40	.0022

Explanations:

[1] Resources that are currently available typically include the current value of all of your investment-related assets that are not expected to be used before retirement. Don't include the value of your home unless you expect to sell it to raise money for retirement. Don't include any vested pension benefits if you have already factored them in on Line 2 of Part II of this work sheet.

[2] The appreciation factor is used to estimate what your currently available retirement resources will be worth when you retire. The appreciation factor assumes a 7.5% after-tax rate of appreciation.

[3] The annual savings factor computes the amount you will need to save during the next year in order to begin accumulating the retirement fund needed by retirement age as indicated on Line 5. The annual savings factor assumes a 7.5% after-tax rate of return.

[4] The annual savings needed to accumulate your retirement nest egg assumes that you will increase the amount of money you save by 5% each year until retirement.

Retirement Action Plan *Work Sheet*

Retirement Action Plan

Current Status		
Needs Action	**OK or Not Applicable**	
		1. You must begin to plan for retirement now—it's never too early. Begin by preparing projections of your retirement income and expenses. If you are within 10 years of retirement, prepare these projections annually.
		2. You cannot rely on pension and Social Security benefits alone to provide for adequate retirement income. Therefore, get into the habit of setting aside some money each year that is earmarked for retirement. An IRA (whether or not it is deductible) is an inexpensive and effective means of getting into this habit.
		3. If you change jobs, roll over any vested pension benefits into an IRA immediately—no matter how small the amount may be and no matter how badly you want to use the money to buy something.
		4. If you are self-employed, set up a retirement plan that is appropriate to your circumstances and needs.
		5. If you have any net income from moonlighting (even if you are covered by a pension plan where you work), set up a simplified employee pension (SEP) plan or a Keogh plan to contribute tax-deductible money for retirement.
		6. One of the best things you can do during your working years to prepare for retirement is to be mortgage free by retirement age. If you are a renter or will still have a large mortgage when you retire, remember that you will need a considerably larger nest egg to cover your housing costs.
		7. Periodically review your retirement plan investments. Be sure to consider them in conjunction with your entire investment portfolio, personal investments, and retirement plan investments.

Comments:

Will Planning/Review Checklist

Use this checklist either to plan a new will or to review an existing will.

Current Status

Yes	No	Unsure	N/A	
☐	☐	☐	☐	1. If there is an existing will, does it reflect the current situation, including birth of heirs and changes in the tax laws, and not contain obsolete sections, including state or residence and inappropriate selection?
☐	☐	☐	☐	2. Will any specific bequests or legacies be made?
☐	☐	☐	☐	3. Are there any bequests to charity, either outright or in trust?
☐	☐	☐	☐	4. Has the disposition of personal property—furniture, jewelry, and automobiles, for example—been planned?
☐	☐	☐	☐	5. Has provision been made for the disposition of real estate?
☐	☐	☐	☐	6. Does the will provide for the disposition of property if an heir predeceases you?
☐	☐	☐	☐	7. Will trusts be established for certain beneficiaries, or will they receive the assets outright?
☐	☐	☐	☐	8. Will certain beneficiaries be provided with periodic payments of income?
☐	☐	☐	☐	9. Does the will take advantage of the unlimited marital deduction to the most effective and practical extent allowed?
☐	☐	☐	☐	10. Has consideration been given to providing for marital and nonmarital trusts in the will?
☐	☐	☐	☐	11. Is the custody of minors satisfactorily addressed?
☐	☐	☐	☐	12. Has consideration been given to appointing a "financial" guardian for the children in addition to a personal guardian?
☐	☐	☐	☐	13. Does the will specify that any minor beneficiary's share of the estate will be held until he or she reaches maturity?
☐	☐	☐	☐	14. Does the will provide for a guardianship or trust to protect the inheritance of disabled or incompetent beneficiaries?
☐	☐	☐	☐	15. Have provisions been made to dispose of business interests?
☐	☐	☐	☐	16. Have appropriate and capable persons or institutions been appointed to serve as executor, trustee, and/or guardian?
☐	☐	☐	☐	17. Does the will name an alternate or successor executor, trustee, and/or guardian?
☐	☐	☐	☐	18. Should any special powers be given to or taken away from the executor?
☐	☐	☐	☐	19. Has the executor's bond requirement been waived?

(Continued on the next page)

Will Planning/Review Checklist *Continued*

Current Status

Yes	No	Unsure	N/A	
☐	☐	☐	☐	20. Are specific powers granted to the executor, as necessary, such as to retain or sell property, to invest trust and estate assets, to allocate receipts and disbursements to income and principal, to make loans and borrow funds, or to settle claims?
☐	☐	☐	☐	21. Is the ownership of the assets complementary to the provisions of the will (i.e., some assets may pass outside of the will by contract or by type of ownership)?
☐	☐	☐	☐	22. Does the will state who will receive property if the beneficiary disclaims it? (Disclaimers can be an effective postmortem planning device.)
☐	☐	☐	☐	23. Have any special directions for the funeral or memorial been provided?
☐	☐	☐	☐	24. Have sources been identified from which debts, funeral expenses, and estate administrative costs will be paid?
☐	☐	☐	☐	25. Will the survivors have enough cash to pay ordinary family living expenses while the estate is in probate?

Letter of Instructions Checklist

A letter of instructions is not a legal document like a will. You have a lot more leeway in both the language and content. Your letter is a good place to put personal wishes and final comments, but your heirs will be very grateful if you include details about important financial matters.

☐ First Things to Do
- Acquaintances and organizations to be called, including Social Security, the bank, and your employer
- Arrangements to be made with funeral home
- Lawyer's name and telephone number
- Newspapers to receive obituary information
- Location of insurance policies

☐ Cemetery and Funeral
- Details of your wishes and any arrangements you have made

☐ Facts for Funeral Director
- Vital statistics, including your full name, residence, marital status, spouse's name, date of birth, birthplace, father's and mother's names and birthplaces, length of residence in state and in United States, military records/history, Social Security number, occupation, and life insurance information

☐ Information for Death Certificate and Filing for Benefits
- Citizen of, race, marital status, name of next of kin (other than spouse), relationship, address, and birthplace

☐ Expected Death Benefits
- Information about any potential death benefits from your employer (including life insurance, profit sharing, pension plan, or accident insurance), life insurance companies, Social Security, the Veterans Administration, or any other source

☐ Special Wishes
- Anything you want them to know

☐ Personal Effects
- A list of who is to receive certain personal effects, usually including details of who is to receive items such as golf clubs or some other special item and it could include autos, etc., in some states

☐ Personal Papers
- Locations of important personal documents, including your will, birth and baptismal certificates, communion and confirmation certificates, diplomas, marriage certificate, military records, naturalization papers, and any other documents (e.g., adoption, divorce)

☐ Safe-Deposit Box*
- Location and number of box and key and an inventory of contents

☐ Post Office Box
- Location and number of box and key (or combination)

☐ Income Tax Returns
- Location of all previous returns
- Location of your estimated tax file
- Tax preparer's name

☐ Loans Outstanding
- Information for loans other than mortgages, including bank name and address, name on loan, account number, monthly payment, location of papers and payment book, collateral, and information on any life insurance on the loan

☐ Debts Owed to the Estate
- Debtor, description, terms, balance, location of documents, and comments on loan status/discharge

---

* State law may require a bank to seal the deceased's safe-deposit box as soon as notified of his or her death, even if the box is jointly owned.

(Continued on the next page)

Letter of Instructions Checklist *Continued*

☐ Social Security
- Full name, Social Security number, and the location of Social Security cards

☐ Life Insurance
- Policy numbers and amounts, location of policy, whose life is insured, insurer's name and address, kind of policy, beneficiaries, issue and maturity date, payment options, and any special facts

☐ Veterans Administration
- If you are a veteran, give information on collecting benefits from local Veterans Administration office

☐ Other Insurance
- If any other insurance benefits or policies are in force, including accident, homeowners/renters, automobile, disability, medical, personal, or professional liability, give insurer's name and address, policy number, beneficiary, coverage, location of policy, term, how acquired (if through employer or other group), agent

☐ Investments
- Stocks: Company, name on certificates, number of shares, certificate numbers, purchase price and date, and location of certificates
- Bonds/notes/bills: Issuer, issued to, face amount, bond number, purchase price and date, maturity date, and location of certificates

- Mutual funds: Company, name on account, number of shares or units, and location of statements and certificates
- Other investments: For each investment, list amount invested, to whom issued, maturity date, issuer, and other applicable data, and location of certificates and other vital papers

☐ Household Contents
- List of contents with name of owners, form of ownership, and location of documents, inventory, and appraisals

☐ Automobiles
- For each car: Year, make, model, color, identification number, title in name(s) of, and location of title and registration

☐ Important Warranties and Receipts
- Location and description

☐ Doctors' Names, Addresses, and Telephone Numbers
- Including dentist, and children's pediatrician and dentist

☐ Checking Accounts
- Name of bank, name on account, account number, and location of passbook (or receipt) for all accounts

☐ Credit Cards
- For each card: company (including telephone and address), name on card, number, and location of card

(Continued on the next page)

Letter of Instructions Checklist *Continued*

☐ House, Condo, or Co-Op
- About the home: in whose name, address, legal description, other descriptions needed, lawyer at closing, and locations of statement of closing, policy of title insurance, deed, and land survey
- About the mortgage: held by, amount of original mortgage, date taken out, amount owed now, method of payment, and location of payment book, if any (or payment statements)
- About life insurance on mortgage: policy number, location of policy, and annual amount
- About property taxes: amount and location of receipts
- About the cost of house: initial buying price, purchase closing fee, other buying costs (real estate agent, legal, taxes), and home improvements
- About improvements: what each consisted of, cost, date, and location of bills

- For renters: lease location and expiration date

☐ Funeral Preferences
- Specify whether *or not* you would like to have any of the following done: Donate organs, autopsy if requested, simple arrangements, embalming, public viewing, least expensive burial or cremation container, or immediate disposition. Remains should be: donated (details of arrangements made), cremated (and the ashes: scattered, buried at), disposed of as follows (details), or buried (at)
- Specify which of the following services should be performed: memorial (after disposition), funeral (before disposition), or graveside to be held at: church, mortuary, or other
- Specify where memorial gifts should be given or whether to omit flowers
- If prearrangements have been made with a mortuary, give details

☐ Signature and date

Estate Planning Action Plan *Work Sheet*

The following action plan is designed to help you jump-start your estate planning.

Estate Planning Action Plan

Current Status		
Needs Action	**OK or Not Applicable**	
		1. Decide how you want your estate to be distributed.
		2. Have an attorney prepare a will that is consistent with your personal wishes and circumstances.
		3. Name an appropriate executor.
		4. Establish a durable power of attorney or living trust that protects you in the event of incapacity.
		5. Prepare and keep up-to-date a letter of instructions.
		6. Designate guardians for your children and, if applicable, disabled adults.
		7. Prepare a living will and a health care proxy.
		8. Prepare an estimate of your taxable estate so that you can determine the type of estate planning techniques that will be appropriate.
		9. Make sure sufficient cash will be able to be raised from your estate to meet the needs of your survivors; if not, take appropriate action to increase your estate liquidity.

(Continued on the next page)

Estate Planning Action Plan *Work Sheet Continued*

Estate Planning Action Plan

Current Status		
Needs Action	**OK or Not Applicable**	
		10. Make sure that the title in which you hold property (single name, jointly with your spouse, etc.) is appropriate for estate planning purposes.
		11. Any gifts to relatives and/or charitable contributions should take into consideration your financial condition and overall estate planning objectives.
		12. If you own property in more than one state, take appropriate action to minimize eventual probate problems.
		13. Consider the use of revocable and irrevocable trusts as part of your estate planning.
		14. If you own your own business, make provisions for its disposition in the event of your death.
		15. Inform your family and any other beneficiaries of your plans.

Comments:

Letter of Instructions *Work Sheet*

Letter of Instructions

A letter of instructions is an informal document that tells your survivors what to do upon your death. The work sheet that follows will help you figure out what to tell your survivors so that they can make your funeral arrangements and settle your other affairs as you wish. A letter of instructions is not a substitute for a will: you should treat it as a supplement to your will. Unlike your will, a letter of instructions—which is not legally binding—can be easily changed and updated.

Expected Death Benefits

1. From employer:

   • Person to contact: Telephone: (   )

   • Life insurance: $

   • Profit sharing: $

   • Pension plan: $

   • Accident insurance: $

   • Other benefits:

2. From insurance companies—total amount: $

3. From Social Security—lump sum plus monthly benefits: $

4. From the Veterans Administration—amount: $
   (Note: The VA must be informed of the death for benefits to be disbursed.)

5. From other sources:

First Things to Do

1. Call:

2. Notify employer. Name and telephone:

3. Make arrangements with the funeral home. (See the "Cemetery and Funeral" section.)

4. Request at least 10 copies of the death certificate. (Usually, the funeral director will get them.)

5. Call lawyer. Name and telephone:

6. Provide the following newspapers with obituary information:

7. Contact the local Social Security office. (See the "Social Security" section.)

8. Retrieve and process insurance policies. (Policy locations are listed in the "Life Insurance" section.)

9. Notify the bank that holds the home mortgage.

10. Notify the following acquaintances and organizations:

(Continued on the next page)

Letter of Instructions *Work Sheet Continued*

Letter of Instructions

Cemetery and Funeral

Cemetery Plot

1. Location:

2. Date purchased: 19

3. Deed number:

4. Location of deed:

5. Other information (e.g., perpetual care):

Facts for the Funeral Director
   This list should be brought to the funeral home with the cemetery deed, if possible.

1. Full name:

2. Residence:

3. Marital status: Spouse's name:

4. Date of birth: 19   Birthplace:

5. Father's name and birthplace:

6. Mother's maiden name and birthplace:

7. Length of residence in state: In United States:

8. Military record:

   When:
   (Bring veterans discharge papers, if possible.)

9. Social Security number: Occupation:

10. Life insurance
    (Bring policy if proceeds will be used for funeral expenses.)

Insurer	Policy Number

Special Wishes

1.

2.

3.

(Continued on the next page)

Letter of Instructions *Work Sheet Continued*

Letter of Instructions

Personal Effects

The following personal effects should be given to the named person:

Item	Person

Funeral Preferences

1. Donate these organs:

2. Autopsy if doctor or family requests: ☐ Yes ☐ No

3. Simple arrangements:
   - ☐ No embalming
   - ☐ No public viewing
   - ☐ The least expensive burial or cremation container
   - ☐ Immediate disposition

4. Remains should be:
   - ☐ Donated: Arrangements made on _____, 19____ with_____
   - ☐ Cremated and the ashes ☐ Scattered ☐ Buried at_____
   - ☐ Disposed of as follows:_____
   - ☐ Buried at _____

5. The following services:
   - ☐ Memorial (after disposition)
   - ☐ Funeral (before disposition)
   - ☐ Graveside

   To be held at: ☐ Church ☐ Mortuary ☐ Other:

6. Memorial gift to: _____ Omit flowers: ☐ Yes ☐ No

7. Prearrangements have been made with the following mortuary:

Location of Personal Papers

1. Last will and testament:

2. Birth and baptismal certificates:

3. Communion, confirmation certificates:

4. School diplomas:

5. Marriage certificate:

6. Military records:

7. Naturalization papers:

8. Other (e.g., adoption, divorce):

(Continued on the next page)

Letter of Instructions *Work Sheet Continued*

Letter of Instructions

Safe-Deposit Box
Note: In the event of the death of a safe-deposit box owner, state law may require the bank to seal the deceased's box as soon as notified of the death, even if the box is jointly owned.

1. Bank name and address:

2. In whose name: Number:

3. Location of key:

4. List of contents (if extensive, attach separate inventory):

Post Office Box

1. Address:

2. Owners:

3. Box number:

4. Location of key or combination:

Income Tax Returns

1. Location of all previous returns (federal, state, local):

2. Tax preparer's name: Telephone:

3. Location of estimated tax file:
   (Check to see if any estimated quarterly taxes are due.)

Doctors' Names and Addresses

1. Doctor's name: Telephone:

   Address:

2. Dentist's name: Telephone:

   Address:

3. Children's pediatrician's name: Telephone:

   Address:

4. Children's dentist's name: Telephone:

   Address:

(Continued on the next page)

Letter of Instructions *Work Sheet Continued*

Letter of Instructions

Checking Accounts
Attach a separate summary if there are multiple accounts.

1. Bank name and address:

2. Name(s) on account:

3. Account number: Type:

4. Location of passbook (or certificate receipt):

5. Special instructions:

Credit Cards
All credit cards in the deceased's name should be cancelled or converted to the survivor's name. Provide the following information for each card:

1. Company: Telephone:

   Address:

2. Name on card: Number:

3. Location of card:

Loans Outstanding
Provide the following information for each loan other than mortgages:

1. Bank name and address:

2. Name on loan:

3. Account number:

4. Monthly payment:

5. Location of papers and payment book (if any):

6. Collateral (if any):

7. Is there life insurance on the loan?   ☐ Yes   ☐ No

Debts Owed to the Estate

1. Debtor:

2. Description:

3. Terms:

4. Balance: $

5. Location of documents:

6. Comments on loan status/discharge:

(Continued on the next page)

Letter of Instructions *Work Sheet Continued*

Letter of Instructions

Social Security

1. Name: Number:

   Location of Social Security cards:

2. File a claim immediately to avoid possibility of losing any benefit checks. Call local Social Security Administration (SSA) office for appointment and follow SSA's instructions as to what to bring. SSA telephone:

3. Expect a lump sum of about $_____, plus continuing benefits for children under age 18, or for full-time students until age 22. A spouse may receive benefits until children reach age 18, between ages 50 and 60 if disabled, or if over age 60.

Life Insurance

To collect benefits, a copy of the death certificate must be sent to each insurance company. Provide the following information for each policy:

1. Policy number: Amount: $

2. Location of policy:

3. Whose life is insured:

4. Insurer's name and address:

5. Kind of policy:

6. Beneficiaries:

7. Issue date: , 19   Maturity date: , 19

8. How paid out:

9. Other options on payout:

10. Other special facts:

11. For $_____ in veterans insurance, call the local Veterans Administration office. Telephone:

(Continued on the next page)

Letter of Instructions *Work Sheet Continued*

Letter of Instructions

Other Insurance

Accident

1. Insurer's name and address:

2. Policy number:

3. Beneficiary:

4. Coverage:

5. Location of policy:

6. Agent (if any):

Homeowners/Renters and Automobile

Provide the following information for each policy:

1. Coverage:

2. Insurer's name and address:

3. Policy number:

4. Location of policy:

5. Term (when to renew):

6. Agent (if any):

Medical

Provide the following information for each policy:

1. Coverage:

2. Insurer's name and address:

3. Policy number:

4. Location of policy:

5. Through employer or other group:

6. Agent (if any):

(Continued on the next page)

Letter of Instructions *Work Sheet Continued*

Letter of Instructions

House, Condo, or Co-Op

Contact the local tax assessor for documentation needed or for more information.

1. In whose name:

2. Address:

3. Lot: Block: On map called:

4. Other descriptions needed:

5. Lawyer at closing:

    Address:

6. Location of statement of closing, policy of title insurance, deed, land survey, and the like:

7. Mortgage:

   a. Held by:

   b. Amount of original mortgage: $

   c. Date taken out: , 19

   d. Amount owed now: $

   e. Method of payment:

   f. Location of payment book, if any (or payment statements):

   g. Is there life insurance on mortgage? ☐ Yes ☐ No

     • If so, policy number:

     • Location of policy:

     • Annual amount: $

8. House taxes

   a. Amount: $

   b. Location of receipts:

9. Cost of house

   a. Initial buying price: $

   b. Purchase closing fee: $

   c. Other costs to buy (e.g., real estate agent, legal, taxes):

   d. Improvements: Total: $

(Continued on the next page)

Letter of Instructions *Work Sheet Continued*

House, Condo, or Co-Op Continued

10. House improvements
    Provide the following information for each improvement:

    a. Improvement:

    b. Cost: $ Date: , 19

    c. Location of bills:

11. If renting, is there a lease: ☐ Yes   ☐ No

    a. Lease location:

    b. Expiration date: , 19

Household Contents

1. Name of owners:

2. Form of ownership:

3. Location of documents:

4. Location of inventory:

5. Location of appraisals:

Automobiles

Provide the following information for each car:

1. Year, make, and model:

2. Body type:

3. Cylinders:

4. Color:

5. Identification number:

6. Title in name(s) of:
   Title to automobiles held in the deceased's name must be changed.

7. Location of papers (e.g., title, registration):

Important Warranties and Receipts

Item	Location

(Continued on the next page)

Letter of Instructions *Work Sheet Continued*

Letter of Instructions

Investments

Provide the following information (if necessary, attach a separate sheet):

Stocks

1. Company:

2. Name on certificate(s):

3. Number of shares: Certificate number(s):

4. Purchase price and date:

5. Location of certificate(s):

Bonds, Notes, and Bills

1. Issuer:

2. Issued to:

3. Face amount: $ Bond number:

4. Purchase price and date:

5. Maturity date:

6. Location of certificate:

Mutual Funds

1. Company:

2. Name on account:

3. Number of shares or units:

4. Location of statements, certificates:

Other Investments

For each investment, list the amount invested, to whom it is issued, the issuer, the maturity date, other applicable data, and the location of certificates and other vital papers.

Estate Planning *Questionnaire*

The following should make it easier for you to create an effective estate plan. Your goal is to make it as easy as possible for your loved ones to activate your estate plan. To ensure that your plan achieves this goal in fact as well as in spirit, review the following and revise your current plan accordingly.

Estate Planning

	Yes	No	NA
1. Have you clearly articulated your wishes regarding the ultimate disposition of your estate?			
2. Do you have an up-to-date will that is consistent with your personal wishes and individual circumstances?			
3. Have you named an appropriate executor?			
4. Have you designated an appropriate adult to be responsible for your financial affairs should you become incapacitated?			
5. Have you prepared a living will and health care proxy?			
6. Has an estimate been made of the size of your taxable estate?			
7. Have you calculated the impact of both federal estate taxes and state death taxes on your estate?			
8. Have provisions been made to provide adequate cash reserves upon your death to provide for your family?			
9. Have you made appropriate provisions in your overall estate planning for property owned in other states?			
10. Are trusts included in your current plan?			
11. Have the effects of current tax regulations on estate planning been evaluated and incorporated into your plan?			
12. Have you informed your family about your funeral plans?			

Comments:

Will Preparation *Checklist*

Will Preparation Checklist

The following items should be included in a will:

	Your full name and location of principal residence.
	Statement that the document is a will.
	Date.
	Statement revoking all previous wills.
	Instructions with respect to disposal of your body and funeral arrangements.
	Specific bequests with provisions for the death of the named beneficiaries. Specific bequests are for the transfer of a particular piece of property to a named beneficiary.
	General bequest, which does not specify from which part of the estate the property is to be taken, with provisions for the death of the named beneficiaries.
	Instructions for dividing the residuary, which is the amount of the estate remaining after these specific and general bequests have been made.
	Provisions for trusts, including the names of selected trustees and successor trustees.
	Statement of who should be presumed to have died first (either husband or wife) should both die in a common accident. This allows both wills to be processed without undue complications or tax effects.
	Names of guardians and alternate guardians for minor children, if necessary, or for a handicapped adult, child, or other relative under your care.
	Designation of what resources or assets are to be used to pay death taxes.
	Names of the executor and substitute executor.
	Signature. The will should be signed in the presence of all of the witnesses.
	Any major changes in the form of codicils. These, too, must be witnessed and signed, as was the original will.

Comments:

Use the order form below to order additional copies of *The ABCs of Managing Your Money*. Or call (303) 220-1200 to place your order with VISA or MasterCard.

Order Form

THE ABCs OF MANAGING YOUR MONEY (BK9305)

Copies at $26.95	$	
Shipping Charge*	$	
Total Enclosed	$	

*Basic shipping and handling charge is $3.50, plus $.50 for each book up to 100 copies. For each 100 books, or part thereof, over the initial 100 ordered, add $20.00 to the $53.50 for the first 100 books. For example, the shipping charge for orders of 101 to 200 books is $73.50; for 201 to 300 books, the shipping charge is $93.50, etc. This is for ground transportation. Individuals who live abroad or require shipment to a post office box will be subject to an additional charge.

* * * * * * BULK ORDER INQUIRIES INVITED * * * * * *

Name

Address

City   State   Zip

(   )
Daytime Telephone

Method of Payment: (check one) _____Check _____VISA _____MasterCard
(Make checks payable to NEFE.)

Account Number   Expiration Date

Signature   Date

Return order and payment to:

      Order Services Department
      NEFE
      4695 South Monaco Street
      Denver, Colorado 80237-3403

Telephone orders may be placed using VISA or MasterCard. Call the Order Services department of NEFE at (303) 220-1200.

No returns can be accepted or refunds issued.